I0447075

Individual Liberty

Selections From the Writings of

BENJAMIN R. TUCKER

EDITED BY C. L. S.

NEW YORK
VANGUARD PRESS
MCMXXVI

Originally published in 1926.

Large Print Edition published 2012 by Skyler J. Collins.
Visit: www.skylerjcollins.com

Cover image by StockFreeImages.com.

ISBN-13: 978-1479307081
ISBN-10: 1479307084

PUBLISHER'S NOTE

C. L. S., the editor and compiler of this book, has known Benjamin R. Tucker personally since 1891, having entered his employ at that time in the mechanical department of *Liberty*, Mr. Tucker's journal for the exposition of Individualist Anarchism. After that time and until the final suspension of publication of *Liberty*, C. L. S. contributed many articles to the columns of that periodical, both signed and unsigned, usually in the editorial department. For a considerable period he had complete editorial charge, during Mr. Tucker's absence. Thus the present work has been performed by one who has entire familiarity with *Liberty's* philosophy and who perhaps at present has a closer sympathy with Mr. Tucker's ideas than any other person in America.

Mr. Tucker has written that "the editor is well chosen, and his qualifications for the job undeniable." He does, however, request that the volume shall be prefaced by a statement that he, "while gratefully acknowledging the good will that has inspired the publication," has had no hand in the work of abridgment, and that the project has been executed without his express sanction or approval, although the publisher's action is "above reproach."

In justice to Mr. Tucker, however, it should be stated that he emphatically protested against the elimination of the words of his opponents in the controversies, since he had always been scrupulously exact in presenting their ideas in full; but the limited scope of this volume made such omission imperative.

A word as to the title of this book. Tucker's lifework is devoted to the exposition of the rights of the

Individual.   As a title for the journal which he used as a medium of expression for thirty years, he chose *Liberty*.   It seems fitting that these two words, standing as they do for the highest aspirations of mankind, should be joined together in a title for this compilation of Tucker's libertarian and anarchistic teachings.

EDITOR'S FOREWORD

For a number of years practically all of the literature of Individualist Anarchism has been out of print. The great bulk of whatever matter there was had, of course, been in the hands of Benjamin R. Tucker, and up to 1908 it was being constantly augmented by him. But when, in January of that year, his entire wholesale stock of publications, manuscripts, etc., and nearly all of his plates were wiped out by fire, the loss was irreparable, and little attempt has been made to replace any of the material destroyed.

The demand for something representative of Individualist Anarchism has become so insistent that it has been determined to produce at least one volume of the best matter available, and in that volume to attempt to cover the whole subject.

The nearest that any book ever came to answering that description is Tucker's "Instead of a Book," first published in 1893, culled from his writings in his periodical, *Liberty*, and out of print since 1908. This closely printed volume of nearly 500 pages was composed of questions and criticisms by his correspondents and by writers in other periodicals, all answered by the editor of *Liberty* in that keen, clear-cut style that was the delight of his adherents and the despair of his opponents.

In casting about for material for the proposed volume, therefore, no other writings than those of Benjamin R. Tucker could for a moment be considered, and it is no exaggeration to say that they stand high above everything else that has been written on the subject, not even excepting the works of Josiah Warren, Proudhon, and Lysander Spooner, or of any other person who has ever attempted to expound the principles of Individualist Anarchism.

Mr. Tucker is an educated and cultured man. His

literary style is both fluent and elegant, his statements concise and accurate, his arguments logical and convincing, and his replies terse yet courteous. The reader is never at a loss to know what he means. There is not a word too much or too little. Every sentence is rounded and complete—not a redundant syllable or a missing punctuation mark. What he writes is a joy to read, even when the reader himself is the victim of his withering sarcasm or caustic satire.

A brief *résumé* of Mr. Tucker's life will serve to indicate the background of his remarkable personality. He was born in South Dartmouth, Massachusetts, April 17, 1854, the son of Abner R. Tucker, owner and outfitter of whale ships and later a grocer in New Bedford. His mother was Caroline A. Cummings, his father's second wife, and Benjamin was their only child. The father was of Quaker parents and the mother was a Unitarian, and an able, progressive and radical woman, her father having been a pronounced admirer of Thomas Paine.

At two years Tucker was reading English fluently and at four gleefully discovered that the Episcopal Prayer Book had misquoted the Bible. At sixteen he had finished the course at the Friends' Academy, and, while at first refusing to go to any college, he finally spent two years at the Massachusetts Institute of Technology (Boston). After hearing Josiah Warren speak and Col. William B. Greene quote Proudhon at a convention of the New England Labor Reform League in Boston in 1872, he soon became an Anarchist and translated Proudhon's "What Is Property?" from the French. In 1877 he edited *The Word* in Princeton, Massachusetts, while its editor, Ezra H. Heywood, was in prison. In 1878 he established and conducted for a year *The Radical Review* in New Bedford. In the same year he joined the editorial staff of the *Boston Daily Globe*, remaining for eleven years.

In 1881 he founded *Liberty*, which he continued to publish, with some irregularity and several suspensions, until 1908, the last issue appearing in April of that year, a few months after the disastrous fire. In 1892, when he assumed editorial duties on *The Engineering Magazine*, he removed *Liberty* to New York, where it was published until its final suspension. Since that time Tucker has been living in France.

"Instead of a Book" was deemed unsuitable for reproduction in its present form because it contains so many articles dealing with local and current events. It was decided that Individualist Anarchism could better be expounded by presenting the words of Mr. Tucker alone, eliminating the voluminous letters of his correspondents and many more or less personal matters that crept into the discussions, with just enough explanatory matter written by the editor to indicate what drew forth the arguments advanced by *Liberty*'s editor and to connect up the loose ends. In many cases Mr. Tucker has so carefully restated the position of his adversary that it has been unnecessary for the editor to repeat it.

The compiler has therefore merely attempted to weld together the different sections and weave the various articles into a more or less continuous whole. The task has proved to be difficult beyond all preconception, and that it has been performed with complete success it would be presumptuous to assert.

In Mr. Tucker's controversies with his correspondents and others, occasional allusions to persons and matters not involved in the discussion have entered. These, while perfectly pertinent when his opponents' remarks were given, add little to the force of the arguments for the Anarchistic position which it is the purpose of this volume exclusively to set forth, and they have therefore generally been excised, in spite of the fact that they constitute some of Mr. Tucker's most pungent writing.

In some places this method of treatment has made it necessary to eliminate parts of paragraphs and even parts of sentences. This elision has not been indicated by asterisks or otherwise, because the frequency of such instances would have made the matter too disconnected; while the main object of this volume is to present, as nearly as possible, an unbroken exposition. It is considered that this proceeding is entirely unobjectionable, since the essential arguments are thus expressed just as clearly, and of course more concisely, than in the complete original.

"Instead of a Book" contained only material published in *Liberty* previous to 1893, so the columns of *Liberty* since that date have been resorted to for some additional material.

The editor wishes to acknowledge his indebtedness to those comrades, all plumb-liners of the period when *Liberty* was the venerated medium for the exchange of their ideas, who have aided him, by advice and hard work, in the preparation of this volume, the index thereto having been prepared by the same person who performed that service for "Instead of a Book."

C. L. S.

Los Angeles, California.
August, 1926.

CONTENTS

ix

CONTENTS

INDIVIDUAL LIBERTY

SOCIOLOGY

I—STATE SOCIALISM AND ANARCHISM:

HOW FAR THEY AGREE, AND WHEREIN THEY DIFFER

This essay, which is the clearest statement on the subject that has ever been produced, was written by Mr. Tucker in 1886, in response to an invitation from the editor of the *North American Review* to furnish him a paper on Anarchism. It was accepted, announced for publication, and was paid for; but it was never printed in that magazine, and, after numerous letters of inquiry had been sent, the manuscript was returned to the author, although the editor of the *Review* volunteered the declaration that it was the ablest article that he had received during his editorship. It appeared as the leading article in "Instead of a Book," and, after forty years, it is still easily the most important thing in the present volume:

PROBABLY no agitation has ever attained the magnitude, either in the number of its recruits or the area of its influence, which has been attained by Modern Socialism, and at the same time been so little understood and so misunderstood, not only by the hostile and the indifferent, but by the friendly, and even by the great mass of its adherents themselves. This unfortunate and highly dangerous state of things is due partly to the fact that the human relationships which this move-ment—if anything so chaotic can be called a movement—aims to transform, involve no special class or classes, but literally all mankind; partly to the fact that these relationships are infinitely more varied and complex in their nature than those with which any special reform has ever been called upon to deal; and partly to the fact that the great moulding forces of society, the channels of information and enlightenment, are well-nigh exclusively under the control of those whose immediate pecuniary interests are antagonistic to the bottom claim of Socialism that labor should be put in possession of its own.

Almost the only persons who may be said to comprehend even approximately the significance, principles, and purposes of Socialism are the chief leaders of the extreme wings of the Socialistic forces, and perhaps a few of the money kings themselves. It is a subject of which it has lately become quite the fashion for preacher, professor, and penny-a-liner to treat, and, for the most part, woful work they have made with it, exciting the derision and pity of those competent to judge. That those prominent in the intermediate Socialistic divisions do not fully understand what they are about is evident from the positions they occupy. If they did; if they were consistent, logical thinkers; if they were what the French call *conse-quent* men,—their reasoning faculties would long since have driven them to one extreme or the other.

For it is a curious fact that the two extremes of the vast army now under consideration, though united, as has been hinted above, by the common claim that labor shall be put in possession of its own, are more diametrically opposed to each other in their fundamental principles of social action and their methods of reaching the ends aimed at than either is to their common enemy, the existing society. They are based on two principles the history of whose conflict is almost equivalent to the history of the world since man came into it; and all intermediate parties, including that of the upholders of the existing society, are based upon a compromise between them. It is clear, then, that any intelligent, deep-rooted opposition to the prevailing order of things must come from one or the other of these extremes, for anything from any other source, far from being revolutionary in character, could be only in the nature of such superficial modification as would be utterly unable to concentrate upon itself the degree of attention and interest now bestowed upon Modern Socialism.

The two principles referred to are *Authority* and *Liberty*, and the names of the two schools of Socialistic thought which fully and unreservedly represent one or the other of them are, respectively, State Socialism and Anarchism. Whoso knows what these two schools want and how they propose to get it understands the Socialistic movement. For, just as it has been said that there is no half-way house between Rome and Reason, so it may be said that there is no half-way house between State Socialism and Anarchism. There are, in fact, two currents steadily flowing from the centre of the Socialistic forces which are concentrating them on the left and on the right; and, if Socialism is to prevail, it is among the possibilities that, after this movement of separation has been completed and the existing order has been crushed out between the two camps, the ultimate and bitterer conflict will be still to come. In that case all the eight-hour men, all the trades-unionists, all the Knights of Labor, all the land nationalization-ists, all the greenbackers, and, in short, all the members of the thousand and one different battalions belonging to the great army of Labor, will have deserted their old posts, and, these being arrayed on the one side and the other, the great battle will begin. What a final victory for the State Socialists will mean, and what a final victory for the Anarchists will mean, it is the purpose of this paper to briefly state.

To do this intelligently, however, I must first describe the ground common to both, the features that make Socialists of each of them.

The economic principles of Modern Socialism are a logical deduction from the principle laid down by Adam Smith in the early chapters of his "Wealth of Nations,"—namely, that labor is the true measure of price. But Adam Smith, after stating this principle most clearly and concisely, immediately abandoned all further consideration of it to devote himself to showing what actually does measure price, and how, therefore, wealth is at present distributed. Since his day nearly all the political economists have followed his example by confining their function to the description of society as it is, in its industrial and commercial phases. Socialism, on the contrary, extends its function to the description of society as it should be, and the discovery of the means of making it what it should be. Half a century or more after Smith enunciated the principle above stated, Socialism picked it up where he had dropped it, and in following it to its logical conclusions, made it the basis of a new economic philosophy.

This seems to have been done independently by three different men, of three different nationalities, in three different languages: Josiah Warren, an American; Pierre J. Proudhon, a Frenchman; Karl Marx, a German Jew. That Warren and Proudhon arrived at their conclusions singly and unaided is certain; but whether Marx was not largely indebted to Proudhon for his economic ideas is questionable. However this may be, Marx's presentation of the ideas was in so many respects peculiarly his own that he is fairly entitled to the credit of originality. That the work of this interesting trio should have been done so nearly simultaneously would seem to indicate that Socialism was in the air, and that the time was ripe and the conditions favorable for the appearance of this new school of thought. So far as priority of time is concerned, the credit seems to belong to Warren, the American,—a fact which should be noted by the stump orators who are so fond of declaiming against Socialism as an imported article. Of the purest revolutionary blood, too, this Warren, for he descends from the Warren who fell at Bunker Hill.

From Smith's principle that labor is the true measure of price—or, as Warren phrased it, that cost is the proper limit of price—these three men made the following deductions: that the natural wage of labor is its product; that this wage, or product, is the only just source of income (leaving out, of course, gift, inheritance, etc.) ; that all who derive income from any other source abstract it directly or indirectly from the natural and just wage of labor; that this abstracting process generally takes one of three forms,—interest, rent, and profit; that these three constitute the trinity of usury, and are simply different methods of levying tribute for the use of capital; that, capital being simply stored-up labor which has already received its pay in full, its use ought to be gratuitous, on the principle that labor is the only basis of price; that the lender of capital is entitled to its return intact, and nothing more; that the only reason why the banker, the stockholder, the landlord, the manufacturer, and the merchant are able to exact usury from labor lies in the fact that they are backed by legal privilege, or monopoly; and that the only way to secure labor the enjoyment of its entire product, or natural wage, is to strike down monopoly.

It must not be inferred that either Warren, Proudhon, or Marx used exactly this phraseology, or followed exactly this line of thought, but it indicates definitely enough the fundamental ground taken by all three, and their substantial thought up to the limit to which they went in common. And, lest I may be accused of stating the positions and arguments of these men incorrectly, it may be well to say in advance that I have viewed them broadly, and that, for the purpose of sharp, vivid, and emphatic comparison and contrast, I have taken considerable liberty with their thought by rearranging it in an order, and often in a phraseology, of my own, but, I am satisfied, without, in so doing, misrepresenting them in any essential particular.

It was at this point—the necessity of striking down monopoly—that came the parting of their ways. Here the road forked. They found that they must turn either to the right or to the left,—follow either the path of Authority or the path of Liberty. Marx went one way; Warren and Proudhon the other. Thus were born State Socialism and Anarchism.

First, then, State Socialism, which may be described as *the doctrine that all the affairs of men should be managed by the government, regardless of individual choice.*

Marx, its founder, concluded that the only way to abolish the class monopolies was to centralize and consolidate all industrial and commercial interests, all productive and distributive agencies, in one vast monopoly in the hands of the State. The government must become banker, manufacturer, farmer, carrier, and merchant, and in these capacities must suffer no competition. Land, tools, and all instruments of production must be wrested from individual hands, and made the property of the collectivity. To the individual can belong only the products to be consumed, not the means of producing them. A man may own his clothes and his food, but not the sewing-machine which makes his shirts or the spade which digs his potatoes. Product and capital are essentially different things; the former belongs to individuals, the latter to society. Society must seize the capital which belongs to it, by the ballot if it can, by revolution if it must. Once in possession of it, it must administer it on the majority principle, through its organ, the State, utilize it in production and distribution, fix all prices by the amount of labor involved, and employ the whole people in its workships, farms, stores, etc. The nation must be transformed into a vast bureaucracy, and every individual into a State official. Everything must be done on the cost principle, the people having no motive to make a profit out of themselves. Individuals not being allowed to own capital, no one can employ another, or even himself. Every man will be a wage-receiver, and the State the only wage-payer. He who will not work for the State must starve, or, more likely, go to prison. All freedom of trade must disappear. Competition must be utterly wiped out. All industrial and commercial activity must be centred in one vast, enormous, all-inclusive monopoly. The remedy for *monopolies* is *monopoly*.

Such is the economic programme of State Socialism as adopted from Karl Marx. The history of its growth and progress cannot be told here. In this country the parties that uphold it are known as the Socialistic Labor Party, which pretends to follow Karl Marx; the Nationalists, who follow Karl Marx filtered through Edward Bellamy; and the Christian Socialists, who follow Karl Marx filtered through Jesus Christ.

What other applications this principle of Authority, once adopted in the economic sphere, will develop is very evident. It means the absolute control by the majority of all individual conduct. The right of such control is already admitted by the State Socialists, though they maintain that, as a matter of fact, the individual would be allowed a much larger liberty than he now enjoys. But he would only be allowed it; he could not claim it as his own. There would be no foundation of society upon a guaranteed equality of the largest possible liberty. Such liberty as might exist would exist by sufferance and could be taken away at any moment. Constitutional guarantees would be of no avail. There would be but one article in the constitution of a State Socialistic country: "The right of the majority is absolute."

The claim of the State Socialists, however, that this right would not be exercised in matters pertaining to the individual in the more intimate and private relations of his life is not borne out by the history of governments. It has ever been the tendency of power to add to itself, to enlarge its sphere, to encroach beyond the limits set for it; and where the habit of resisting such encroachment is not fostered, and the individual is not taught to be jealous of his rights, individuality gradually disappears and the government or State becomes the all-in-all. Control naturally accompanies responsibility. Under the system of State Socialism, therefore, which holds the community responsible for the health, wealth, and wisdom of the individual, it is evident that the community, through its majority expression, will insist more and more on prescribing the conditions of health, wealth, and wisdom, thus impairing and finally destroying individual independence and with it all sense of individual responsibility.

Whatever, then, the State Socialists may claim or disclaim, their system, if adopted, is doomed to end in a State religion, to the expense of which all must contribute and at the altar of which all must kneel; a State school of medicine, by whose practitioners the sick must invariably be treated; a State system of hygiene, prescribing what all must and must not eat, drink, wear, and do; a State code of morals, which will not content itself with punishing crime, but will prohibit what the majority decide to be vice; a State system of instruction, which will do away with all private schools, academies, and colleges; a State nursery, in which all children must be brought up in common at the public expense; and, finally, a State family, with an attempt at stirpiculture, or scientific breeding, in which no man and woman will be allowed to have children if the State prohibits them and no man and woman can refuse to have children if the State orders them. Thus will Authority achieve its acme and Monopoly be carried to its highest power.

Such is the ideal of the logical State Socialist, such the goal which lies at the end of the road that Karl Marx took. Let us now follow the fortunes of Warren and Proudhon, who took the other road,—the road of Liberty.

This brings us to Anarchism, which may be described as *the doctrine that all the affairs of men should be managed by individuals or voluntary associations, and that the State should be abolished.*

When Warren and Proudhon, in prosecuting their search

for justice to labor, came face to face with the obstacle of class monopolies, they saw that these monopolies rested upon Authority, and concluded that the thing to be done was, not to strengthen this Authority and thus make monopoly universal, but to utterly uproot Authority and give full sway to the opposite principle, Liberty, by making competition, the antithesis of monopoly, universal. They saw in competition the great leveller of prices to the labor cost of production. In this they agreed with the political economists. The query then naturally presented itself why all prices do not fall to labor cost; where there is any room for incomes acquired otherwise than by labor; in a word, why the usurer, the receiver of interest, rent, and profit, exists. The answer was found in the present one-sidedness of competition. It was discovered that capital had so manipulated legislation that unlimited competition is allowed in supplying productive labor, thus keeping wages down to the starvation point, or as near it as practicable; that a great deal of competition is allowed in supplying distributive labor, or the labor of the mercantile classes, thus keeping, not the prices of goods, but the merchants' actual profits on them down to a point somewhat approximating equitable wages for the merchants' work; but that almost no competition at all is allowed in supplying capital, upon the aid of which both productive and distributive labor are dependent for their power of achievement, thus keeping the rate of interest on money and of house-rent and ground-rent at as high a point as the necessities of the people will bear.

On discovering this, Warren and Proudhon charged the political economists with being afraid of their own doctrine. The Manchester men were accused of being inconsistent. They believed in liberty to compete with the laborer in order to reduce his wages, but not in liberty to compete with the capitalist in order to reduce his usury. *Laissez faire* was very good sauce for the goose, labor, but very poor sauce for the gander, capital. But how to correct this inconsistency, how to serve this gander with this sauce, how to put capital at the service of business men and laborers at cost, or free of usury, —that was the problem.

Marx, as we have seen, solved it by declaring capital to be a different thing from product, and maintaining that it belonged to society and should be seized by society and employed for the benefit of all alike. Proudhon scoffed at this distinction between capital and product. He maintained that capital and product are not different kinds of wealth, but simply alternate conditions or functions of the same wealth; that all wealth undergoes an incessant transformation from capital into product and from product back into capital, the process repeating itself interminably; that capital and product are purely social terms; that what is product to one man immediately becomes capital to another, and *vice versa*; that if there were but one person in the world, all wealth would be to him at once capital and product; that the fruit of A's toil is his product, which, when sold to B, becomes B's capital (unless B is an unproductive consumer, in which case it is merely wasted wealth, outside the view of social economy); that a steam-engine is just as much product as a coat, and that a coat is just as much capital as a steam-engine; and that the same laws of equity govern the possession of the one that govern the possession of the other.

For these and other reasons Proudhon and Warren found themselves unable to sanction any such plan as the seizure of capital by society. But, though opposed to socializing the ownership of capital, they aimed nevertheless to socialize its effects by making its use beneficial to all instead of a means of impoverishing the many to enrich the few. And when the light burst in upon them, they saw that this could be done by subjecting capital to the natural law of competition, thus bringing the price of its own use down to cost,—that is, to nothing beyond the expenses incidental to handling and transferring it. So they raised the banner of Absolute Free Trade; free trade at home, as well as with foreign countries; the logical carrying out of the Manchester doctrine; *laissez faire* the universal rule. Under this banner they began their fight upon monopolies, whether the all-inclusive monopoly of the State Socialists, or the various class monopolies that now prevail.

Of the latter they distinguished four of principal importance: the money monopoly, the land monopoly, the tariff monopoly, and the patent monopoly.

First in the importance of its evil influence they considered the money monopoly, which consists of the privilege given by the government to certain individuals, or to indivduals holding certain kinds of property, of issuing the circulating medium, a privilege which is now enforced in this country by a national tax of ten per cent. upon all other persons who attempt to furnish a circulating medium, and by State laws making it a criminal offence to issue notes as currency. It is claimed that the holders of this privilege control the rate of interest, the rate of rent of houses and buildings, and the prices of goods,—the first directly, and the second and third indirectly. For, say Proudhon and Warren, if the business of banking were made free to all, more and more persons would enter into it until the competition should become sharp enough to reduce the price of lending money to the labor cost, which statistics show to be less than three-fourths of one per cent. In that case the thousands of people who are now deterred from going into business by the ruinously high rates which they must pay for capital with which to start and carry on business will find their difficulties removed. If they have property which they do not desire to convert into money by sale, a bank will take it as collateral for a loan of a certain proportion of its market value at less than one per cent. discount. If they have no property, but are industrious, honest, and capable, they will generally be able to get their individual notes endorsed by a sufficient number of known and solvent parties; and on such business paper they will be able to get a loan at a bank on similarly favorable terms. Thus interest will fall at a blow. The banks will really not be lending capital at all, but will be doing business on the capital of their customers, the business consisting in an exchange of the known and widely available credits of the banks for the unknown and unavailable, but equally good, credits of the customers, and a charge therefor of less than one per cent., not as interest for the use of capital, but as pay for the labor of running the banks. This facility of acquiring capital will give an unheard of impetus to business, and consequently create an unprecedented demand for labor,—a demand which will always be in excess of the supply, directly the contrary of the present condition of the labor market. Then will be seen an exemplification of the words of Richard Cobden that, when two laborers are after one employer, wages fall, but when two employers are after one laborer, wages rise. Labor will then be in a position to dictate its wages, and will thus secure its natural wage, its entire product. Thus the same blow that strikes interest down will send wages up. But this is not all. Down will go profits also. For merchants, instead of buying at high prices on credit, will borrow money of the banks at less than one per cent., buy at low prices for cash, and correspondingly reduce the prices of their goods to their customers. And with the rest will go house-rent. For no one who can borrow capital at one per cent. with which to build a house of his own will consent to pay rent to a landlord at a higher rate than that. Such is the vast claim made by Proudhon and Warren as to the results of the simple abolition of the money monopoly.

Second in importance comes the land monopoly, the evil effects of which are seen principally in exclusively agricultural countries, like Ireland. This monopoly consists in the enforcement by government of land titles which do not rest upon personal occupancy and cultivation. It was obvious to Warren and Proudhon that, as soon as individualists should no longer be protected by their fellows in anything but personal occupancy and cultivation of land, ground-rent would disappear, and so usury have one less leg to stand on. Their followers of to-day are disposed to modify this claim to the extent of admitting that the very small fraction of ground-rent which rests, not on monopoly, but on superiority of soil or site, will continue to exist for a time and perhaps forever, though tending constantly to a minimum under conditions of freedom. But the inequality of soils which gives rise to the economic rent of land, like the inequality of human skill which gives rise to the economic rent of ability, is not a cause for serious alarm even to the most thorough opponent of usury, as its nature is not that of a germ from which other and graver inequalities may spring, but rather that of a decaying branch which may finally wither and fall.

Third, the tariff monopoly, which consists in fostering production at high prices and under unfavorable conditions by visiting with the penalty of taxation those who patronize production at low prices and under favorable conditions. The evil to which this monopoly gives rise might more properly be called *mis*usury than usury, because it compels labor to pay, not exactly for the use of capital, but rather for the misuse of capital. The abolition of this monopoly would result in a great reduction in the prices of all articles taxed, and this saving to the laborers who consume these articles would be another step toward securing to the laborer his natural wage, his entire product. Proudhon admitted, however, that to abolish this monopoly before abolishing the money monopoly would be a cruel and disastrous policy, first, because the evil of scarcity of money, created by the money monopoly, would be intensified by the flow of money out of the country which would be involved in an excess of imports over exports, and, second, because that fraction of the laborers of the country which is now employed in the protected industries would be turned adrift to face starvation without the benefit of the insatiable demand for labor which a competitive money system would create. Free trade in money at home, making money and work abundant, was insisted upon by Proudhon as a prior condition of free trade in goods with foreign countries.

Fourth, the patent monopoly, which consists in protecting inventors and authors against competition for a period long enough to enable them to extort from the people a reward enormously in excess of the labor measure of their services,— in other words, in giving certain people a right of property for a term of years in laws and facts of Nature, and the power to exact tribute from others for the use of this natural wealth, which should be open to all. The abolition of this monopoly would fill its beneficiaries with a wholesome fear of competition which would cause them to be satisfied with pay for their services equal to that which other laborers get for theirs, and to secure it by placing their products and works on the market at the outset at prices so low that their lines of business would be no more tempting to competitors than any other lines.

The development of the economic programme which consists in the destruction of these monopolies and the substitution for them of the freest competition led its authors to a perception of the fact that all their thought rested upon a very fundamental principle, the freedom of the individual, his right of sovereignty over himself, his products, and his affairs, and of rebellion against the dictation of external authority. Just as the idea of taking capital away from individuals and giving it to the government started Marx in a path which ends in making the government everything and the individual nothing, so the idea of taking capital away from government-protected monopolies and putting it within easy reach of all individuals started Warren and Proudhon in a path which ends in making the individual everything and the government nothing. If the individual has a right to govern himself, all external government is tyranny. Hence the necessity of abolishing the State. This was the logical conclusion to which Warren and Proudhon were forced, and it became the fundamental article of their political philosophy. It is the doctrine which Proudhon named An-archism, a word derived from the Greek, and meaning, not necessarily absence of order, as is generally supposed, but absence of rule. The Anarchists are simply unterrified Jeffersonian Democrats. They believe that "the best government is that which governs least," and that that which governs least is no government at all. Even the simple police function of protecting person and property they deny to governments supported by compulsory taxation. Protection they look upon as a thing to be secured, as long as it is necessary, by voluntary association and coöperation for self-defence, or as a commodity to be purchased, like any other commodity, of those who offer the best article at the lowest price. In their view it is in itself an invasion of the individual to compel him to pay for or suffer a protection against invasion that he has not asked for and does not desire. And they further claim that protection will become a drug in the market, after poverty and consequently crime have disappeared through the realization of their economic programme. Compulsory taxation is to them the life-principle of all the monopolies, and passive, but organized, resistance to the tax-collector they contemplate, when the proper time comes, as one of the most effective methods of accomplishing their purposes.

Their attitude on this is a key to their attitude on all other questions of a political or social nature. In religion they are atheistic as far as their own opinions are concerned, for they look upon divine authority and the religious sanction of morality as the chief pretexts put forward by the privileged classes for the exercise of human authority. "If God exists," said Proudhon, "he is man's enemy." And in contrast to Voltaire's famous epigram, "If God did not exist, it would be necessary to invent him," the great Russian Nihilist, Michael Bakounine, placed this antithetical proposition: "If God existed, it would be necessary to abolish him." But although, viewing the divine hierarchy as a contradiction of Anarchy, they do not believe in it, the Anarchists none the less firmly believe in the liberty to believe in it. Any denial of religious freedom they squarely oppose.

Upholding thus the right of every individual to be or select his own priest, they likewise uphold his right to be or select his own doctor. No monopoly in theology, no monopoly in medicine. Competition everywhere and always; spiritual advice and medical advice alike to stand or fall on their own merits. And not only in medicine, but in hygiene, must this principle of liberty be followed. The individual may decide for himself not only what to do to get well, but what to do to keep well. No external power must dictate to him what he must and must not eat, drink, wear, or do.

Nor does the Anarchistic scheme furnish any code of morals to be imposed upon the individual. "Mind your own business" is its only moral law. Interference with another's business is a crime and the only crime, and as such may properly be resisted. In accordance with this view the Anarchists look upon attempts to arbitrarily suppress vice as in themselves crimes. They believe liberty and the resultant social well-being to be a sure cure for all the vices. But they recognize the right of the drunkard, the gambler, the rake, and the harlot to live their lives until they shall freely choose to abandon them.

In the matter of the maintenance and rearing of children the Anarchists would neither institute the communistic nursery which the State Socialists favor nor keep the communistic school system which now prevails. The nurse and the teacher, like the doctor and the preacher, must be selected voluntarily, and their services must be paid for by those who patronize them. Parental rights must not be taken away, and parental responsibilities must not be foisted upon others.

Even in so delicate a matter as that of the relations of the sexes the Anarchists do not shrink from the application of their principle. They acknowledge and defend the right of any man and woman, or any men and women, to love each other for as long or as short a time as they can, will, or may.

To them legal marriage and legal divorce are equal absurdities. They look forward to a time when every individual, whether man or woman, shall be self-supporting, and when each shall have an independent home of his or her own, whether it be a separate house or rooms in a house with others; when the love relations between these independent individuals shall be as varied as are individual inclinations and attractions; and when the children born of these relations shall belong exclusively to the mothers until old enough to belong to themselves.

Such are the main features of the Anarchistic social ideal. There is wide difference of opinion among those who hold it as to the best method of obtaining it. Time forbids the treatment of that phase of the subject here. I will simply call attention to the fact that it is an ideal utterly inconsistent with that of those Communists who falsely call themselves Anarchists while at the same time advocating a *régime* of Archism fully as despotic as that of the State Socialists themselves. And it is an ideal that can be as little advanced by the forcible expropriation recommended by John Most and Prince Kropotkine as retarded by the brooms of those Mrs. Partingtons of the bench who sentence them to prison; an ideal which the martyrs of Chicago did far more to help by their glorious death upon the gallows for the common cause of Socialism than by their unfortunate advocacy during their lives, in the name of Anarchism, of force as a revolutionary agent and authority as a safeguard of the new social order. The Anarchists believe in liberty both as end and means, and are hostile to anything that antagonizes it.

I should not undertake to summarize this altogether too summary exposition of Socialism from the standpoint of Anarchism, did I not find the task already accomplished for me by a brilliant French journalist and historian, Ernest Lesigne, in the form of a series of crisp antitheses; by reading which to you as a conclusion of this lecture I hope to deepen the impression which it has been my endeavor to make.

"There are two Socialisms.

"One is communistic, the other solidaritarian.

"One is dictatorial, the other libertarian.

"One is metaphysical, the other positive.

"One is dogmatic, the other scientific.

"One is emotional, the other reflective.

"One is destructive, the other constructive.

"Both are in pursuit of the greatest possible welfare for all.

"One aims to establish happiness for all, the other to enable each to be happy in his own way.

"The first regards the State as a society *sui generis*, of an especial essence, the product of a sort of divine right outside of and above all society, with special rights and able to exact special obediences; the second considers the State as an association like any other, generally managed worse than others.

"The first proclaims the sovereignty of the State, the second recognizes no sort of sovereign.

"One wishes all monopolies to be held by the State; the other wishes the abolition of all monopolies.

"One wishes the governed class to become the governing class; the other wishes the disappearance of classes.

"Both declare that the existing state of things cannot last.

"The first considers revolution as the indispensable agent of evolution; the second teaches that repression alone turns evolution into revolution.

"The first has faith in a cataclysm.

"The second knows that social progress will result from the free play of individual efforts.

"Both understand that we are entering upon a new historic phase.

"One wishes that there should be none but proletaires.

"The other wishes that there should be no more proletaires.

"The first wishes to take everything from everybody.

"The second wishes to leave each in possession of its own.

"The one wishes to expropriate everybody.

"The other wishes everybody to be a proprietor.

"The first says: 'Do as the government wishes.'

"The second says: 'Do as you wish yourself.'

"The former threatens with despotism.

"The latter promises liberty.

"The former makes the citizen the subject of the State.

"The latter makes the State the employee of the citizen.

"One proclaims that labor pains will be necessary to the birth of the new world.

"The other declares that real progress will not cause suffering to any one.

"The first has confidence in social war.

"The other believes only in the works of peace.

"One aspires to command, to regulate, to legislate.

"The other wishes to attain the minimum of command, of regulation, of legislation.

"One would be followed by the most atrocious of reactions.

"The other opens unlimited horizons to progress.

"The first will fail; the other will succeed.

"Both desire equality.

"One by lowering heads that are too high.

"The other by raising heads that are too low.

"One sees equality under a common yoke.

"The other will secure equality in complete liberty.

"One is intolerant, the other tolerant.

"One frightens, the other reassures.

"The first wishes to instruct everybody.

"The second wishes to enable everybody to instruct himself.

"The first wishes to support everybody.

"The second wishes to enable everybody to support himself.

"One says:

"The land to the State.

"The mine to the State.

"The tool to the State.

"The product to the State.

"The other says:

"The land to the cultivator.

"The mine to the miner.

"The tool to the laborer.

"The product to the producer.

"There are only these two Socialisms.

"One is the infancy of Socialism; the other in its manhood.

"One is already the past; the other is the future.

"One will give place to the other.

"To-day each of us must choose for one or the other of these two Socialisms, or else confess that he is not a Socialist."

POSTSCRIPT

Forty years ago, when the foregoing essay was written, the denial of competition had not yet effected the enormous concentration of wealth that now so gravely threatens social order. It was not yet too late to stem the current of accumulation by a reversal of the policy of monopoly. The Anarchistic remedy was still applicable.

Today the way is not so clear. The four monopolies, unhindered, have made possible the modern development of the trust, and the trust is now a monster which, I fear, even the freest banking, could it be instituted, would be unable to destroy. As long as the Standard Oil group controlled only fifty millions of dollars, the institution of free competition would have crippled it hopelessly; it needed the money monopoly for its sustenance and its growth. Now that it controls, directly and indirectly, perhaps ten thousand millions, it sees in the money monopoly a convenience, to be sure, but no longer a necessity. It can do without it. Were all restrictions upon banking to be removed, concentrated capital could meet successfully the new situation by setting aside annually for sacrifice a sum that would remove every competitor from the field.

If this be true, then monopoly, which can be controlled permanently only by economic forces, has passed for the moment beyond their reach, and must be grappled with for a time solely by forces political or revolutionary. Until measures of forcible confiscation, through the State or in defiance of it, shall have abolished the concentrations that monopoly has created, the economic solution proposed by Anarchism and outlined in the foregoing pages—*and there is no other solution*—will remain a thing to be taught to the rising generation, that conditions may be favorable to its application after the great levelling. But education is a slow process, and for this reason we must hope that the day of readjustment may not come too quickly. Anarchists who endeavor to hasten it by joining in the propaganda of State Socialism or revolution make a sad mistake indeed. They help to so force the march of events that the people will not have time to find out, by the study of their experience, that their troubles have been due to the rejection of competition. If this lesson shall not be learned in season, the past will be repeated in the future, in which case we shall have to turn for consolation to the doctrine of Nietzsche that this is bound to happen anyhow, or to the reflection of Renan that, from the point of view of Sirius, all these matters are of little moment.

B. R. T.

August 11, 1926.

The foregoing postscript was originally written in 1911. Today Mr. Tucker sees fit to modify it to its present form, which makes it unavoidably imply that the abolition of *all four* of the great monopolies could even now loosen the grip of capitalism. His statement amounts to the prediction that the inauguration of free banking, which Individualist Anarchists commonly anticipate as the first step in the realization of freedom, would not alone achieve that result. But it should be recorded that the editor of this book, and those other adherents to the ideas set forth in it, who by their advice and otherwise have aided him in the task, do not share Mr. Tucker's pessimism. Unlike him, they have been in intimate contact with the industrial and commercial life of the United States for the past two decades and have therefore been able to observe that the trend of events is not now inevitably toward either State confiscation or revolution. The enormous strides made by voluntary association, especially among those opposed to the domination of capitalism, point the way clearly to the peaceful elimination of the financial oligarchy which now rules the nation.—The Editor.

II—THE INDIVIDUAL, SOCIETY, AND THE STATE

THE RELATION OF THE STATE TO THE INDIVIDUAL

The following is an address by Mr. Tucker delivered before the Unitarian Ministers' Institute, at the annual session held in Salem, Mass., October 14, 1890. On account of the clear and concise manner in which the subject is treated, it may well engage the attention of any student seeking to understand Anarchism:

LADIES AND GENTLEMEN:—Presumably the honor which you have done me in inviting me to address you to-day upon "The Relation of the State to the Individual" is due principally to the fact that circumstances have combined to make me somewhat conspicuous as an exponent of the theory of Modern Anarchism,—a theory which is coming to be more and more regarded as one of the few that are tenable as a basis of political and social life. In its name, then, I shall speak to you in discussing this question, which either underlies or closely touches almost every practical problem that confronts this generation. The future of the tariff, of taxation, of finance, of property, of woman, of marriage, of the family, of the suffrage, of education, of invention, of literature, of science, of the arts, of personal habits, of private character, of ethics, of religion, will be determined by the conclusion at which mankind shall arrive as to whether and how far the individual owes allegiance to the State.

Anarchism, in dealing with this subject, has found it necessary, first of all, to define its terms. Popular conceptions of the terminology of politics are incompatible with the rigorous exactness required in scientific investigation. To be sure, a departure from the popular use of language is accompanied by the risk of misconception by the multitude, who persistently ignore the new definitions; but, on the other hand, conformity thereto is attended by the still more deplorable alternative of confusion in the eyes of the competent, who would be justified in attributing inexactness of thought where there is inexactness of expression. Take the term "State," for instance, with which we are especially concerned to-day. It is a word that is on every lip. But how many of those who use it have any idea of what they mean by it? And, of the few who have, how various are their conceptions! We designate by the term "State" institutions that embody absolutism in its extreme form and institutions that temper it with more or less liberality. We apply the word alike to institutions that do nothing but aggress and to institutions that, besides aggressing, to some extent protect and defend. But which is the State's essential function, aggression or defence, few seem to know or care. Some champions of the State evidently consider aggression its principle, although they disguise it alike from themselves and from the people under the term "administration," which they wish to extend in every possible direction. Others, on the contrary, consider defence its principle, and wish to limit it accordingly to the performance of police duties. Still others seem to think that it exists for both aggression and defence, combined in varying proportions according to the momentary interests, or maybe only whims, of those happening to control it. Brought face to face with these diverse views, the Anarchists, whose mission in the world is the abolition of aggression and all the evils that result therefrom, perceived that, to be understood, they must attach some definite and avowed significance to the terms which they are obliged to employ, and especially to the words "State" and "government." Seeking, then, the elements common to all the institutions to which the name "State" has been applied, they have found them two in number: first, agression; second, the assumption of sole authority over a given area and all within it, exercised generally for the double purpose of more complete oppression of its subjects and extension of its boundaries. That this second element is common to all States, I think, will not be denied,—at least, I am not aware that any State has ever tolerated a rival State within its borders; and it seems plain that any State which should do so would thereby cease to be a State and to be considered as such by any. The exercise of authority over the same area by two States is a contradiction. That the first element, aggression, has been and is common to all States will probably be less generally admitted. Nevertheless, I shall not attempt to re-enforce here the conclusion of Spencer, which is gaining wider acceptance daily,—that the State had its origin in aggression, and has continued as an aggressive institution from its birth. Defence was an afterthought, prompted by necessity; and its introduction as a State function, though effected doubtless with a view to the strengthening of the State, was really and in principle the initiation of the State's destruction. Its growth in importance is but an evidence of the tendency of progress toward the abolition of the State. Taking this view of the matter, the Anarchists contend that defence is not an essential of the State, but that aggression is. Now what is aggression? Aggression is simply another name for government. Aggression, invasion, government, are interconvertible terms. The essence of government is control, or the attempt to control. He who attempts to control another is a governor, an aggressor, an invader; and the nature of such invasion is not changed, whether it is made by one man upon another man, after the manner of the ordinary criminal, or by one man upon all other men, after the manner of an absolute monarch, or by all other men upon one man, after the manner of a modern democracy. On the other hand, he who resists another's attempt to control is not an aggressor, an invader, a governor, but simply a defender, a protector; and the nature of such resistance is not changed whether it be offered by one man to another man, as when one repels a criminal's onslaught, or by one man to all other men, as when one declines to obey an oppressive law, or by all men to one man, as when a subject people rises against a despot, or as when the members of a community voluntarily unite to restrain a criminal. This distinction between invasion and resistance, between government and defence, is vital. Without it there can be no valid philosophy of politics. Upon this distinction and the other considerations just outlined, the Anarchists frame the desired definitions. This, then, is the Anarchistic definition of government: the subjection of the non-invasive individual to an external will. And this is the Anarchistic definition of the State: the embodiment of the principle of invasion in an individual, or a band of individuals, assuming to act as representatives or masters of the entire people within a given area. As to the meaning of the remaining term in the subject under discussion, the word "individual," I think there is little difficulty. Putting aside the subtleties in which certain metaphysicians have indulged, one may use this word without danger of being misunderstood. Whether the definitions thus arrived at prove generally acceptable or not is a matter of minor consequence. I submit that they are reached scientifically, and serve the purpose of a clear conveyance of thought. The Anarchists, having by their adoption taken due care to be explicit, are entitled to have their ideas judged in the light of these definitions.

Now comes the question proper: What relations should exist between the State and the Individual? The general method of determining these is to apply some theory of ethics involving a basis of moral obligation. In this method the Anarchists have no confidence. The idea of moral obligation, of inherent rights and duties, they totally discard. They look upon all obligations, not as moral, but as social, and even then not really as obligations except as these have been consciously and voluntarily assumed. If a man makes an agreement with men, the latter may combine to hold him to his agreement; but, in the absence of such agreement, no man, so far as the Anarchists are aware, has made any agreement with God or with any other power of any order whatsoever. The Anarchists are not only utilitarians, but egoists in the farthest and fullest sense. So far as inherent right is concerned, might is its only measure. Any man, be his name Bill Sykes or Alexander Romanoff, and any set of men, whether the Chinese highbinders or the Congress of the United States, have the right, if they have the power, to kill or coerce other men and to make the entire world subservient to their ends. Society's right to enslave the individual and the individual's right to enslave society are unequal only because their powers are unequal. This position being subversive of all systems of religion and morality, of course I cannot expect to win immediate assent thereto from the audience which I am addressing to-day; nor does the time at my disposal allow me to sustain it by an elaborate, or even a summary, examination of the foundations of ethics. Those who desire a greater familiarity with this particular phase of the subject should read a profound German work, "Der Einzige und sein Eigenthum," written years ago by a comparatively unknown author, Dr. Caspar Schmidt, whose *nom de plume* was Max Stirner. Read only by a few scholars, the book is buried in obscurity, but is destined to a resurrection that perhaps will mark an epoch.

If this, then, were a question of right, it would be, according to the Anarchists, purely a question of strength. But, fortunately, it is not a question of right: it is a question of expediency, of knowledge, of science,—the science of living together, the science of society. The history of humanity has been largely one long and gradual discovery of the fact that the individual is the gainer by society exactly in proportion as society is free, and of the law that the condition of a permanent and harmonious society is the greatest amount of individual liberty compatible with equality of liberty. The average man of each new generation has said to himself more clearly and consciously than his predecessor: "My neighbor is not my enemy, but my friend, and I am his, if we would but mutually recognize the fact. We help each other to a better, fuller, happier living; and this service might be greatly increased if we would cease to restrict, hamper, and oppress each other. Why can we not agree to let each live his own life, neither of us transgressing the limit that separates our individualities?" It is by this reasoning that mankind is approaching the real social contract, which is not, as Rousseau thought, the origin of society, but rather the outcome of a long social experience, the fruit of its follies and disasters. It is obvious that this contract, this social law, developed to its perfection, excludes all aggression, all violation of equality of liberty, all invasion of every kind. Considering this contract in connection with the Anarchistic definition of the State as the embodiment of the principle of invasion, we see that the State is antagonistic to society; and, society being essential to individual life and development, the conclusion leaps to the eyes that the relation of the State to the individual and of the individual to the State must be one of hostility, enduring till the State shall perish.

"But," it will be asked of the Anarchists at this point in the argument, "what shall be done with those individuals who undoubtedly will persist in violating the social law by invading their neighbors?" The Anarchists answer that the abolition of the State will leave in existence a defensive association, resting no longer on a compulsory but on a voluntary basis, which will restrain invaders by any means that may prove necessary. "But that is what we have now," is the rejoinder. "You really want, then, only a change of name?" Not so fast, please. Can it be soberly pretended for a moment that the State, even as it exists here in America, is purely a defensive institution? Surely not, save by those who see of the State only its most palpable manifestation,—the policeman on the street-corner. And one would not have to watch him very closely to see the error of this claim. Why, the very first act of the State, the compulsory assessment and collection of taxes, is itself an aggression, a violation of equal liberty, and, as such, vitiates every subsequent act, even those acts which would be purely defensive if paid out of a treasury filled by voluntary contributions. How is it possible to sanction, under the law of equal liberty, the confiscation of a man's earnings to pay for protection which he has not sought and does not desire? And, if this is an outrage, what name shall we give to such confiscation when the victim is given, instead of bread, a stone, instead of protection, oppression? To force a man to pay for the violation of his own liberty is indeed an addition of insult to injury. But that is exactly what the State is doing. Read the "Congressional Record"; follow the proceedings of the State legislatures; examine our statute-books; test each act separately by the law of equal liberty,—you will find that a good nine-tenths of existing legislation serves, not to enforce that fundamental social law, but either to prescribe the individual's personal habits, or, worse still, to create and sustain commercial, industrial, financial, and proprietary monopolies which deprive labor of a large part of the reward that it would receive in a perfectly free market. "To be governed," says Proudhon, "is to be watched, inspected, spied, directed, law-ridden, regulated, penned up, indoctrinated, preached at, checked, appraised, sized, censured, commanded, by beings who have neither title nor knowledge nor virtue. To be governed is to have every operation, every transaction every movement noted, registered, counted, rated, stamped, measured, numbered, assessed, licensed, refused, authorized, indorsed, admonished, prevented, reformed, redressed, corrected. To be governed is, under pretext of public utility and in the name of the general interest, to be laid under contribution, drilled, fleeced, exploited, monopolized, extorted from, exhausted, hoaxed, robbed; then, upon the slightest resistance, at the first word of complaint, to be repressed, fined, vilified, annoyed, hunted down, pulled about, beaten, disarmed, bound, imprisoned, shot, mitrailleused, judged, condemned, banished, sacrificed, sold, betrayed, and, to crown all, ridiculed, derided, outraged, dishonored." And I am sure I do not need to point out to you the existing laws that correspond to and justify nearly every count in Proudhon's long indictment. How thoughtless, then, to assert that the existing political order is of a purely defensive character instead of the aggressive State which the Anarchists aim to abolish!

This leads to another consideration that bears powerfully upon the problem of the invasive individual, who is such a bugbear to the opponents of Anarchism. Is it not such treatment as has just been described that is largely responsible for his existence? I have heard or read somewhere of an inscription written for a certain charitable institution:

> "This hospital a pious person built,
> But first he made the poor wherewith to fill't."

And so, it seems to me, it is with our prisons. They are filled with criminals which our virtuous State has made what they are by its iniquitous laws, its grinding monopolies, and the horrible social conditions that result from them. We enact many laws that manufacture criminals, and then a few that punish them. Is it too much to expect that the new social conditions which must follow the abolition of all interference with the production and distribution of wealth will in the end so change the habits and propensities of men that our jails and prisons, our policemen and our soldiers,—in a word, our whole machinery and outfit of defence,—will be superfluous? That, at least, is the Anarchists' belief. It sounds Utopian, but it really rests on severely economic grounds. To-day, however, time is lacking to explain the Anarchistic view of the dependence of usury, and therefore of poverty, upon monopolistic privilege, especially the banking privilege, and to show how an intelligent minority, educated in the principle of Anarchism and determined to exercise that right to ignore the State upon which Spencer, in his "Social Statics," so ably and admirably insists, might, by setting at defiance the National and State banking prohibitions, and establishing a Mutual Bank in competition with the existing monopolies, take the first and most important step in the abolition of usury and of the State. Simple as such a step would seem, from it all the rest would follow.

A half-hour is a very short time in which to discuss the relation of the State to the individual, and I must ask your pardon for the brevity of my dealing with a succession of considerations each of which needs an entire essay for its development. If I have outlined the argument intelligibly, I have accomplished all that I expected. But, in the hope of impressing the idea of the true social contract more vividly upon your minds, in conclusion I shall take the liberty of reading another page from Proudhon, to whom I am indebted for most of what I know, or think I know, upon this subject. Contrasting authority with free contract, he says, in his "General Idea of the Revolution of the Nineteenth Century":—

"Of the distance that separates these two *régimes*, we may judge by the difference in their styles.

"One of the most solemn moments in the evolution of the principle of authority is that of the promulgation of the Decalogue. The voice of the angel commands the People, prostrate at the foot of Sinai:—

"Thou shalt worship the Eternal, and only the Eternal.

"Thou shalt swear only by him.

"Thou shalt keep his holidays, and thou shalt pay his tithes.

"Thou shalt honor thy father and thy mother.

"Thou shalt not kill.

"Thou shalt not steal.

"Thou shalt not commit adultery.

"Thou shalt not bear false witness.

"Thou shalt not covet or calumniate.

"For the Eternal ordains it, and it is the Eternal who has made you what you are. The Eternal is alone sovereign, alone wise, alone worthy; the Eternal punishes and rewards. It is in the power of the Eternal to render you happy or unhappy at his will.

"All legislations have adopted this style; all, speaking to man, employ the sovereign formula. The Hebrew commands in the future, the Latin in the imperative, the Greek in the infinitive. The moderns do not otherwise. The tribune of the parliament-house is a Sinai as infallible and as terrible as that of Moses; whatever the law may be, from whatever lips it may come, it is sacred once it has been proclaimed by that prophetic trumpet, which with us is the majority.

"Thou shalt not assemble.

"Thou shalt not print.

"Thou shalt not read.

"Thou shalt respect thy representatives and thy officials, which the hazard of the ballot or the good pleasure of the State shall have given you.

"Thou shalt obey the laws which they in their wisdom shall have made.

"Thou shalt pay thy taxes faithfully.

"And thou shalt love the Government, thy Lord and thy God, with all thy heart and with all thy soul and with all thy mind, because the Government knows better than thou what thou art, what thou art worth, what is good for thee, and because it has the power to chastise those who disobey its commandments, as well as to reward unto the fourth generation those who make themselves agreeable to it.

"With the Revolution it is quite different.

"The search for first causes and for final causes is eliminated from economic science as from the natural sciences.

"The idea of Progress replaces, in philosophy, that of the Absolute.

"Revolution succeeds Revelation.

"Reason, assisted by Experience, discloses to man the laws of Nature and Society; then it says to him:—

"These laws are those of necessity itself. No man has made them; no man imposes them upon you. They have been gradually discovered, and I exist only to bear testimony to them.

"If you observe them, you will be just and good.

"If you violate them, you will be unjust and wicked.

"I offer you no other motive.

"Already, among your fellows, several have recognized that justice is better, for each and for all, than iniquity; and they have agreed with each other to mutually keep faith and right, —that is, to respect the rules of transaction which the nature of things indicates to them as alone capable of assuring them, in the largest measure, well-being, security, peace.

"Do you wish to adhere to their compact, to form a part of their society?

"Do you promise to respect the honor, the liberty, and the goods of your brothers?

"Do you promise never to appropriate, either by violence, or by fraud, or by usury, or by speculation, the product or the possession of another?

"Do you promise never to lie and deceive, either in justice, or in business, or in any of your transactions?

"You are free to accept or to refuse.

"If you refuse, you become a part of the society of savages. Outside of the communion of the human race, you become an object of suspicion. Nothing protects you. At the slightest insult, the first comer may lift his hand against you without incurring any other accusation than that of cruelty needlessly practiced upon a brute.

"On the contrary, if you swear to the compact, you become a part of the society of free men. All your brothers enter into an engagement with you, promise you fidelity, friendship, aid, service, exchange. In case of infraction, on their part or on yours, through negligence, passion, or malice, you are responsible to each other for the damage as well as the scandal and the insecurity of which you have been the cause: this responsibility may extend, according to the gravity of the perjury or the repetitions of the offence, even to excommunication and to death.

"The law is clear, the sanction still more so. Three articles, which make but one,—that is the whole social contract. Instead of making oath to God and his prince, the citizen swears upon his conscience, before his brothers, and before Humanity. Between these two oaths there is the same difference as between slavery and liberty, faith and science, courts and justice, usury and labor, government and economy, non-existence and being, God and man."

LIBERTY'S DECLARATION OF PURPOSE

Volume I, No. 1, of *Liberty* appeared on August 6, 1881, and here is its salutatory:

LIBERTY enters the field of journalism to speak for herself because she finds no one willing to speak for her. She hears no voice that always champions her; she knows no pen that always writes in her defence; she sees no hand that is always lifted to avenge her wrongs or vindicate her rights. Many claim to speak in her name, but few really understand her. Still fewer have the courage and the opportunity to consistently fight for her. Her battle, then, is her own, to wage and win. She accepts it fearlessly and with a determined spirit.

Her foe, Authority, takes many shapes, but, broadly speaking, her enemies divide themselves into three classes: first, those who abhor her both as a means and as an end of progress, opposing her openly, avowedly, sincerely, consistently, universally; second, those who profess to believe in her as a means of progress, but who accept her only so far as they think she will subserve their own selfish interests, denying her and her blessings to the rest of the world; third, those who distrust her as a means of progress, believing in her only as an end to be obtained by first trampling upon, violating, and outraging her. These three phases of opposition to Liberty are met in almost every sphere of thought and human activity. Good representatives of the first are seen in the Catholic Church and the Russian autocracy; of the second, in the Protestant Church and the Manchester school of politics and political economy; of the third, in the atheism of Gambetta and the socialism of Karl Marx.

Through these forms of authority another line of demarcation runs transversely, separating the divine from the human;

or better still, the religious from the secular. Liberty's victory over the former is well-nigh achieved. Last century Voltaire brought the authority of the supernatural into disrepute. The Church has been declining ever since. Her teeth are drawn, and though she seems still to show here and there vigorous signs of life, she does so in the violence of the death-agony upon her, and soon her power will be felt no more. It is human authority that hereafter is to be dreaded, and the State, its organ, that in the future is to be feared. Those who have lost their faith in gods only to put it in governments; those who have ceased to be Church-worshippers only to become State-worshippers; those who have abandoned pope for king or czar, and priest for president or parliament,—have indeed changed their battle-ground, but none the less are foes of Liberty still. The Church has become an object of derision; the State must be made equally so. The State is said by some to be a "necessary evil"; it must be made unnecessary. This century's battle, then, is with the State: the State, that debases man; the State, that prostitutes woman; the State, that corrupts children; the State, that trammels love; the State, that stifles thought; the State, that monopolizes land; the State, that limits credit; the State, that restricts exchange; the State, that gives idle capital the power of increase, and, through interest, rent, profit, and taxes, robs industrious labor of its products.

How the State does these things, and how it can be prevented from doing them, Liberty proposes to show in more detail hereafter in the prosecution of her purpose. Enough to say now that monopoly and privilege must be destroyed, opportunity afforded, and competition encouraged. This is Liberty's work, and "Down with Authority" her war-cry.

ANARCHISM AND THE STATE

Mr. Henry Appleton, one of *Liberty's* original editorial contributors, was obliged to cease to act in that capacity when he took a position not in harmony with that of the editor on a point of great importance, whereat he later complained, and tried to explain his view of the controversy.   In answering him Mr. Tucker dealt with some essential questions of principle:

I DO NOT admit anything except the existence of the individual, as a condition of his sovereignty.   To say that the sovereignty of the individual is conditioned by *Liberty* is simply another way of saying that it is conditioned by itself. To condition it by the cost principle is equivalent to instituting the cost principle by authority,—an attempted fusion of Anarchism with State Socialism which I have always understood Mr. Appleton to rebel against.

It is true that the affirmation of individual sovereignty is *logically* precedent to protest against authority as such.   But in practice they are inseparable.   To protest against the invasion of individual sovereignty is necessarily to affirm individual sovereignty.   The Anarchist always carries his base of supplies with him.   He cannot fight away from it.   The moment he does so he becomes an Archist.   This protest contains all the affirmation that there is.   As I have pointed out to Comrade Lloyd, Anarchy has no side that is affirmative in the sense of constructive.   Neither as Anarchists nor—what is practically the same thing—as individual sovereigns have we any constructive work to do, though as progressive beings we have plenty of it.   But, if we had perfect liberty, we might, if we chose, remain utterly inactive and still be individual sovereigns.   Mr. Appleton's unenviable experiences are due to no mistake of mine, but to his own folly in acknowledging the pertinence of the hackneyed cry for construction, which loses none of its nonsense on the lips of a Circuit Court Judge.

I base my assertion that the Chicago Communists are not Anarchists entirely on the ground that Anarchism means a protest against every form of invasion.   (Whether this definition is etymologically correct I will show in the next paragraph.)   Those who protest against the existing political State, with emphasis on the *existing*, are not Anarchists, but Archists.   In objecting to a special form or method of invasion, they tacitly acknowledge the rightfulness of some other form or method of invasion.   Proudhon never fought any particular State; he fought the institution itself, as necessarily negative of individual sovereignty, whatever form it may take. His use of the word Anarchism shows that he considered it coextensive with individual sovereignty. If his applications of it were directed against political government, it was because he considered political government the only invader of individual sovereignty worth talking about, having no knowledge of Mr. Appleton's "comprehensive philosophy," which thinks it takes cognizance of a "vast mountain of government outside of the organized State." The reason why Most and Parsons are not Anarchists, while I am one, is because their Communism is another State, while my voluntary co-operation is not a State at all. It is a very easy matter to tell who is an Anarchist and who is not. One question will always readily decide it. Do you believe in any form of imposition upon the human will by force? If you do, you are not an Anarchist. If you do not, you are an Anarchist. What can any one ask more reliable, more scientific, than this?

Anarchy does not mean simply opposed to the *archos*, or political leader. It means opposed to *archē*. Now, *archē*, in the first instance, means *beginning, origin*. From this it comes to mean *a first principle, an element;* then *first place, supreme power, sovereignty, dominion, command, authority;* and finally *a sovereignty, an empire, a realm, a magistracy, a governmental office*. Etymologically, then, the word anarchy may have several meanings, among them, as Mr. Appleton says, *without guiding principle*, and to this use of the word I have never objected, always striving, on the contrary, to interpret in accordance with their definition the thought of those who so use it. But the word Anarchy as a philosophical term and the word Anarchist as the name of a philosophical sect were first appropriated in the sense of opposition to dominion, to authority, and are so held by right of occupancy, which fact makes any other philosophical use of them improper and confusing. Therefore, as Mr. Appleton does not make the political sphere coextensive with dominion or authority, he cannot claim that Anarchy, when extended beyond the political sphere, necessarily comes to mean *without guiding principle*, for it may mean, and by appropriation does mean, *without dominion, without authority*. Consequently it is a term which completely and scientifically covers the individualistic protest.

I could scarcely name a word that has been more abused, misunderstood, and misinterpreted than Individualism. Mr. Appleton makes so palpable a point against himself in instancing the Protestant sects that it is really laughable to see him try to use it against me. However it may be with the Protestant sects, the one great Protestant body itself was born of protest, suckled by protest, *named after protest*, and lived on protest until the days of its usefulness were over. If such instances proved anything, plenty of them might be cited against Mr. Appleton. For example, taking one of more recent date, I might pertinently inquire which contributed most to the freedom of the negro,—those who defined themselves through their affirmations as the Liberty Party or as Colonizationists, or those who defined themselves through their protests as the Anti-Slavery Society or as Abolitionists. Unquestionably the latter. And when human slavery in all its forms shall have disappeared, I fancy that the credit of the victory will be given quite as exclusively to the Anarchists, and that these latter-day Colonizationists, of whom Mr. Appleton has suddenly become so enamored, will be held as innocent of its overthrow as are their predecessors and namesakes of the overthrow of chattel slavery.

It is to be regretted that Mr. Appleton took up so much space with other matters that he could not turn his "flood of light" into my "delusion" that the State is the efficient cause of tyranny over individuals; for the question whether this is a delusion or not is the very heart of the issue between us. He has asserted that there is a vast mountain of government outside of the organized State, and that our chief battle is with that; I, on the contrary, have maintained that practically almost all the authority against which we have to contend is exercised by the State, and that, when we have abolished the State, the struggle for individual sovereignty will be well-nigh over. I have shown that Mr. Appleton, to maintain his position, must point out this vast mountain of government and tell us definitely what it is and how it acts, and this is what the readers of *Liberty* have been waiting to see him do. But he no more does it in his last article than in his first. And his only attempt to dispute my statement that the State is the *efficient* cause of tyranny over individuals is confined to two or three sentences which culminate in the conclusion that the *initial* cause is the surrendering individual. I have never denied it, and am charmed by the air of innocence with which this substitution of *initial* for *efficient* is effected. Of initial causes finite intelligence knows nothing; it can only know causes as more or less remote. But using the word initial in the sense of remoter, I am willing to admit, for the sake of the argument (though it is not a settled matter), that the initial cause was the surrendering individual. Mr. Appleton doubtless means voluntarily surrendering individual, for compulsory surrender would imply the prior existence of a power to exact it, or a primitive form of State. But the State, having come into existence through such voluntary surrender, becomes a positive, strong, growing, encroaching institution, which expands, not by further voluntary surrenders, but by exacting surrenders from its individual subjects, and which contracts only as they successfully rebel. That, at any rate, is what it is to-day, and hence it is the *efficient* cause of tyranny. The only sense, then, in which it is true that "the individual is the proper objective point of reform" is this,—that he must be penetrated with the Anarchistic idea and taught to rebel. But this is not what Mr. Appleton means. If it were, his criticism would not be pertinent, for I have never advocated any other method of abolishing the State. The logic of his position compels another interpretation of his words,—namely that the State cannot disappear until the individual is perfected. In saying which, Mr. Appleton joins hands with those wise persons who admit that Anarchy will be practicable when the millennium arrives. It is an utter abandonment of Anarchistic Socialism. No doubt it is true that, if the individual could perfect himself while the barriers to his perfection are standing, the State would afterwards disappear. Perhaps, too, he could go to heaven, if he could lift himself by his boot-straps.

If one must favor colonization, or localization, as Mr. Appleton calls it, as a result of looking "seriously" into these matters, then he must have been trifling with them for a long time. He has combated colonization in these columns more vigorously than ever I did or can, and not until comparatively lately did he write anything seeming to favor it. Even then he declared that he was not given over to the idea, and seemed only to be making a tentative venture into a region which he had not before explored. If he has since become a settler, it only indicates to my mind that he has not yet fathomed the real cause of the people's wretchedness. That cause is State interference with natural economic processes. The people are poor and robbed and enslaved, not because "industry, commerce, and domicile are centralized,"—in fact, such centralization has, on the whole, greatly benefited them,—but because the control of the conditions under which industry, commerce, and domicile are exercised and enjoyed is centralized. The localization needed is not the localization of persons in space, but of powers in persons,—that is, the restriction of power to self and the abolition of power over others. Government makes itself felt alike in country and in city, capital has its usurious grip on the farm as surely as on the workshop, and the oppressions and exactions of neither government nor capital can be avoided by migration. The State is the enemy, and the best means of fighting it can only be found in communities already existing. If there were no other reason for opposing colonization, this in itself would be sufficient.

RESISTANCE TO GOVERNMENT

In 1888 Mr. John Beverley Robinson (who just before his death in 1923 translated Proudhon's "General Idea of the Revolution in the Nineteenth Century," published by Freedom Press, London) entered into a discussion with the editor of *Liberty* on the question of non-resistance, which enabled Mr. Tucker to make clear the attitude of Anarchism toward aggression and in its manner of treating aggressors:

MR. ROBINSON says that the essence of government is compulsion by violence. If it is, then of course Anarchists, always opposing government, must always oppose violence. But Anarchists do not so define government. To them the essence of government is invasion. From the standpoint of this definition, why should Anarchists, protesting against invasion and determined not to be invaded, not use violence against it, provided at any time violence shall seem the most effective method of putting a stop to it?

But it is not the most effective method, insists Mr. Robinson; "it does not accomplish its purpose." Ah, here we are on quite another ground. The claim no longer is that it is necessarily un-Anarchistic to use violence, but that other influences than violence are more potent to overcome invasion. Exactly; that is the gospel which *Liberty* has always preached. I have never said anything to the contrary, and Mr. Robinson's criticism, so far as it lies in this direction, seems to me *mal à propos*. His article is prompted by my answers to Mr. Blodgett in No. 115. Mr. Blodgett's questions were not as to what Anarchists would find it best to do, but as to what their Anarchistic doctrine logically binds them to do and avoid doing. I confined my attention strictly to the matter in hand, omitting extraneous matters. Mr. Robinson is not justified in drawing inferences from my omissions, especially inferences that are antagonistic to my definite assertions at other times.

Perhaps he will answer me, however, that there are certain circumstances under which I think violence advisable. Granted; but, according to his article, so does he. These circumstances, however, he distinguishes from the social state as a state of warfare. But so do I. The question comes up of what you are to do when a man makes war upon you. Ward him off, says Mr. Robinson, but do not attack him in turn to prevent a repetition of his attack. As a general policy, I agree; as a rule without exceptions, I dissent. Suppose a man tries to knock me down. I will parry his blows for a while, meanwhile trying to dissuade him from his purpose. But suppose he does not desist, and I have to take a train to reach the bedside of my dying child. I straightway knock him down and take the train. And if afterwards he repeats his attack again and again, and thereby continually takes my time away from the business of my life, I put him out of my way, in the most decent manner possible, but summarily and forever. In other words, it is folly for people who desire to live in society to put up with the invasions of the incorrigible. Which does not alter the fact that with the corrigible it is not only good policy, but in accordance with the sentiments of highly-developed human beings, to be as gentle and kind as possible.

To describe such dealing with the incorrigible as the exercise of "our liberty to compel others" denotes an utter misconception. It is simply the exercise of our liberty to keep others from compelling us.

But who is to judge where invasion begins? asks Mr. Robinson. Each for himself, and those to combine who agree, I answer. It will be perpetual war, then? Not at all; a war of short duration, at the worst. I am well aware that there is a border-land between legitimate and invasive conduct over which there must be for a time more or less trouble. But it is an ever-decreasing margin. It has been narrowing ever since the idea of equal liberty first dawned upon the mind of man, and in proportion as this idea becomes clearer and the new social conditions which it involves become real will it contract towards the geometrical conception of a line. And then the world will be at peace. Meanwhile, if the pick-pocket continues his objectionable business, it will not be because of any such reasoning as Mr. Robinson puts into his mouth. He may so reason, but as a matter of fact he never does. Or, if he does, he is an exceptional pick-pocket. The normal pick-pocket has no idea of equal liberty. Whenever the idea dawns upon him, he will begin to feel a desire for its realization and to acquire a knowledge of what equal liberty is. Then he will see that it is exclusive of pocket-picking. And so with the people who hanged the Chicago martyrs. I have never blamed them in the usual sense of the word blame. I charge them with committing gross outrage upon the principle of equal liberty, but not with knowing what they did. When they become Anarchists, they will realize what they did, and will do so no more. To this end my comrades and I are trying to enlighten them concerning the principle of equal liberty. But we shall fail if we obscure the principle by denying or concealing the lengths to which, in case of need, it allows us to go lest people of tender sensibilities may infer that we are in favor of always going to such lengths, regardless of circumstances.

While I should like to see the line between liberty and aggression drawn with scientific exactness, I cannot admit that such rigor of definition is essential to the realization of Anarchism. If, in spite of the lack of such a definition, the history of liberty has been, as Mr. Robinson truly says, "a record of the continual widening of this limit," there is no reason why this widening process should not go on until Anarchy becomes a fact. It is perfectly thinkable that, after the last inch of debatable ground shall have been adjudged to one side or the other, it may still be found impossible to scientifically formulate the rule by which this decision and its predecessors were arrived at.

The chief influence in narrowing the strip of debatable land is not so much the increasing exactness of the knowledge of what constitutes aggression as the growing conception that aggression is an evil to be avoided and that liberty is the condition of progress. The moment one abandons the idea that he was born to discover what is right and enforce it upon the rest of the world, he begins to feel an increasing disposition to let others alone and to refrain even from retaliation or resistance except in those emergencies which immediately and imperatively require it. This remains true even if aggression be defined in the extremely broad sense of the infliction of pain; for the individual who traces the connection between liberty and the general welfare will be pained by few things so much as by the consciousness that his neighbors are curtailing their liberties out of consideration for his feelings, and such a man will never say to his neighbors, "Thus far and no farther," until they commit acts of direct and indubitable interference and trespass. The man who feels more pained at seeing his neighbor bathe naked than he would at the knowledge that he refrained from doing so in spite of his preference is invariably the man who believes in aggression and government as the basis of society and has not learned the lesson that "liberty is the mother of order."

This lesson, then, rather than an exact definition of aggression, is the essential condition of the development of Anarchism. Liberty has steadily taught this lesson, but has never professed an ability to define aggression, except in a very general way. We must trust to experience and the conclusions therefrom for the settlement of all doubtful cases.

As for States and Churches, I think there is more foundation than Mr. Robinson sees for the claim that they are conspiracies. Not that I fail to realize as fully as he that there are many good men in both whose intent is not at all to oppress or aggress. Doubtless there are many good and earnest priests whose sole aim is to teach religious truth as they see it and elevate human life, but has not Dr. McGlynn conclusively shown that the real power of control in the Church is always vested in an unscrupulous machine? That the State originated in aggression Herbert Spencer has proved. If it now pretends to exist for purposes of defence, it is because the advance of sociology has made such a pretence necessary to its preservation. Mistaking this pretense for reality, many good men enlist in the work of the State. But the fact remains that the State exists mainly to do the will of capital and secure it all the privileges it demands, and I cannot see that the combinations of capitalists who employ lobbyists to buy legislators deserve any milder title than "conspirators," or that the term "conspiracy" inaccurately expresses the nature of their machine, the State.

I think it accurate to say that Anarchism contemplates anything and everything that does not contradict Anarchism. The writer whom *Liberty* criticised had virtually made it appear that police and jails do contradict Anarchism. *Liberty* simply denies this, and in that sense contemplates police and jails. Of course it does not contemplate the compulsory support of such institutions by non-invasive persons.

When I describe a man as an invader, I cast no reflection upon him; I simply state a fact. Nor do I assert for a moment the moral inferiority of the invader's desire. I only declare the impossibility of simultaneously gratifying the invader's desire to invade and my desire to be let alone. That these desires are morally equal I cheerfully admit, but they cannot be equally realized. Since one must be subordinated to the other, I naturally prefer the subordination of the invader's, and am ready to co-operate with non-invasive persons to achieve that result. I am not wedded to the term "justice," nor have I any objection to it. If Mr. Robinson doesn't like it, let us say "equal liberty" instead. Does he maintain that the use of force to secure equal liberty is precisely parallel to the use of force to destroy equal liberty? If so, I can only hope, for the sake of those who live in the houses which he builds, that his appreciation of an angle is keener in architecture than it is in sociology.

If the invader, instead of chaining me to a post, barricades the highway, do I any the less lose my liberty of locomotion? Yet he has ceased to be violent. We obtain liberty, not by the cessation of violence, but by the recognition, either voluntary or enforced, of equality of liberty.

We are to establish the contrary by persistent inculcation of the doctrine of equality of liberty, whereby finally the majority will be made to see in regard to existing forms of invasion what they have already been made to see in regard to its obsolete forms,—namely, that they are not seeking equality of liberty at all, but simply the subjection of all others to themselves. Our sense of what constitutes invasion has been acquired by experience. Additional experience is continually sharpening that sense. Though we still draw the line by rule of thumb, we are drawing it more clearly every day. It would be an advantage if we could frame a clear-cut generalization whereby to accelerate our progress. But though we have it not, we still progress.

Must I consent to be trampled upon simply because no contract has been made?

So the position of the non-resistant is that, when nobody attacks him, he won't resist. "We are all Socialists now," said some Englishman not long ago. Clearly we are all non-resistants now, according to Mr. Robinson. I know of no one who proposes to resist when he isn't attacked, of no one who proposes to enforce a contract which nobody desires to violate. I tell Mr. Robinson, as I have told Mr. Pentecost, that the believers in equal liberty ask nothing better than that all men should voluntarily act in accordance with the principle. But it is a melancholy fact that many men are not willing so to act. So far as our relations with such men are concerned, it is not a matter of contract, but of force. Shall we consent to be ruled, or shall we refuse to be ruled? If we consent, are we Anarchists? If we refuse, are we Archists? The whole question lies there, and Mr. Robinson fails to meet it.

The chief difference between passive resistance and non-resistance is this: passive resistance is regarded by its champions as a mere policy, while non-resistance is viewed by those who favor it as a principle or universal rule. Believers in passive resistance consider it as generally more effective than active resistance, but think that there are certain cases in which the opposite is true; believers in non-resistance consider either that it is immoral to actively resist or else that it is *always* unwise to do so.

Because violence, like every other policy, is advisable when it will accomplish the desired end and inadvisable when it will not.

Anarchism is philosophical, but it is not a system of philosophy. It is simply the fundamental principle in the science of political and social life. The believers in government are not as easily to be satisfied as Mr. Robinson thinks; and it is well that they are not. The considerations upon which he relies may convince them that government does not exist to suppress robbery, but will not convince them that abolition of the State will obviate the necessity of dealing violently with the other and more ordinary kinds of government of which common robbery is one. For, even though they be led to admit that the disappearance of the robber State must eventually induce the disappearance of all other robbers, they will remember that effects, however certain, are not always immediate, and that, pending the consummation, there are often serious difficulties that must be confronted.

If Mr. Robinson still maintains that doing violence to those who let us alone is precisely parallel to doing violence to those who assault us, I can only modestly hint once more that I have a better eye for an angle than he has.

As long as nearly all people are agreed in their identification of the great majority of actions as harmonious with or counter to equal liberty, and as long as an increasing number of people are extending this agreement in identification over a still larger field of conduct, the definition of invasion as the infringement of equal liberty, far from being vain, will remain an important factor in political progress.

It seems that there are cases in which, according to Mr. Robinson, we may resort to violence. It is now my turn to ask, Why? If he favors violence in one case, why not in all? I can see why, but not from his standpoint. For my part, I don't care a straw whether, when Mr. Robinson sees fit to use violence, he acts under protest or from principle. The main question is: Does he think it wise under some circumstances to use violence, or is he so much of a practical Archist that he would not save his child from otherwise inevitable murder by splitting open the murderer's head?

LIBERTY AND ORGANIZATION

Thirty-five years ago the *Personal Rights Journal* of London, at that time edited by J. H. Levy, was a valiant champion of what was then known as Individualism. This latter was practically Anarchism, but that fact was not realized by Levy, Wordsworth Donisthorpe and other contributors to the columns of the *Journal*, which led to discussions between those gentlemen and the editor of *Liberty* concerning Anarchism and organization, taxation, etc. Mr. Tucker's remarks are here set forth:

NAMES aside, the thing that Individualism favors is organization to maintain the widest liberty equally for all citizens. Well, that is precisely what Anarchism favors. Individualism does not want such organization any longer than is necessary. Neither does Anarchism. Mr. Levy's assumption that Anarchism does not want such organization at all arises from his failure to recognize the Anarchistic definition of government. Government has been defined repeatedly in these columns as the subjection of the *non-invasive* individual to a will not his own. The subjection of the *invasive* individual is not government, but resistance to and protection from government. By these definitions government is always an evil, but resistance to it is never an evil or a poison. Call such resistance an antidote if you will, but remember that not all antidotes are poisonous. The worst that can be said of resistance or protection is, not that it is an evil, but that it is a loss of productive force in a necessary effort to overcome evil. It can be called an evil only in the sense that needful and not especially healthful labor can be called a curse.

Government is invasion, and the State is the embodiment

of invasion in an individual, or band of individuals, assuming to act as representatives or masters of the entire people within a given area. The Anarchists are opposed to all government, and especially to the State as the worst governor and chief invader. From *Liberty's* standpoint, there are not three positions, but two: one, that of the authoritarian Socialists, favoring government and the State; the other, that of the Individualists *and* Anarchists, against government and the State.

I may add, in conclusion, that very probably the disposition of the Individualist to give greater prominence than does the Anarchist to the necessity of organization for protection is due to the fact that he seems to see less clearly than the Anarchist that the necessity for defence against individual invaders is largely and perhaps, in the end, wholly due to the oppressions of the invasive State, and that when the State falls, criminals will begin to disappear.

"Whatever else Anarchism may mean, it means that State coercion of peaceable citizens, into co-operation in restraining the activity of Bill Sikes, is to be condemned and ought to be abolished. Anarchism implies the right of an individual to stand aside and see a man murdered or a woman raped. It implies the right of the would-be passive accomplice of aggression to escape all coercion. It is true the Anarchist may voluntarily co-operate to check aggression; but also he may not. *Quâ* Anarchist, he is within his right in withholding such co-operation, in leaving others to bear the burden of resistance to aggression, or in leaving the aggressor to triumph unchecked. Individualism, on the other hand, would not only restrain the active invader up to the point necessary to restore freedom to others, but would also coerce the man who would otherwise be a passive witness of, or conniver at, aggression into co-operation against his more active colleague."

The foregoing paragraph occurs in any ably-written article by Mr. J. H. Levy in the *Personal Rights Journal*. The writer's evident intention was to put Anarchism in an unfavorable light by stating its principles, or one of them, in a very offensive way. At the same time it was his intention also to be fair,—that is, not to distort the doctrine of Anarchism,— and *he has not distorted it*. I reprint the paragraph in editorial type for the purpose of giving it, as an Anarchist, my entire approval, barring the stigma sought to be conveyed by the words "accomplice" and "conniver." If a man will but state the truth as I see it, he may state it as baldly as he pleases; I will accept it still. The Anarchists are not afraid of their principles. It is far more satisfactory to have one's position stated baldly and accurately by an opponent who understands it than in a genial, milk-and-water, and inaccurate fashion by an ignoramus.

It is agreed, then, that, in Anarchism's view, an individual has a right to stand aside and see a man murdered. And pray, why not? If it is justifiable to collar a man who is minding his own business and force him into a fight, why may we not also collar him for the purpose of forcing him to help us to coerce a parent into educating his child, or to commit any other act of invasion that may seem to us for the general good? I can see no ethical distinction here whatever. It is true that Mr. Levy, in the succeeding paragraphs, justifies the collaring of the non-co-operative individual on the ground of necessity. (I note here that this is the same ground on which Citizen Most proposes to collar the non-co-operator in his communistic enterprises and make him work for love instead of wages.) But some other motive than necessity must have been in Mr. Levy's mind, unconsciously, when he wrote the paragraph which I have quoted. Else why does he deny that the non-co-operator is "within his right"? I can understand the man who in a crisis justifies no matter what form of compulsion on the ground of sheer necessity, but I cannot understand the man who denies the right of the individual thus coerced to resist such compulsion and insist on pursuing his own independent course. It is precisely this denial, however, that Mr. Levy makes; otherwise his phrase "within his right" is meaningless.

But however this may be, let us look at the plea of necessity. Mr. Levy claims that the coercion of the peaceful non-co-operator is necessary. Necessary to what? Necessary, answers Mr. Levy, "in order that freedom may be at the maximum." Supposing for the moment that this is true, another inquiry suggests itself: Is the absolute maximum of freedom an end to be attained *at any cost?* I regard liberty as the chief essential to man's happiness, and therefore as the most important thing in the world, and I certainly want as much of it as I can get. But I cannot see that it concerns me much whether the aggregate amount of liberty enjoyed by all individuals added together is at its maximum or a little below it, if I, as one individual, am to have little or none of this aggregate. If, however, I am to have as much liberty as others, and if others are to have as much as I, then, feeling secure in what we have, it will behoove us all undoubtedly to try to attain the maximum of liberty compatible with this condition of equality. Which brings us back to the familiar law of equal liberty,—the greatest amount of individual liberty compatible with the equality of liberty. But this maximum of liberty is a very different thing from that which is to be attained, according to the hypothesis, only by violating equality of liberty. For, certainly, to coerce the peaceful non-co-operator is to violate equality of liberty. If my neighbor believes in co-operation and I do not, and if he has liberty to choose to co-operate while I have no liberty to choose not to co-operate, then there is no equality of liberty between us. Mr. Levy's position is analogous to that of a man who should propose to despoil certain individuals of peacefully and honestly acquired wealth on the ground that such spoliation is necessary in order that wealth may be at the maximum. Of course Mr. Levy would answer to this that the hypothesis is absurd, and that the maximum could not be so attained; but he clearly would have to admit, if pressed, that, even if it could, the end is not important enough to justify such means. To be logical he must make the same admission regarding his own proposition.

But after all, is the hypothesis any more absurd in the one case than in the other? I think not. It seems to me just as impossible to attain the maximum of liberty by depriving people of their liberty as to attain the maximum of wealth by depriving people of their wealth. In fact, it seems to me that in both cases the means is absolutely destructive of the end. Mr. Levy wishes to restrict the functions of government; now, the compulsory co-operation that he advocates is the chief obstacle in the way of such restriction. To be sure, government restricted by the removal of this obstacle would no longer be government, as Mr. Levy is "quick-witted enough to see" (to return the compliment which he pays the

Anarchists). But what of that? It would still be a power for preventing those invasive acts which the people are practically agreed in wanting to prevent. If it should attempt to go beyond this, it would be promptly checked by a diminution of the supplies. The power to cut off the supplies is the most effective weapon against tyranny. To say, as Mr. Levy does, that "taxation must be coextensive with government" is not the proper way to put it. It is government (or, rather, the State) that must and will be coextensive with taxation. When compulsory taxation is abolished, there will be no State, and the defensive institution that will succeed it will be steadily deterred from becoming an invasive institution through fear that the voluntary contributions will fall off. This constant motive for a voluntary defensive institution to keep itself trimmed down to the popular demand is itself the best possible safeguard against the bugbear of multitudinous rival political agencies which seems to haunt Mr. Levy. He says that the voluntary taxationists are victims of an illusion. The charge might be made against himself with much more reason.

My chief interest in Mr. Levy's article, however, is excited by his valid criticism of those Individualists who accept voluntary taxation, but stop short, or think they stop short, of Anarchism.

LIBERTY AND TAXATION

The power of taxation, being the most vital one to the State, naturally was a prominent subject in *Liberty's* discussions. Mr. F. W. Read, in London *Jus*, attacked the position of Anarchism on this point and was thus answered by Mr. Tucker:

THE idea that the voluntary taxationist objects to the State precisely because it does not rest on contract, and wishes to substitute contract for it, is strictly correct, and I am glad to see (for the first time, if my memory serves me) an opponent grasp it. But Mr. Read obscures his statement by his previous remark that the proposal of voluntary taxation is "the outcome of an idea . . . that the State *is, or* ought to be, founded on contract." This would be true if the words which I have italicized should be omitted. It was the insertion of these words that furnished the writer a basis for his otherwise groundless analogy between the Anarchists and the followers of Rousseau. The latter hold that the State originated in a contract, and that the people of to-day, though they did not make it, are bound by it. The Anarchists, on the contrary, deny that any such contract was ever made; declare that, had one ever been made, it could not impose a shadow of obligation on those who had no hand in making it; and claim the right to contract for themselves as they please. The position that a man may make his own contracts, far from being analogous to that which makes him subject to contracts made by others, is its direct antithesis.

It is perfectly true that voluntary taxation would not necessarily "prevent the existence of five or six 'States' in England," and that "members of all these 'States' might be living in the same house." But I see no reason for Mr. Read's exclamation point after this remark. What of it? There are many more than five or six Churches in England, and it frequently happens that members of several of them live in the same house. There are many more than five or six insurance companies in England, and it is by no means uncommon for members of the same family to insure their lives and goods against accident or fire in different companies. Does any harm come of it? Why, then, should there not be a considerable number of defensive associations in England, in which people, even members of the same family, might insure their lives and goods against murderers or thieves? Though Mr. Read has grasped one idea of the voluntary taxationists, I fear that he sees another much less clearly,——namely, the idea that defence is a service, like any other service; that it is labor both useful and desired, and therefore an economic commodity subject to the law of supply and demand; that in a free market this commodity would be furnished at the cost of production; that, competition prevailing, patronage would go to those who furnished the best article at the lowest price; that the production and sale of this commodity are now monopolized by the State; that the State, like almost all monopolists, charges exorbitant prices; that, like almost all monopolists, it supplies a worthless, or nearly worthless, article; that, just as the monopolist of a food product often furnishes poison instead of nutriment, so the State takes advantage of its monopoly of defence to furnish invasion instead of protection; that, just as the patrons of the one pay to be poisoned, so the patrons of the other pay to be enslaved; and, finally, that the State exceeds all its fellow-monopolists in the extent of its villainy because it enjoys the unique privilege of compelling all people to buy its product whether they want it or not. If, then, five or six "States" were to hang out their shingles, the people, I fancy, would be able to buy the very best kind of security at a reasonable price. And what is more,—the better their services, the less they would be needed; so that the multiplication of "States" involves the abolition of the State.

All these considerations, however, are disposed of, in Mr. Read's opinion, by his final assertion that "the State is a social organism." He considers this "the explanation of the whole matter." But for the life of me I can see in it nothing but another irrelevant remark. Again I ask: What of it? Suppose the State is an organism,—what then? What is the inference? That the State is therefore permanent? But what is history but a record of the dissolution of organisms and the birth and growth of others to be dissolved in turn? Is the State exempt from this order? If so, why? What proves it? The State an organism? Yes; so is a tiger. But unless I meet him when I haven't my gun, his organism will speedily disorganize. The State is a tiger seeking to devour the people, and they must either kill or cripple it. Their own safety depends upon it. But Mr. Read says it can't be done. "By no possibility can the power of the State be restrained." This must be very disappointing to Mr. Donisthorpe and *Jus,* who are working to restrain it. If Mr. Read is right, their occupation is gone. Is he right? Unless he can demonstrate it, the voluntary taxationists and the Anarchists will continue their work, cheered by the belief that the compulsory and invasive State is doomed to die.

In answer to Mr. Read's statement (which, if, with all its implications, it were true, would be a valid and final answer to the Anarchists) that "dissolving an organism is something different from dissolving a collection of atoms with no organic structure," I cannot do better than quote the following passage from an article by J. Wm. Lloyd in No. 107 of *Liberty*:

"It appears to me that this universe is but a vast aggregate of individuals; of individuals simple and primary, and of individuals complex, secondary, tertiary, etc., formed by the aggregation of primary individuals or of individuals of a lesser degree of complexity. Some of these individuals of a high degree of complexity are true individuals, *concrete*, so united that the lesser organisms included cannot exist, apart from the main organism; while others are imperfect, *discrete*, the included organisms existing fairly well, quite as well, or better, apart than united. In the former class are included many of the higher forms of vegetable and animal life, including man, and in the latter are included many lower forms of vegetable and animal life (quack-grass, tape-worms, etc.), and most society organisms, governments, nations, churches, armies, etc."

Taking this indisputable view of the matter, it becomes clear that Mr. Read's statement about "dissolving an organism" is untrue while the word organism remains unqualified by some adjective equivalent to Mr. Lloyd's *concrete*. The question, then, is whether the State is a concrete organism. The Anarchists claim that it is not. If Mr. Read thinks that it is, the *onus probandi* is upon him. I judge that his error arises from a confusion of the State with society. That society is a concrete organism the Anarchists do not deny; on the contrary, they insist upon it. Consequently they have no intention or desire to abolish it. They know that its life is inseparable from the lives of individuals; that it is impossible to destroy one without destroying the other. But, though society cannot be destroyed, it can be greatly hampered and impeded in its operations, much to the disadvantage of the individuals composing it, and it meets its chief impediment in the State. The State, unlike society, is a discrete organism. If it should be destroyed to-morrow, individuals would still continue to exist. Production, exchange, and association would go on as before, but much more freely, and all those social functions upon which the individual is dependent would operate in his behalf more usefully than ever. The individual is not related to the State as the tiger's paw is related to the tiger. Kill the tiger, and the tiger's paw no longer performs its office; kill the State, and the individual still lives and satisfies his wants. As for society, the Anarchists would not kill it if they could, and could not if they would.

Mr. Read finds it astounding that I should "put the State on a level with churches and insurance companies." I find his astonishment amusing. Believers in compulsory religious systems were astounded when it was first proposed to put the church on a level with other associations. Now the only astonishment is—at least in the United States—that the church is allowed to stay at any other level. But the political superstition has replaced the religious superstition, and Mr. Read is under its sway.

I do not think "that five or six 'States' could exist side by side with" *quite* "the same convenience as an equal number of churches." In the relations with which States have to do there is more chance for friction than in the simply religious sphere. But, on the other hand, the friction resulting from a multiplicity of States would be but a mole-hill compared with the mountain of oppression and injustice which is gradually heaped up by a single compulsory State. It would not be necessary for a police officer of a voluntary "State" to know to what "State" a given individual belonged, or whether he belonged to any. Voluntary "States" could, and probably would, authorize their executives to proceed against invasion, no matter who the invader or invaded might be. Mr. Read will probably object that the "State" to which the invader belonged might regard his arrest as itself an invasion, and proceed against the "State" which arrested him. Anticipation of such conflicts would probably result exactly in those treaties between "States" which Mr. Read looks upon as so desirable, and even in the establishment of federal tribunals, as courts of last resort, by the coöperation of the various "States," on the same voluntary principle in accordance with which the "States" themselves were organized.

Voluntary taxation, far from impairing the "State's" credit, would strengthen it. In the first place, the simplification of its functions would greatly reduce, and perhaps entirely abolish, its need to borrow, and the power to borrow is generally inversely proportional to the steadiness of the need. It is usually the inveterate borrower who lacks credit. In the second place, the power of the State to repudiate, and still continue its business, is dependent upon its power of compulsory taxation. It knows that, when it can no longer borrow, it can at least tax its citizens up to the limit of revolution. In the third place, the State is trusted, not because it is over and above individuals, but because the lender presumes that it desires to maintain its credit and will therefore pay its debts. This desire for credit will be stronger in a "State" supported by voluntary taxation than in the State which enforces taxation.

All the objections brought forward by Mr. Read (except the organism argument) are mere difficulties of administrative detail, to be overcome by ingenuity, patience, discretion, and expedients. They are not logical difficulties, not difficulties of principle. They seem "enormous" to him; but so seemed the difficulties of freedom of thought two centuries ago. What does he think of the difficulties of the existing *régime?* Apparently he is as blind to them as is the Roman Catholic to the difficulties of a State religion. All these "enormous" difficulties which arise in the fancy of the objectors to the voluntary principle will gradually vanish under the influence of the economic changes and well-distributed prosperity which will follow the adoption of that principle. This is what Proudhon calls "the dissolution of government in the economic organism." It is too vast a subject for consideration here, but, if Mr. Read wishes to understand the Anarchistic theory of the process, let him study that most wonderful of all the wonderful books of Proudhon, the "Idée Générale de la Révolution au Dix-Neuvième Siècle."

It is true that "history shows a continuous weakening of the State in some directions, and a continuous strengthening in other directions." At least such is the tendency, broadly speaking, though this continuity is sometimes broken by periods of reaction. This tendency is simply the progress of evolution towards Anarchy. The State invades less and less, and protects more and more. It is exactly in the line of this process, and at the end of it, that the Anarchists demand the abandonment of the last citadel of invasion by the substitution of voluntary for compulsory taxation. When this step is taken, the "State" will achieve its maximum strength as a protector against aggression, and will maintain it as long as its services are needed in that capacity.

If Mr. Read, in saying that the power of the State cannot

be restrained, simply meant that it cannot be legally restrained, his remark had no fitness as an answer to Anarchists and voluntary taxationists. They do not propose to legally restrain it. They propose to create a public sentiment that will make it impossible for the State to collect taxes by force or in any other way invade the individual. Regarding the State as an instrument of aggression, they do not expect to convince it that aggression is against its interests, but they do expect to convince individuals that it is against their interests to be invaded. If by this means they succeed in stripping the State of its invasive powers, they will be satisfied, and it is immaterial to them whether the means is described by the word "restraint" or by some other word. In fact, I have striven in this discussion to accommodate myself to Mr. Read's phraseology. For myself I do not think it proper to call voluntary associations States, but, enclosing the word in quotation marks, I have so used it because Mr. Read set the example.

Mr. Frederic A. C. Perrine, of Newark, N. J., asked Mr. Tucker for his reason for refusing to pay poll tax, and incidentally criticised the latter's position on that matter, which brought forth this reply:

MR. PERRINE'S criticism is an entirely pertinent one, and of the sort that I like to answer, though in this instance circumstances have delayed the appearance of his letter. The gist of his position—in fact, the whole of his argument—is based on the assumption that the State is precisely the thing which the Anarchists say it is not,—namely, a voluntary association of contracting individuals. Were it really such, I should have no quarrel with it, and I should admit the truth of Mr. Perrine's remarks. For certainly such voluntary association would be entitled to enforce whatever regulations the contracting parties might agree upon within the limits of whatever territory, or divisions of territory, had been brought into the association by these parties as individual occupiers thereof, and no non-contracting party would have a right to enter or remain in this domain except upon such terms as the association might impose. But if, somewhere between these divisions of territory, had lived, prior to the formation of the association, some individual on his homestead, who for any reason, wise or foolish, had declined to join in forming the association, the contracting parties would have had no right to evict him, compel him to join, make him pay for any incidental benefits that he might derive from proximity to their association, or restrict him in the exercise of any previously-enjoyed right to prevent him from reaping these benefits. Now, voluntary association necessarily involving the right of secession, any seceding member would naturally fall back into the position and upon the rights of the individual above described, who refused to join at all. So much, then, for the attitude of the individual toward any voluntary association surrounding him, his support thereof evidently depending upon his approval or disapproval of its objects, his view of its efficiency in attaining them, and his estimate of the advantages and disadvantages involved in joining, seceding, or abstaining. But no individual to-day finds himself under any such circumstances. The States in the midst of which he lives cover all the ground there is, affording him no escape, and are not voluntary associations, but gigantic usurpations. There is not one of them which did not result from the agreement of a larger or smaller number of individuals, inspired sometimes no doubt by kindly, but oftener by malevolent, designs, to declare all the territory and persons within certain boundaries a nation which every one of these persons must support, and to whose will, expressed through its sovereign legislators and administrators no matter how chosen, every one of them must submit. Such an institution is sheer tyranny, and has no rights which any individual is bound to respect; on the contrary, every individual who understands his rights and values his liberties will do his best to overthrow it. I think it must now be plain to Mr. Perrine why I do not feel bound either to pay taxes or to emigrate. Whether I will pay them or not is another question,—one of expediency. My object in refusing has been, as Mr. Perrine suggests, propagandism, and in the receipt of Mr. Perrine's letter I find evidence of the adaptation of this policy to that end. Propagandism is the only motive that I can urge for isolated individual resistance to taxation. But out of propagandism by this and many other methods I expect there ultimately will develop the organization of a determined body of men and women who will effectively, though passively, resist taxation, not simply for propagandism, but to directly cripple their oppressors. This is the extent of the only "violent substitution of end for beginning" which I can plead guilty of advocating, and, if the end can be "better and more easily obtained" in any other way, I should like to have it pointed out. The "grand race experience" which Mr. Perrine thinks I neglect is a very imposing phrase, on hearing which one is moved to lie down in prostrate submission; but whoever first chances to take a closer look will see that it is but one of those spooks of which Tak Tak [James L. Walker, author of "The Philosophy of Egoism"] tells us. Nearly all the evils with which mankind was ever afflicted were products of this "grand race experience," and I am not aware that any were ever abolished by showing it any unneccessary reverence. We will bow to it when we must; we will "compromise with existing circumstances" when we have to; but at all other times we will follow our reason and the plumb-line.

When I said that voluntary association necessarily involves the right of secession, I did not deny the right of any individuals to go through the form of constituting themselves an association in which each member waives the right of secession. My assertion was simply meant to carry the idea that such a constitution, if any should be so idle as to adopt it, would be a mere *form*, which every decent man who was a party to it would hasten to violate and tread under foot as soon as he appreciated the enormity of his folly. Contract is a very serviceable and most important tool, but its usefulness has its limits; no man can employ it for the abdication of his manhood. To indefinitely waive one's right of secession is to make one's self a slave. Now, no man can make himself so much a slave as to forfeit the right to issue his own emancipation proclamation. Individuality and its right of assertion are indestructible except by death. Hence any signer of such a constitution as that supposed who should afterwards become an Anarchist would be fully justified in the use of any means that would protect him from attempts to coerce him in the name of that constitution. But even if this were not so; if men were really under obligation to keep impossible contracts,—there would still be no inference to be drawn therefrom regarding the relations of the United States to its so-called citizens. To assert that the United States constitution is similar to that of the hypothesis is an extremely wild remark. Mr. Perrine can readily find this out by reading Lysander Spooner's "Letter to Grover Cleveland." That masterly document will tell him what the United States constitution is and just how binding it is on anybody. But if the United States constitution were a voluntary contract of the nature described above, it would still remain for Mr. Perrine to tell us why those who failed to repudiate it are bound, by such failure, to comply with it, or why the assent of those who entered into it is binding upon people who were then unborn, or what right the contracting parties, if there were any, had to claim jurisdiction and sovereign power over that vast section of the planet which has since been known as the United States of America and over all the persons contained therein, instead of over themselves simply and such lands as they personally occupied and used. These are points which he utterly ignores. His reasoning consists of independent propositions between which there are no logical links. Now, as to the "grand race experience." It is perfectly true that, if we have anything grand, it is this, but it is no less true that, if we have anything base, it is this. It is *all* we have, and, being all, includes all, both grand and base. I do not deny man's grandeur, neither do I deny his degradation; consequently I neither accept nor reject all that he has been and done. I try to use my reason for the purpose of discrimination, instead of blindly obeying any divinity, even that of man. We should not worship this race experience by imitation and repetition, but should strive to profit by its mistakes and avoid them in future. Far from believing in any Edenic state, I yield to no man in my strict adherence to the theory of evolution, but evolution is "leading us up to Anarchy" simply because it has already led us in nearly every other direction and made a failure of it. Evolution like nature, of which it is the instrument or process, is extremely wasteful and short-sighted. Let us not imitate its wastefulness or even tolerate it if we can help it; let us rather use our brains for the guidance of evolution in the path of economy. Evolution left to itself will sooner or later eliminate every other social form and leave us Anarchy. But evolution guided will try to discover the common element in its past failures, summarily reject everything having this element, and straightway accept Anarchy, which has it not. Because we are the products of evolution we are not therefore to be its puppets. On the contrary, as our intelligence grows, we are to be more and more its masters. It is just because we let it master us, just because we strive to act with it rather than across its path, just because we dilly-dally and shilly-shally and fritter away our time, for instance, over secret ballots, open ballots, and the like, instead of treating the whole matter of the suffrage from the standpoint of principle, that we do indeed "pave the way," much to our sorrow, "for those great revolutions" and "great epochs" when extremists suddenly get the upper hand. Great epochs, indeed! Great disasters rather, which it behooves us vigilantly to avoid. But how? By being extremists now. If there were more extremists in evolutionary periods, there would be no revolutionary periods. There is no lesson more important for mankind to learn than that. Until it is learned, Mr. Perrine will talk in vain about the divinity of man, for every day will make it more patent that his god is but a jumping-jack.

I have never said that it is "each man's duty to break all contracts as soon as he has become convinced that they were made foolishly." What I said was that, if a man should sign a contract to part with his liberty forever, he would violate it as soon as he saw the enormity of his folly. Because I believe that some promises are better broken than kept, it does not follow that I think it wise always to break a foolish promise. On the contrary, I deem the keeping of promises such an important matter that only in the extremest cases would I approve their violation. It is of such vital consequence that associates should be able to rely upon each other that it is better never to do anything to weaken this confidence except when it can be maintained only at the expense of some consideration of even greater importance. I mean by evolution just what Darwin means by it,—namely, the process of selection by which, out of all the variations that occur from any cause whatever, only those are preserved which are best adapted to the environment. Inasmuch as the variations that perish vastly outnumber those that survive, this process is extremely wasteful, but human intelligence can greatly lessen the waste. I am perfectly willing to admit its optimism if by optimism is meant the doctrine that everything is for the best *under the circumstances*. Optimism so defined is nothing more than the doctrine of necessity. As to the word "degradation," evidently Mr. Perrine is unaware of all its meanings. By its derivation it implies descent from something higher, but it is also used by the best English writers to express a low condition regardless of what preceded it. It was in the latter sense that I used it.

ANARCHISM AND CRIME

Mr. B. W. Ball wrote an article in the *Index* criticizing Anarchism without having familiarized himself with the groundwork of that philosophy. Hence the following reply:

Mr. Ball's central argument against us, stated briefly, is this: Where crime exists, force must exist to repress it. Who denies it? Certainly not *Liberty*; certainly not the Anarchists. Anarchism is not a revival of non-resistance, although there may be non-resistants in its ranks. The direction of Mr. Ball's attack implies that we would let robbery, rape, and murder make havoc in the community without lifting a finger to stay their brutal, bloody work. On the contrary, we are the sternest enemies of invasion of person and property, and, although chiefly busy in destroying the causes thereof, have no scruples against such heroic treatment of its immediate manifestations as circumstances and wisdom may dictate. It is true that we look forward to the ultimate disappearance of the necessity of force even for the purpose of repressing crime, but this, though involved in it as a necessary result, is by no means a necessary condition of the abolition of the State.

In opposing the State, therefore, we do not deny Mr. Ball's proposition, but distinctly affirm and emphasize it. We make war upon the State as the chief invader of person and property, as the cause of substantially all the crime and misery that exist, as itself the most gigantic criminal extant. It manufactures criminals much faster than it punishes them. It exists to create and sustain the privileges which produce economic and social chaos. It is the sole support of the monopolies which concentrate wealth and learning in the hands of a few and disperse poverty and ignorance among the masses, to the increase of which inequality the increase of crime is directly proportional. It protects a minority in plundering the majority by methods too subtle to be understood by the victims, and then punishes such unruly members of the majority as attempt to plunder others by methods too simple and straightforward to be recognized by the State as legitimate, crowning its outrages by deluding scholars and philosophers of Mr. Ball's stamp into pleading, as an excuse for its infamous existence, the necessity of repressing the crime which it steadily creates.

Mr. Ball,—to his honor be it said,—during anti-slavery days, was a steadfast abolitionist. He earnestly desired the abolition of slavery. Doubtless he remembers how often he was met with the argument that slavery was necessary to keep the unlettered blacks out of mischief, and that it would be unsafe to give freedom to such a mass of ignorance. Mr. Ball in those days saw through the sophistry of such reasoning, and knew that those who urged it did so to give some color of moral justification to their conduct in living in luxury on the enforced toil of slaves. He probably was wont to answer them something after this fashion: "It is the institution of slavery that keeps the blacks in ignorance, and to justify slavery on the ground of their ignorance is to reason in a circle and beg the very question at issue."

To-day Mr. Ball—again to his honor be it said—is a religious abolitionist. He earnestly desires the abolition, or at least the disappearance, of the Church. How frequently he must meet or hear of priests who, while willing to privately admit that the doctrines of the Church are a bundle of delusions, argue that the Church is necessary to keep the superstition-ridden masses in order, and that their release from the mental subjection in which it holds them would be equivalent to their precipitation into unbridled dissipation, libertinism, and ultimate ruin. Mr. Ball sees clearly through the fallacy of all such logic, and knows that those who use it do so to gain a moral footing on which to stand while collecting their fees from the poor fools who know no better than to pay them. We can fancy him replying with pardonable indignation: "Cunning knaves, you know very well that it is your Church that saturates the people with superstition, and that to justify its existence on the ground of their superstition is to put the cart before the horse and assume the very point in dispute."

Now, we Anarchists are political abolitionists. We earnestly desire the abolition of the State. Our position on this question is parallel in most respects to those of the Church abolitionists and the slavery abolitionists. But in this case Mr. Ball—to his disgrace be it said—takes the side of the tyrants against the abolitionists, and raises the cry so frequently raised against him: The State is necessary to keep thieves and murderers in subjection, and, were it not for the State, we should all be garroted in the streets and have our throats cut in our beds. As Mr. Ball saw through the sophistry of his opponents, so we see through his, precisely similar to theirs, though we know that not he, but the capitalists use it to blind the people to the real object of the institution by which they are able to extort from labor the bulk of its products. We answer him as he did them, and in no very patient mood: Can you not see that it is the State that creates the conditions which give birth to thieves and murderers, and that to justify its existence on the ground of the prevalence of theft and murder is a logical process every whit as absurd as those used to defeat your efforts to abolish slavery and the Church?

Once for all, then, we are not opposed to the punishment of thieves and murderers; we are opposed to their manufacture. Right here Mr. Ball must attack us, or not at all.

The makers of party platforms, the writers of newspaper editorials, the pounders of pulpit-cushions, and the orators of the stump, who are just now blending their voices in frantic chorus to proclaim the foreign origin of evil and to advocate therefore the exclusion of the foreign element from American soil, should study the figures compiled by the Rev. Frederick Howard Wines from the tenth census reports and presented by him to the congress of the National Prison Association lately held in Boston. Such of these shriekers as are provided with thinkers may find in these statistics food for thought. From them it appears that, though the ratio of crime among our foreign-born population is still very much higher than the ratio among our native population, the former ratio, which in 1850 was more than five times as high as the latter, in 1880 was less than twice as high. And it further appears that, if crimes against person and property are alone considered, the two ratios stand almost exactly on a level, and that the ratio of foreign-born criminals tends to exceed that of native criminals in proportion as the catalogue of "crimes" is extended to cover so-called offences against public morals, public policy, and society. In other words, the percentage of natives who steal, damage, burn, assault, kidnap, rape, and kill is about as large as the percentage of foreigners of similarly invasive tendencies, and the percentage of foreign-born law-breakers exceeds that of native law-breakers only because the foreign-born are less disposed than the natives to obey those laws which say that people shall not drink this or eat that or smoke the other; that they shall not love except under prescribed forms and conditions; that they shall not dispose or expose their persons except as their rulers provide; that they shall not work or play on Sunday or blaspheme the name of the Lord; that they shall not gamble or swear; that they shall not sell certain articles at all, or buy certain others without paying a tax for the privilege; and that they shall not mail, own, or read any obscene literature except the Bible. That is to say, again, people who happen to have been born in Europe are no more determined to invade their fellow-men than are people who happen to have been born in America, but that the latter are much more willing to be invaded and trampled upon than any other people on earth. Which speaks very well, in *Liberty's* opinion, for the foreigners, and makes it important for our own liberty and welfare to do everything possible to encourage immigration.

But, say the shriekers, these foreigners are Anarchists and Socialists. Well, there's some truth in that; as a general rule, the better people are, the more Anarchists and Socialists will be found among them. This, too, is a fact which the tenth census proves.

Now, in what class of foreigners *in this country* do the Anarchists and Socialists figure most largely? Certainly not among the Chinese or the Irish or the Cubans or the Spaniards or the Italians or the Australians or the Scotch or the French or the English or the Canadians. But these are the only foreigners except the Russians who make a poorer showing in point of criminality than the native Americans. To find in this country any considerable number of Anarchists and Socialists of foreign birth, we must go to the Russians, the Germans, the Poles, the Hungarians, and the Bohemians. The statistics show, however, that the Russians are almost as orderly as Americans, the Germans exactly as orderly, the Poles more orderly, and the Hungarians and Bohemians more than twice as orderly.

Moral: If the defenders of privilege desire to exclude from this country the opponents of privilege, they should see to it that Congress omits the taking of the eleventh census. For the eleventh census, if taken, will undoubtedly emphasize these two lessons of the tenth: first, that foreign immigration does not increase dishonesty and violence among us, but does increase the love of liberty; second, that the population of the world is gradually dividing into two classes,—Anarchists and criminals.

LIBERTY AND POLITICS

CONNECTED with the Massachusetts branch of the National Woman Suffrage Association is a body of women calling itself the Boston Political Class, the object of which is the preparation of its members for the use of the ballot. On May 30, 1889, this class was addressed in public by Dr. Wm. T. Harris, the Concord philosopher, on the subject of State Socialism, Anarchism, and free competition. Let me say, parenthetically, to these ladies that, if they really wish to learn how to use the ballot, they would do well to apply for instruction, not to Dr. Harris, but to ex-Supervisor Bill Simmons, or Johnny O'Brien of New York, or Senator Matthew Quay, or some leading Tammany brave, or any of the "bosses" who rule city, State, and Nation; for, the great object of the ballot being to test truth by counting noses and to prove your opponents wrong by showing them to be less numerous than your friends, and these men having practically demonstrated that they are masters of the art of rolling up majorities at the polls, they can teach the members of the Boston Political Class a trick or two by which they can gain numerical supremacy, while Dr. Harris, in the most favorable view of the case, can only elevate their intelligence and thereby fix them more hopelessly in a minority that must be vanquished in a contest where ballots instead of brains decide the victory.

But let that pass. I am not concerned now with these excellent ladies, but with Dr. Harris's excellent address; for it was excellent, notwithstanding the fact that he intended it partly as a blow at Anarchism. Instead of being such a blow, the discourse was really an affirmation of Anarchism almost from beginning to end, at least in so far as it dealt with principles, and departed from Anarchism only in two or three mistaken attempts to illustrate the principles laid down and to identify existing society with them as expressive of them.

After positing the proposition that the object of society is the production of self-conscious intelligence in its highest form, or, in other words, the most perfect individuality, the lecturer spent the first half of his time in considering State Socialism from this standpoint. He had no difficulty in showing that the absorption of enterprise by the State is indeed a "looking backward,"—a very long look backward at that communism which was the only form of society known to primitive man; at that communism which purchases material equality at the expense of the destruction of liberty; at that communism out of which evolution, with its tendency toward individuality, has been gradually lifting mankind for thousands of years; at that communism which, by subjecting the individual rights of life and property to industrial tyranny, thereby renders necessary a central political tyranny to at least partially secure the right to life and make possible the continuance of some semblance of social existence. The lecturer took the position that civil society is dependent upon freedom in production, distribution, and consumption, and that such freedom is utterly incompatible with State Socialism, which in its ultimate implies the absolute control of all these functions by arbitrary power as a substitute for economic law. Therefore Dr. Harris, setting great value upon civil society, has no use for State Socialism. Neither have the Anarchists. Thus far, then, the Anarchists and the teacher of the Boston Political class walk hand in hand.

Dr. Harris, however, labors under a delusion that just at this point he parts company with us. As we follow his argument further, we shall see if this be true. The philosophy of society, he continued in substance, is coextensive with a ground covered by four institutions,—namely, the family, civil society, the State, and the Church. Proceeding then to define the specific purposes of these institutions, he declared that the object of the family is to assure the reproduction of individuals and prepare them, by guidance through childhood, to become reasonable beings; that the object of civil society is to enable each individual to reap advantage from the powers of all other individuals through division of labor, free exchange, and other economic means; that the object of the State is to protect each individual against aggression and secure him in his freedom as long as he observes the equal freedom of others; and that the object of the Church (using the term in its broadest sense, and not as exclusively applicable to the various religious bodies) is to encourage the investigation and perfection of science, literature, the fine arts, and all those higher humanities that make life worth living and tend to the elevation and completion of self-conscious intelligence or individuality. Each of these objects, in the view of the lecturer, is necessary to the existence of any society worthy of the name, and the omission of any one of them disastrous. The State Socialists, he asserted truthfully, would ruin the whole structure by omitting civil society, whereas the Anarchists, he asserted erroneously, would equally ruin it by omitting the State. Right here lies Dr. Harris's error, and it is the most vulgar of all errors in criticism,—that of treating the ideas of others from the standpoint, not of their definitions, but of your own. Dr. Harris hears that the Anarchists wish to abolish the State, and straightway he jumps to the conclusion that they wish to abolish what he defines as the State. And this, too, in spite of the fact that, to my knowledge, he listened not long ago to the reading of a paper by an Anarchist from which it was clearly to be gathered that the Anarchists have no quarrel with any institution that contents itself with enforcing the law of equal freedom, and that they oppose the State only after first defining it as an institution that claims authority over the *non-aggressive* individual and enforces that authority by physical force or by means that are effective only because they can and will be backed by physical force if necessary. Far from omitting the State *as Dr. Harris defines it*, the Anarchists expressly favor such an institution, by whatever name it may be called, as long as its *raison d'être* continues; and certainly Dr. Harris would not demand its preservation after it had become superfluous.

In principle, then, are not the Anarchists and Dr. Harris in agreement at every essential point? It certainly seems so. I do not know an Anarchist that would not accept every division of his social map.

Defining the object of the family as he defines it, the Anarchists believe in the family; they only insist that free competition and experiment shall always be allowed in order that it may be determined *what form* of family best secures this object.

Defining the object of civil society as he defines it, the Anarchists believe in civil society; only they insist that the freedom of civil society shall be complete instead of partial.

Defining the object of the State as he defines it, the Anarchists believe in the State; only they insist that the greater part, if not all, of the necessity for its existence is the result of an artificial limitation of the freedom of civil society, and that the completion of industrial freedom may one day so harmonize individuals that it will no longer be necessary to provide a guarantee of political freedom.

Defining the object of the Church as he defines it, the Anarchists most certainly believe in the Church; only they insist that all its work shall be purely voluntary, and that its discoveries and achievements, however beneficial, shall not be imposed upon the individual by authority.

But there is a point, unhappily, where the Anarchists and Dr. Harris do part company, and that point is reached when he declares or assumes or leaves it to be inferred that the present form of the family is the form that best secures the objects of the family, and that no attempt at any other form is to be tolerated, although evidence of the horrors engendered by the prevailing family life is being daily spread before our eyes in an ever-increasing volume; that the present form of civil society is the embodiment of complete economic freedom, although it is undeniable that the most important freedoms, those without which all other freedoms are of little or no avail,

—the freedom of banking and the freedom to take possession of unoccupied land,—exist nowhere in the civilized world; that the existing State does nothing but enforce the law of equal freedom, although it is unquestionably based upon a compulsory tax that is itself a denial of equal freedom, and is daily adding to ponderous volumes of statutes the bulk of which are either sumptuary and meddlesome in character or devised in the interest of privilege and monopoly; and that the existing Church carries on its work in accordance with the principle of free competition, in spite of the indubitable fact that, in its various fields of religion, science, literature, and the arts, it is endowed with innumerable immunities, favors, prerogatives, and licenses, with the extent and stringency of which it is still unsatisfied.

All these assumptions clearly show that Dr. Harris is a man of theory, and not of practice. He knows nothing but disembodied principles. Consequently, when the State Socialist proposes to embody a principle antagonistic to his, he recognizes it as such and demolishes it by well-directed arguments. But this same antagonistic principle, so far as it is already embodied, is unrecognizable by him. As soon as it becomes incarnate, he mistakes it for his own. No matter what shape it has taken, be it a banking monopoly, or a land monopoly, or a national post-office monopoly, or a common school system, or a compulsory tax, or a setting-up of non-aggressive individuals to be shot at by an enemy, he hastens to offer it one hand, while he waves the flag of free competition with the other. In consequence of its fleshly wrappings, he is constitutionally incapable of combating the *status quo*. For this reason he is not an altogether competent teacher, and is liable to confuse the minds of the ambitious ladies belonging to the Boston Political Class.

LIBERTY AND PROHIBITION

Mr. Lucian V. Pinney, a protectionist and a greenbacker—but an anti-prohibitionist—made the following statement in his paper, the Winsted (Conn.) *Press:*

"There is nothing any better than Liberty and nothing any worse than despotism, be it theological despotism of the skies, the theocratic despotism of kings, or the democratic despotism of majorities; and the labor reformer who starts out to combat the despotism of capitalism with other despotism no better lacks only power to be worse than the foe he encounters." Mr. Tucker then took him to task for his inconsistency:

MR. PINNEY is a man who combats the despotism of capital with that despotism which denies the liberty to buy foreign goods untaxed and that despotism which denies the liberty to issue notes to circulate as currency. Mr. Pinney is driven into this inconsistency by his desire for high wages and an abundance of money, which he thinks it impossible to get except through tariff monopoly and money monopoly. But religious despotism pleads a desire for salvation, and moral despotism pleads a desire for purity, and prohibitory despotism pleads a desire for sobriety. Yet all these despotisms lead to hell, though all these hells are paved with good intentions; and Mr. Pinney's hells are just as hot as any. The above extract shows that he knows Liberty to be the true way of salvation. Why, then, does he not steadily follow it?

Mr. Pinney combats prohibition in the name of Liberty. Thereupon I showed him that his argument was equally good against his own advocacy of a tariff on imports and an exclusive government currency. Carefully avoiding any illusion to the analogy, Mr. Pinney now rejoins: "In brief, we are despotic because we believe it is our right to defend ourselves from foreign invaders on the one side and wild-cat swindlers on the other." Yes, just as despotic as the prohibtionists who believe it is their right to defend themselves from drunkards and rumsellers."

Continuing his controversy with me regarding the logic of the principle of liberty, Mr. Pinney says:

"There is no analogy between prohibition and the tariff; the tariff prohibits no man from indulging his desire to trade where he pleases. It is simply a tax. It is slightly analogous to a license tax for the privilege of selling liquor in a given territory, but prohibition, in theory if not in practice, is an entirely different matter."

This is a distinction without a difference. The so-called prohibitory liquor law prohibits no man, even theoretically, from indulging his desire to sell liquor; it simply subjects the man so indulging to fine and imprisonment. The tax imposed by the tariff law and the fine imposed by the prohibitory law share alike the nature of a penalty, and are equally invasive of liberty. Mr. Pinney's argument, though of no real validity in any case, would present at least a *show* of reason in the mouth of a "revenue reformer"; but, coming from one who scorns the idea of raising revenue by the tariff and who has declared explicitly that he desires the tariff to be so effectively prohibitory that it shall yield no revenue at all, it lacks even the appearance of logic.

Equally lame is Mr. Pinney's apology for a compulsory money system:

"As for the exclusive government currency which we advocate, and which Mr. Tucker tortures into prohibition of individual property scrip, there is just as much analogy as there is between prohibition and the exclusive law-making, treaty-making, war-declaring, or any other powers delegated to government because government better than the individual can be intrusted with and make use of these powers."

Just as much, I agree; and in this I can see a good reason why Mr. Pinney, who started out with the proposition that "there is nothing better than liberty and nothing any worse than despotism," should oppose law-making, treaty-making, war-declaring, etc., but none whatever why he should favor an exclusive government currency. How much "torture" it requires to extract the idea of "prohibition of individual property scrip" from the idea of an *"exclusive* government currency" our readers will need no help in deciding, unless the word "exclusive" has acquired some new meaning as unknown to them as it is to me.

But Mr. Pinney's brilliant ideas are not exhausted yet. He continues:

"Government prohibits the taking of private property for public uses without just compensation. Therefore, if we fit Mr. Tucker's Procrustean bed, we cannot sustain this form of prohibition and consistently oppose prohibition of liquor drinking! This is consistency run mad, 'analogy' reduced to an absurdity. We are astonished that Mr. Tucker can be guilty of it."

So am I. Or rather, I should be astonished if I had been guilty of it. But I haven't. To say nothing of the fact that the governmental prohibition here spoken of is a prohibition laid by government upon itself, and that such prohibitions can never be displeasing to an Anarchist, it is clear that the taking of private property from persons who have violated the rights of nobody is invasion, and to the prohibition of invasion no friend of liberty has any objection. Mr. Pinney has already resorted to the plea of invasion as an excuse for his advocacy of a tariff, and it would be a good defence if he could establish it. But I have pointed out to him that the pretence that the foreign merchant who sells goods to American citizens or the individual who offers his I O U are invaders is as flimsy as the prohibitionist's pretence that the rumseller and the drunkard are invaders. Neither invasion nor evasion will relieve Mr. Pinney of his dilemma.

In an unguarded moment of righteous impatience with the folly of the prohibitionists Mr. Pinney had given utterance to some very extreme and Anarchistic doctrine. I applauded him, and ventured to call his attention to one or two forms of prohibition other than that of the liquor traffic, equally repugnant to his theory of liberty and yet championed by him. One of these was the tariff. He answered me that "there is no analogy between prohibition and the tariff; the tariff prohibits no man from indulging his desire to trade where he pleases." Right here logomachy made its first appearance, over the word "prohibit." I had cited two forms of State interference with trade, each of which in practice either annoys it or hampers it or effectively prevents it, according to circumstances. This analogy in substantial results presented a difficulty, which Mr. Pinney tried to overcome by beginning a dispute over the meaning of the word "prohibit,"—a matter of only formal moment so far as the present discussion is concerned. He declared that the tariff is not like the prohibitory liquor law, inasmuch as it prohibits nobody from trading where he pleases. A purely nominal distinction, if even that; consequently Mr. Pinney, in passing it off as a real one, was guilty of quibbling.

But I met Mr. Pinney on his own ground, allowing that, speaking exactly, the tariff does not prohibit, but adding, on the other hand, that neither does the so-called prohibitory liquor law; that both simply impose penalties on traders, in the one case as a condition, in the other as a consequence, of carrying on their trades. Hence my analogy still stood, and I expected it to be grappled with. But no. Mr. Pinney, in the very breath that he protests against quibbling, insists on his quibble by asking if prison discipline is, then, so lax that convicted liquor sellers can carry on their business within the walls, and by supposing that I would still think prohibition did not prohibit, if the extreme penalty for liquor selling were decapitation. I do not dispute the fact that a man cannot carry on the liquor business as long as he is in prison, nor can Mr. Pinney dispute the fact that a man cannot sell certain foreign goods in this country as long as he cannot raise the money to pay the tariff; and while I am confident that decapitation, if rigorously enforced, would stop the liquor traffic, I am no less sure that the effect on foreign traffic would be equally disastrous were decapitation to be enforced as a tax upon importers. On Mr. Pinney's theory the prohibitory liquor laws could be made non-prohibitory simply by changing the penalties from imprisonments to fines. The absurdity of this is evident.

But, if I were to grant that Mr. Pinney's quibble shows that there is no analogy between a prohibitory liquor law and a revenue tariff (which I do not grant, but deny), it would still remain for him to show that there is no analogy between a prohibitory liquor law and such a tariff as he favors,—one so high as to be absolutely prohibitory and yield no revenue at all,—or else admit his inconsistency in opposing the former and not the latter. He has not attempted to meet this point, even with a quibble.

One other point, however, he does try to meet. To my statement that his position on the abstract question of liberty involves logically opposition to government in all its functions he makes this answer:

"Between puritan meddling with a man's domestic affairs, and necessary government regulation of matters which the individual is incompetent to direct, yet which must be directed in order to secure to the individual his rightful liberty, there is a distance sufficiently large to give full play to our limited faculties."

But who is to judge what government regulation is "necessary" and decide what matters "the individual is incompetent to direct"? The majority? But the majority are just as likely to decide that prohibition is necessary and that the individual is incompetent to direct his appetite as that a tariff is necessary and that the individual is incompetent to make his own contracts. Mr. Pinney, then, must submit to the will of the majority. His original declaration, however, was that despotism was despotism, whether exercised by a monarch or a majority. This drives him back upon liberty in all things. For just as he would object to the reign of a monarch disposed to administer affairs rationally and equitably simply because he was a monarch, so he must object to the reign of a majority, even though its administration were his ideal, simply because it is a majority. Mr. Pinney is trying to serve both liberty and authority, and is making himself ridiculous in the attempt.

ANARCHISM AND CAPITAL PUNISHMENT

SINCE the execution of Kemmler, I have seen it stated repeatedly in the press, and especially in the reform press, and even in the Anarchistic press, that that execution was a murder. I have also seen it stated that capital punishment is murder in its worst form. I should like to know upon what principle of human society these assertions are based and justified.

If they are based on the principle that punishment inflicted by a compulsory institution which manufactures the criminals is worse than the crime punished, I can understand them and in some degree sympathize with them. But in that case I cannot see why *capital* punishment should be singled out for emphatic and exceptional denunciation. The same objection applies as clearly to punishment that simply takes away liberty as to punishment that takes away life.

The use of the word *capital* makes me suspect that this denunciation rests on some other ground than that which I have just suggested. But what is this ground?

If society has a right to protect itself against such men as Kemmler, as is admitted, why may it not do so in whatever way proves most effective? If it is urged that capital punishment is not the most effective way, such an argument, well sustained by facts, is pertinent and valid. This position also I can understand, and with it, if not laid down as too absolute a rule, I sympathize. But this is not to say that the society which inflicts capital punishment commits murder. Murder is an offensive act. The term cannot be applied legitimately to any defensive act. And capital punishment, however ineffective it may be and through whatever ignorance it may be resorted to, is a strictly defensive act,—at least in theory. Of course compulsory institutions often make it a weapon of offence, but that does not affect the question of capital punishment *per se* as distinguished from other forms of government.

For one, I object to this distinction unless it is based on rational grounds. In doing so, I am not moved by any desire to defend the horrors of the gallows, the guillotine, or the electric chair. They are as repulsive to me as to any one. And the conduct of the physicians, the ministers, the newspapers, and the officials disgusts me. These horrors all tell most powerfully against the expediency and efficiency of capital punishment. But nevertheless they do not make it murder. I insist that there is nothing sacred in the life of an invader, and there is no valid principle of human society that forbids the invaded to protect themselves in whatever way they can.

LIBERTY AND PROPERTY

Mr. Hugo Bilgram of Philadelphia, author of "Involuntary Idleness" and "The Cause of Business Depressions," contributed an article to *Liberty* on "The Right of Ownership," in which he defined that right as "that relation between a thing and a person created by the social promise to guarantee possession"; and then propounded to the editor of *Liberty* the following question:

"Has Anarchism a different conception of the right of ownership, or is this right altogether repudiated, or is it assumed that out of the ruins of government another social organization, wielding a supreme power, will arise?" Mr. Tucker replied:

IN DISCUSSING such a question as this, it is necessary at the start to put aside, as Mr. Bilgram doubtless does put aside, the intuitive idea of right, the conception of right as a standard which we are expected to observe from motives supposed to be superior to the consideration of our interests. When I speak of the "right of ownership," I do not use the word "right" in that sense at all. In the thought that I take to be fundamental in Mr. Bilgram's argument—namely, that there is no right, from the standpoint of society, other than social expediency—I fully concur. But I am equally certain that the standard of social expediency—that is to say, the facts as to what really is socially expedient, and the generalizations from those facts which we may call the laws of social expediency —exists apart from the decree of any social power whatever. In accordance with this view, the Anarchistic definition of the right of ownership, while closely related to Mr. Bilgram's, is such a modification of his that it does not carry the implication which his carries and which he points out. From an Anarchistic standpoint, the right of ownership is that control of a thing by a person which will receive either social sanction, or else unanimous individual sanction, when the laws of social expediency shall have been finally discovered. (Of course I might go farther and explain that Anarchism considers the greatest amount of liberty compatible with equality of liberty the fundamental law of social expediency, and that nearly all Anarchists consider labor to be the only basis of the right of ownership in harmony with that law; but this is not essential to the definition, or to the refutation of Mr. Bilgram's point against Anarchism.)

It will be seen that the Anarchistic definition just given does not imply necessarily the existence of an organized or instituted social power to enforce the right of ownership. It contemplates a time when social sanction shall be superseded by unanimous individual sanction, thus rendering enforcement needless.   But in such an event, by Mr. Bilgram's definition, the right of ownership would cease to exist.   In other words, he seems to think that, if all men were to agree upon a property standard and should voluntarily observe it, property would then have no existence simply because of the absence of any institution to protect it.   Now, in the view of the Anarchists, property would then exist in its perfection.

So I would answer Mr. Bilgram's question, as put in his concluding paragraph, as follows: Anarchism does not repudiate the right of ownership, but it has a conception thereof sufficiently different from Mr. Bilgram's to include the possibility of an end of that social organization which will arise, not out of the ruins of government, but out of the transformation of government into voluntary association for defence.

ANARCHISM AND FORCE

BECAUSE I claim and teach that Anarchism justifies the application of force to invasive men and condemns force only when applied to non-invasive men, Mr. Hugh O. Pentecost declares that the only difference between Anarchism on the one hand and Monarchism or Republicanism on the other is the difference between the popular conception of invasion and my own.   If I were to assert that biology is the science which deals with the phenomena of living matter and excludes all phenomena of matter that is not living, and if Mr. Pentecost were to say that, assuming this, the only difference between the biological sciences and the abiological is the difference between the popular conception of life and my own, he would take a position precisely analogous to that which he takes on the subject of Anarchism, and the one position would be every whit as sensible and every whit as foolish as the other. The limit between invasion and non-invasion, like the limit between life and non-life, is not, at least in our present comprehension of it, a hard and fast line.   But does it follow from this that invasion and non-invasion, life and non-life, are identical?   Not at all.   The indefinite character of the boundary does no more than show that a small proportion of the phenomena of society, like a small proportion of the phenomena of matter, still resists the respective distinguishing tests to which by far the greater portion of such phenomena have yielded and by which they have been classified. And however embarrassing in practice may be the reluctance of frontier phenomena to promptly arrange themselves on either side of the border in obedience to the tests, it is still more embarrassing in theory to attempt to frame any rational view of society or life without recognition of these tests, by which, broadly speaking, distinctions have been established. Some of the most manifest distinctions have never been sharply drawn.

If Mr. Pentecost will view the subject in this light and follow out the reasoning thus entered upon, he will soon discover that my conception or misconception of what constitutes invasion does not at all affect the scientific differentiation of Anarchism from Archism. I may err grievously in attributing an invasive or a non-invasive character to a given social phenomenon, and, if I act upon my error, I shall act Archistically; but the very fact that I am acting, not blindly and at hap-hazard, but in furtherance of an endeavor to conform to a generalization which is the product of long experience and accumulating evidence, adds infinitely to the probability that I shall discover my error. In trying to draw more clearly the line between invasion and non-invasion, all of us, myself included, are destined to make many mistakes, but by our very mistakes we shall approach our goal. Only Mr. Pentecost and those who think with him take themselves out of the path of progress by assuming that it is possible to live in harmony simply by ignoring the fact of friction and the causes thereof. The no-rule which Mr. Pentecost believes in would amount in practice to submission to the rule of the invasive man. No-rule, in the sense of no-force-in-any-case, is a self-contradiction. The man who attempts to practice it becomes an abettor of government by declining to resist it. So long as Mr. Pentecost is willing to let the criminal ride roughshod over him and me, his "preference not to be ruled at all" is nothing but a beatific revelling in sheerest moonshine and Utopia.

METHODS

PASSIVE RESISTANCE

How are you going to put your theories into practice? is the eternal question propounded by students of sociology to the expounders of Anarchism. To one of those inquirers the editor of *Liberty* made this reply:

"EDGEWORTH" makes appeal to me through *Lucifer* to know how I propose to "starve out Uncle Sam." Light on this subject he would "rather have than roast beef and plum pudding for dinner *in sæculâ sæculorum.*" It puzzles him to know whether by the clause "resistance to taxation" on the "sphynx head of *Liberty* on 'God and the State'" I mean that "true Anarchists should advertise their principles by allowing property to be seized by the sheriff and sold at auction, in order by such personal sacrifices to become known to each other as men and women of a common faith, true to that faith in the teeth of their interests and trustworthy for combined action." If I do mean this, he ventures to "doubt the policy of a test which depletes, not that enormous vampire, Uncle Sam, but our own little purses, so needful for our propaganda of ideas, several times a year, distrainment by the sheriff being in many parts of the country practically equivalent to tenfold taxes." If, on the other hand, I have in view a minority capable of "successfully withdrawing the supplies from Uncle Sam's treasury," he would like to inquire "how any minority, however respectable in numbers and intelligence, is to withstand the sheriff backed by the army, and to withhold tribute to the State."

Fair and pertinent questions these, which I take pleasure in answering. In the first place, then, the policy to be pursued by individual and isolated Anarchists is dependent upon circumstances. I, no more than "Edgeworth," believe in any foolish waste of needed material. It is not wise warfare to throw your ammunition to the enemy unless you throw it from the cannon's mouth. But if you can compel the enemy to waste his ammunition by drawing his fire on some thoroughly protected spot; if you can, by annoying and goading and harassing him in all possible ways, drive him to the last resort of stripping bare his tyrannous and invasive purposes and put him in the attitude of a designing villain assailing honest men for purposes of plunder,—there is no better strategy. Let no Anarchist, then, place his property within reach of the sheriff's clutch. But some year, when he feels exceptionally strong and independent, when his conduct can impair no serious personal obligations, when on the whole he would a little rather go to jail than not, and when his property is in such shape that he can successfully conceal it, let him declare to the assessor property of a certain value, and then defy the collector to collect. Or, if he have no property, let him decline to pay his poll tax. The State will then be put to its trumps. Of two things one,—either it will let him alone, and then he will tell his neighbors all about it, resulting the next year in an alarming disposition on their part to keep their own money in their own pockets; or else it will imprison him, and then by the requisite legal processes he will demand and secure all the rights of a civil prisoner and live thus a decently comfortable life until the State shall get tired of supporting him and the increasing number of persons who will follow his example. Unless, indeed, the State, in desperation, shall see fit to make its laws regarding imprisonment for taxes more rigorous, and then, if our Anarchist be a determined man, we shall find out how far a republican government, "deriving its just powers from the consent of the governed," is ready to go to procure that "consent,"—whether it will stop at solitary confinement in a dark cell or join with the Czar of Russia in administering torture by electricity. The farther it shall go the better it will be for Anarchy, as every student of the history of reform well knows. Who can estimate the power for propagandism of a few cases of this kind, backed by a well-organized force of agitators without the prison walls? So much, then, for individual resistance.

But, if individuals can do so much, what shall be said of the enormous and utterly irresistible power of a large and intelligent minority, comprising say one-fifth of the population in any given locality? I conceive that on this point I need do no more than call "Edgeworth's" attention to the wonderfully instructive history of the Land League movement in Ireland, the most potent and instantly effective revolutionary force the world has ever known so long as it stood by its original policy of "Pay No Rent," and which lost nearly all its strength the day it abandoned that policy. "Oh, but it did abandon it?" "Edgeworth" will exclaim. Yes, but why? Because there the peasantry, instead of being an intelligent minority following the lead of principles, were an ignorant, though enthusiastic and earnest, body of men following blindly the lead of unscrupulous politicians like Parnell, who really wanted anything but the abolition of rent, but were willing to temporarily exploit any sentiment or policy that would float them into power and influence. But it was pursued far enough to show that the British government was utterly powerless before it; and it is scarcely too much to say, in my opinion, that, had it been persisted in, there would not to-day be a landlord in Ireland. It is easier to resist taxes in this country than it is to resist rent in Ireland; and such a policy would be as much more potent here than there as the intelligence of the people is greater, providing always that you can enlist in it a sufficient number of earnest and determined men and women. If one-fifth of the people were to resist taxation, it would cost more to collect their taxes, or try to collect them, than the other four-fifths would consent to pay into the treasury, The force needed for this bloodless fight *Liberty* is slowly but surely recruiting, and sooner or later it will organize for action. Then, Tyranny and Monopoly, down goes your house!

"Passive resistance," said Ferdinand Lassalle, with an obtuseness thoroughly German, "is the resistance which does not resist." Never was there a greater mistake. It is the only resistance which in these days of military discipline resists with any result. There is not a tyrant in the civilized world to-day who would not do anything in his power to precipitate a bloody revolution rather than see himself confronted by any large fraction of his subjects determined not to obey. An insurrection is easily quelled; but no army is willing or able to train its guns on inoffensive people who do not even gather in the streets but stay at home and stand back on their rights. Neither the ballot nor the bayonet is to play any great part in the coming struggle; passive resistance is the instrument by which the revolutionary force is destined to secure in the last great conflict the people's rights forever.

The idea that Anarchy can be inaugurated by force is as fallacious as the idea that it can be sustained by force. Force cannot preserve Anarchy; neither can it bring it. In fact, one of the inevitable influences of the use of force is to postpone Anarchy. The only thing that force can ever do for us is to save us from extinction, to give us a longer lease of life in which to try to secure Anarchy by the only methods that can ever bring it. But this advantage is always purchased at immense cost, and its attainment is always attended by frightful risk. The attempt should be made only when the risk of any other course is greater. When a physician sees that his patient's strength is being exhausted so rapidly by the intensity of his agony that he will die of exhaustion before the medical processes inaugurated have a chance to do their curative work, he administers an opiate. But a good physician is always loth to do so, knowing that one of the influences of the opiate is to interfere with and defeat the medical processes themselves. He never does it except as a choice of evils. It is the same with the use of force, whether of the mob or of the State, upon diseased society; and not only those who prescribe its indiscriminate use as a sovereign remedy and a permanent tonic, but all who ever propose it as a cure, and even all who would lightly and unnecessarily resort to it, not as a cure, but as an expedient, *are social quacks.*

The power of passive resistance has been strikingly illustrated in Russia [1905-6]. She has had three "general strikes," and only the first one was truly, magnificently successful. It was absolutely pacific; it was of the sort that Tolstoi has been urging for years. Workmen, clerks, professional men, even government employees and *dvorniks* (janitors converted into spies and informers), simply dropped their tools, briefs, documents, and what not, and refused to carry on the activities of industrial and political life. The result, on the government's side, was panic. A constitution was granted; a whole series of reforms—on paper—followed.

The second strike was called when the circumstances were unfavorable and the causes distinctly doubtful in the opinion of the majority of the government's enemies. It failed, and the consequent bitterness and apprehension led to a third strike, with an appeal to arms at Moscow. That appeal was most unfortunate; the revolutionary elements had overestimated their strength, and greatly underestimated that of the autocratic-bureaucratic machine. The army was loyal, and the "revolution" was crushed. Now the government has regained its confidence, and is reviving the Plehve tactics. It is suppressing not merely revolutionary bodies and manifestations, but liberal and constitutional ones as well. Reaction is admittedly a strong probability, and the really substantial victories of October may be forfeited.

Of course, human nature is human nature, and it were both idle and unfair to blame the distracted and exasperated Russian radicals for the turn events have taken. Witte has not been honest; the Bourbons were at no time in actual fear of his liberalism. Quite likely any other body of men would have acted as the Russian intellectuals and proletariat committees have acted. Still the fact remains that, had the policy of strictly passive resistance been continued, and had not the strike and boycott weapon been too recklessly used, the cause of freedom and progress in Russia would to-day rejoice in much brighter prospects. Whatever reform Russia shall be shown by developments to have secured she will certainly owe to the peaceful demonstration of the "Red Sunday" and to the passive strike.

Passive resistance and boycotting are now prominent features of every great national movement. Hungary having been threatened with absolutism, and being, probably, too weak to risk war with Austria, what does she do? Her national leaders talk about a boycott against Austrian products and passive resistance to the collection of taxes and the recruiting of troops. In some localities the resistance has already been attempted, with results as painful as demoralizing to the agents of the Austrian government. The boycotting of Austrian products may or may not be irrational, but this tendency to resort to boycotting is a sign of the times.

Of the superior effectiveness of passive resistance to arbitrary and invasive policies it is hardly necesary to speak. It may be noted, however, that the labor members of the British Parliament seem to appreciate the full power of this method of defence. The Balfour-clerical education bill, a reactionary measure, has largely been nullified in Wales by the refusal of its opponents to pay the school rates. The labor group demands legislation throwing the burden of school support and maintenance on the national treasury. Under such a system, passive resistance to the school act would be rendered almost impossible, for national taxation is largely indirect. The reactionaries perceive this, and are not at all averse to the proposal. Local autonomy in taxation and direct local rates are very advantageous to passive resisters, and labor is short-sighted in giving up the adavantage.

THE FUTILITY OF THE BALLOT

No superstition was so tirelessly and so mercilessly attacked by the editor of *Liberty* as that of the ballot. To those who defended it and advocated it as a means of securing liberty he was always ready with a biting answer. Here are some samples of such:

GENERAL BUTLER'S long-expected letter [in acceptance of the nomination for the presidency given him by the labor party] is out at last. The question now is how many it will hoodwink. Among these at least will not be *Liberty*. Would that as much could be asserted of all who think they believe in *Liberty*. But the political habit is a clinging one; the fascinations of political warfare seldom altogether lose their charm over those who have once been under its influence; traces of faith in its efficacy still linger in the minds of those who suppose themselves emancipated; the old majority superstition yet taints the reformer's blood, and, in face of the evils that threaten society's life, he appeals to its saving grace with the same curious mixture of doubt and confidence that sometimes leads a wavering and timorous Infidel, when brought face to face with the fancied terrors of death, to re-embrace the theological superstition from which his good sense has once revolted and to declare his belief on the Lord Jesus, lest, as one of them is said to have profanely put it, "there may be, after all, a God, or a Christ, or a Hell, or some damned thing or other." To such as these, then, Butler will look for some of his strength, and not be disappointed.

The audacity of this demagogue's utterances, the fearlessness with which he exposes such shams and frauds and tyrannies as he does not himself champion, the fury of his onslaught on those hypocrites in high places to dislodge whom for his own benefit and glory he himself hypocritically espouses the cause of the people, all tend to fire such radical hearts as have no radical heads to guide them, and accordingly we see on every hand reformers of every stripe, through their press and on their platforms, enlisting in the service of this incarnation of reaction, this personification of absolutism, this total stranger to the principle of Liberty, this unscrupulous plunderer of labor, this servant of the fearful trinity of the people's enemies, being at once an insincere devotee of the Church, a steadfast lover of a mammoth and omnipotent State, and a bloated beneficiary of the exactions of Capital.

The platform announced in his letter is a ridiculous tissue of contradictions and absurdities. Anti-monopoly only in name, it sanctions innumerable monopolies and privileges, and avowedly favors class legislation. As far as it is not nondescript, it is the beginning of State Socialism,—that is, a long step towards the realization of the most gigantic and appalling monopoly ever conceived by the mind of man. One sentence in it, however, commands my approbation "The laboring man votes for his Fetich, the Democratic party, and the farmer votes for his Fetich, the Republican party, and the result is that both are handed over as captives to the corruptionists and monopolists, whichever side wins. *Mark this: the laborers and the people never win!*" True, every word of it! But why not go a little farther? Suppose both laborer and farmer vote for their new Fetich, Ben Butler and his party of State Socialism, what will be the result then? Will not both be handed over as captives to a band of corruptionists as much larger and greedier as the reach and resources of the government are made vaster, all in the service and pay, not of a number of distinct and relatively weak monopolies, but of one consolidated monopoly whose rapacity will know no bounds? No doubt about it whatever. Let those who will, then, bow before this idol,—no Anarchistic knee shall bend. We Anarchists have not come for that. We come to shatter Fetiches, not to kneel before them,—no more before Fetich Butler than Fetich Blaine or Fetich Cleveland or Fetich St. John. We are here to let in the light of Liberty upon political superstition, and from that policy can result no captivity to corruption, no subserviency to monopoly, only a *world of free laborers controlling the products of their labor and growing richer every day.*

I greatly admire Hugh O. Pentecost. He is a growing and a fair-minded man. His *Twentieth Century*, now published weekly in an enlarged form, is doing a useful work. He already accepts Anarchy as an ultimate, and the whole tenor of his writings is leading him on, it seems to me, to a casting-off of his devotion to the single-tax movement and to reforms still more distinctly State Socialistic, and to a direct advocacy of Anarchistic principles and methods. It is because I believe this that I feel like reasoning with him regarding a vital inconsistency in his discourse of January 13 on "Ballots or Bullets?" in which, moreover, the tendency referred to is marked.

After laying it down as a principle that force is never justifiable (and, by the way, I cannot accept so absolute a denial of force as this, though I heartily agree that force is futile in *almost all* circumstances), he goes on as follows: "If it is not justifiable for the establishment and maintenance of government, neither is it justifiable for the overthrow or modification of government. . . . The intellectual and moral process of regeneration is slower than force, but it is right; and when the work is thus done, it has the merit of having been done properly and thoroughly." So far, excellent. But mark the next sentence: "The ballot is the people's agency even for correcting its own evils, and it seems to me a social crime to refrain from its use for regenerative purposes until it is absolutely demonstrated that it is a failure as an instrument for freedom."

Now, what is the ballot? It is neither more nor less than a paper representative of the bayonet, the billy, and the bullet. It is a labor-saving device for ascertaining on which side force lies and bowing to the inevitable. The voice of the majority saves bloodshed, but it is no less the arbitrament of force than is the decree of the most absolute of despots backed by the most powerful of armies. Of course it may be claimed that the struggle to attain to the majority involves an incidental use of intellectual and moral processes; but these influences would exert themselves still more powerfully in other channels if there were no such thing as the ballot, and, when used as subsidiary to the ballot, they represent only a striving for the time when physical force can be substituted for them. Reason devoted to politics fights for its own dethronement. The moment the minority becomes the majority, it ceases to reason and persuade, and begins to command and enforce and punish. If this be true,—and I think that Mr. Pentecost will have difficulty in gainsaying it,—it follows that to use the ballot for the modification of government is to use force for the modification of government; which sequence makes it at once evident that Mr. Pentecost in his conclusion pronounces it a social crime to avoid that course which in his premise he declares unjustifiable.

It behooves Mr. Pentecost to examine this charge of inconsistency carefully, for his answer to it must deeply affect his career. If he finds that it is well-founded, the sincerity of his nature will oblige him to abandon all such political measures as the taxation of land values and the government ownership of banks and railroads and devote himself to Anarchism, which offers not only the goal that he seeks, but confines itself to those purely educational methods of reaching it with which he finds himself in sympathy.

VOLUNTARY CO-OPERATION A REMEDY

Mr. Wordsworth Donisthorpe, of London, wrote a lengthy plaint in *Liberty*, setting forth his woes as a citizen beset with various difficulties. He wished to be informed if Anarchism could free him from those woes, whereupon Mr. Tucker tried to lead him to the light:

THE Anarchists never have claimed that liberty will bring perfection; they simply say that its results are vastly preferable to those that follow authority. Under liberty Mr. Donisthorpe may have to listen for some minutes every day to the barrel-organ (though I really think that it will never lodge him in the mad-house), but at least he will have the privilege of going to the music-hall in the evening; whereas, under authority, even in its most honest and consistent form, he will get rid of the barrel-organ only at the expense of being deprived of the music-hall, and, in its less honest, less consistent, and more probable form, he may lose the music-hall at the same time that he is forced to endure the barrel-organ. As a choice of blessings, liberty is the greater; as a choice of evils, liberty is the smaller. Then liberty always, say the Anarchists. No use of force, except against the invader; and in those cases where it is difficult to tell whether the alleged offender is an invader or not, still no use of force except where the necessity of immediate solution is so imperative that we must use it to save ourselves. And in these few cases where we must use it, let us do so frankly and squarely, acknowledging it as a matter of necessity, without seeking to harmonize our action with any political ideal or constructing any far-fetched theory of a State or collectivity having prerogatives and rights superior to those of individuals and aggregations of individuals and exempted from the operation of the ethical principles which individuals are expected to observe. But to say all this to Mr. Donisthorpe is like carrying coals to Newcatsle. He knows as well as I do that "liberty is not the daughter, but the mother of order."

I will try to deal briefly with Mr. Donisthorpe's questions. To his first: "How far may voluntary co-operators invade the liberty of others?" I answer: Not at all. Under this head I have previously made answer to Mr. Donisthorpe and this is the best rule that I can frame as a guide to voluntary co-operators. To apply it to only one of Mr. Donisthorpe's cases, I think that under a system of Anarchy, even if it were admitted that there was some ground for considering an unvaccinated person an invader, it would be generally recognized that such invasion was not of a character to require treatment by force, and that any attempt to treat it by force would be regarded as itself an invasion of a less doubtful and more immediate nature, requiring as such to be resisted.

But under a system of Anarchy how is such resistance to be made? is Mr. Donisthorpe's second question. By another band of voluntary co-operators. But are we then, Mr. Donisthorpe will ask, to have innumerable bands of voluntary co-operators perpetually at war with each other? Not at all. A system of Anarchy in actual operation implies a previous education of the people in the principles of Anarchy, and that in turn implies such a distrust and hatred of interference that the only band of voluntary co-operators which could gain support sufficient to enforce its will would be that which either entirely refrained from interference or reduced it to a minimum. This would be my answer to Mr. Donisthorpe, were I to admit his assumption of a state of Anarchy supervening upon a sudden collapse of Archy. But I really scout this assumption as absurd. Anarchists work for the abolition of the State, but by this they mean not its overthrow, but, as Proudhon put it, its dissolution in the economic organism. This being the case, the question before us is not, as Mr. Donisthorpe supposes, what measures and means of interference we are justified in instituting, but which ones of those already existing we should first lop off. And to this the Anarchists answer that unquestionably the first to go should be those that interfere most fundamentally with a free market, and that the economic and moral changes that would result from this would act as a solvent upon all the remaining forms of interference.

"Is compulsory co-operation ever desirable?" Compulsory co-operation is simply one form of invading the liberty of others, and voluntary co-operators will not be justified in resorting to it—that is, in becoming compulsory co-operators—any more than resorting to any other form of invasion.

"How are we to remove the injustice of allowing one man to enjoy what another has earned?" I do not expect it ever to be removed altogether. But I believe that for every dollar that would be enjoyed by tax-dodgers under Anarchy, a thousand dollars are now enjoyed by men who have got possession of the earnings of others through special industrial, commercial, and financial privileges granted them by authority in violation of a free market.

ECONOMICS

I—MONEY AND INTEREST

CAPITAL, PROFITS, AND INTEREST

In the study of the economic question, the first thing that must engage our attention is why the worker fails to get all of the product of his labor. Volumes have been written by economists of various schools in discussion of the problem, most of them muddling about in the mire of their own misconceptions. But the editor of *Liberty* went straight to the heart of the matter and quickly found the answer:

"SOMEBODY gets the surplus wealth that labor produces and does not consume. Who is the Somebody?" Such is the problem recently posited in the editorial columns of the New York *Truth*. Substantially the same question has been asked a great many times before, but, as might have been expected, this new form of putting it has created no small hubbub. *Truth's* columns are full of it; other journals are taking it up; clubs are organizing to discuss it; the people are thinking about it; students are pondering over it. For it is a most momentous question. A correct answer to it is unquestionably the first step in the settlement of the appalling problem of poverty, intemperance, ignorance, and crime. *Truth*, in selecting it as a subject on which to harp and hammer from day to day, shows itself a level-headed, far-sighted newspaper. But, important as it is, it is by no means a difficult question to one who really considers it before giving an answer, though the variety and absurdity of nearly all the replies thus far volunteered certainly tend to give an opposite impression.

What are the ways by which men gain possession of property? Not many. Let us name them: work, gift, discovery, gaming, the various forms of illegal robbery by force or fraud, usury. Can men obtain wealth by any other than one or more of these methods? Clearly, no. Whoever the Somebody may be, then, he must accumulate his riches in one of these ways. We will find him by the process of elimination.

Is the Somebody the laborer? No; at least not as laborer; otherwise the question were absurd. Its premises exclude him. He gains a bare subsistence by his work; no more. We are searching for his surplus product. He has it not.

Is the Somebody the beggar, the invalid, the cripple, the discoverer, the gambler, the highway robber, the burglar, the defaulter, the pickpocket, or the common swindler? None of these, to any extent worth mentioning. The aggregate of wealth absorbed by these classes of our population compared with the vast mass produced is a mere drop in the ocean, unworthy of consideration in studying a fundamental problem of political economy. These people get some wealth, it is true; enough, probably for their own purposes: but labor can spare them the whole of it, and never know the difference.

Then we have found him. Only the usurer remaining, he must be the Somebody whom we are looking for; he, and none other. But who is the usurer, and whence comes his power? There are three forms of usury; interest on money, rent of land and houses, and profit in exchange. Whoever is in receipt of any of these is a usurer. And who is not? Scarcely any one. The banker is a usurer; the manufacturer is a usurer; the merchant is a usurer; the landlord is a usurer; and the workingman who puts his savings, if he has any, out at interest, or takes rent for his house or lot, if he owns one, or exchanges his labor for more than an equivalent,—he too is a usurer. The sin of usury is one under which all are concluded, and for which all are responsible. But all do not benefit by it. The vast majority suffer. Only the chief usurers accumulate: in agricultural and thickly-settled countries, the landlords; in industrial and commercial countries, the bankers. Those are the Somebodies who swallow up the surplus wealth.

And where do the Somebodies get their power? From monopoly. Here, as usual, the State is the chief of sinners. Usury rests on two great monopolies,—the monopoly of land

and the monopoly of credit. Were it not for these, it would disappear. Ground-rent exists only because the State stands by to collect it and to protect land-titles rooted in force or fraud. Otherwise the land would be free to all, and no one could control more than he used. Interest and house-rent exist only because the State grants to a certain class of individuals and corporations the exclusive privilege of using its credit and theirs as a basis for the issuance of circulating currency. Otherwise credit would be free to all, and money, brought under the law of competition, would be issued at cost. Interest and rent gone, competition would leave little or no chance for profit in exchange except in business protected by tariff or patent laws. And there again the State has but to step aside to cause the last vestige of usury to disappear.

The usurer is the Somebody, and the State is his protector. Usury is the serpent gnawing at labor's vitals, and only liberty can detach and kill it. Give laborers their liberty, and they will keep their wealth. As for the Somebody, he, stripped of his power to steal, must either join their ranks or starve.

Mr. J. M. L. Babcock, of Boston, at that time a Greenbacker but later becoming a thorough-going opponent of interest, wrote in the columns of *Liberty* in defense of both interest and profits. Mr. Tucker therefore had to set him right:

"WHATEVER contributes to production is entitled to an equitable share in the distribution!" Wrong! *Whoever* contributes to production is alone so entitled. *What* has no rights that *Who* is bound to respect. *What* is a thing. *Who* is a person. Things have no claims; they exist only to be claimed. The possession of a right cannot be predicated of dead material, but only of a living person. "In the production of a loaf of bread, the plough performs an important service, and equitably comes in for a share of the loaf." Absurd! A plough cannot own bread, and, if it could, would be unable to eat it. A plough is a *What*, one of those things above mentioned, to which no rights are attributable.

Oh! but we see. "Suppose one man spends his life in

making ploughs to be used by others who sow and harvest wheat. If he furnishes his ploughs only on condition that they be returned to him in as good state as when taken away, how is he to get his bread?" It is the maker of the plough, then, and not the plough itself, that is entitled to a reward? *What* has given place to *Who*. Well, we'll not quarrel over that. The maker of the plough certainly is entitled to pay for his work. Full pay, paid once; no more. That pay is the plough itself, or its equivalent in other marketable products, said equivalent being measured by the amount of labor employed in their production. But if he lends his plough and gets only his plough back, how is he to get his bread? asks Mr. Babcock, much concerned. Ask us an easy one, if you please. We give this one up. But why should he lend his plough? Why does he not sell it to the farmer, and use the proceeds to buy bread of the baker? See, Mr. Babcock? If the lender of the plough "receives nothing more than his plough again, he receives nothing for the product of his own labor, and is on the way to starvation." Well, if the fool will not sell his plough, let him starve. Who cares? It's his own fault. How can he expect to receive anything for the product of his own labor if he refuses to permanently part with it? Does Mr. Babcock propose to steadily add to this product at the expense of some laborer, and meanwhile allow this idler, who has only made a plough, to loaf on in luxury, for the balance of his life, on the strength of his one achievement? Certainly not, when our friend understands himself. And then he will say with us that the slice of bread which the plough-lender should receive can be neither large nor small, but must be nothing.

We refer Mr. Babcock to one of his favorite authors, John Ruskin [in "Letters to British Workmen," under the heading, "The Position of William"], who argues this very point on Mr. Babcock's own ground, except that he illustrates his position by a plane instead of a plough.

Mr. Babcock replies by denying the similarity, saying that Ruskin "concludes that the case he examines is one of sale and purchase." Let us see. Ruskin is examining a story told by Bastiat in illustration and defence of usury. After printing Bastiat's version of it, he abridges it thus, stripping away all mystifying clauses:

"James makes a plane, lends it to William on 1st of January for a year. William gives him a plank for the loan of it, wears it out, and makes another for James, which he gives him on 31st December. On 1st January he again borrows the new one; and the arrangement is repeated continuously. The position of William, therefore, is that he makes a plane every 31st of December; lends it to James till the next day, and pays James a plank annually for the privilege of lending it to him on that evening."

Substitute in the foregoing "plough" for "plane," and "loaf" or "slice" for "plank," and the story differs in no essential point from Mr. Babcock's. How monstrously unjust the transaction is can be plainly seen. Ruskin next shows how this unjust transaction may be changed into a just one:

"If James did not lend the plane to William, he could only get his gain of a plank by working with it himself and wearing it out himself. When he had worn it out at the end of the year, he would, therefore, have to make another for himself. William, working with it instead, gets the advantage instead, which he must, therefore, pay James his plank for; and return to James what James would, if he had not lent his plane, then have had—not a new plane, but the worn-out one. James must make a new one for himself, as he would have had to do if no William had existed; and if William likes to borrow it again for another plank, all is fair. That is to say, clearing the story of its nonsense, that James makes a plane annually and sells it to William for its proper price, which, in kind, is a new plank."

It is *this latter transaction,* wholly different from the former, that Ruskin pronounces a "sale," having "nothing whatever to do with principal or with interest." And yet, according to Mr. Babcock, "the case he examines [Bastiat's, of course] is one of sale and purchase."

It is an error common with the economists to assume that an increase of capital decreases the rate of interest and that nothing else can materially decrease it. The facts are just the contrary. The rate of interest may, and often does, decrease when the amount of capital has not increased; the amount of capital may increase without decreasing the rate of interest, which may in fact increase at the same time; and so far from the universalization of wealth being the sole means of abolishing interest, the abolition of interest is the *sine qua non* of the universalization of wealth.

Suppose, for instance, that the banking business of a nation is conducted by a system of banks chartered and regulated by the government, these banks issuing paper money based on specie, dollar for dollar. If now a certain number of these banks, by combining to buy up the national legislature, should secure the exclusive privilege of issuing two paper dollars for each specie dollar in their vaults, could they not afford to, and would they not in fact, materially reduce their rate of discount? Would not the competing banks be forced to reduce their rate in consequence? And would not this reduction lower the rate of interest throughout the nation? Undoubtedly; and yet the amount of capital in the country remains the same as before.

Suppose, further, that during the following year, in consequence of the stimulus given to business and production by this decrease in the rate of interest and also because of unusually favorable natural conditions, a great increase of wealth occurs. If then the banks of the nation, holding from the government a monopoly of the power to issue money, should combine to contract the volume of the currency, could they not, and would they not, raise the rate of interest thereby? Undoubtedly; and yet the amount of capital in the country is greater than it ever was before.

But suppose, on the other hand, that all these banks, chartered and regulated by the government and issuing money dollar for dollar, had finally been allowed to issue paper beyond their capital based on the credit and guaranteed capital of their customers; that their circulation, thus doubly secured, had become so popular that people preferred to pay their debts in coin instead of bank-notes, thus causing coin to flow into the vaults of the banks and add to their reserve; that this additon had enabled them to add further to their circulation, until, by a continuation of the process, it at last amounted to eight times their original capital; that by levying a high rate of interest on this they had bled the people nigh unto death; that then the government had stepped in and said to the banks: "When you began, you received an annual interest of six per cent. on your capital; you now receive nearly that rate on a circulation eight times your capital based really on the people's credit; therefore at one-eighth of the original rate your annual profit would be as great as formerly; henceforth your rate of discount must not exceed three-fourths of one per cent." Had all this happened (and with the exception of the last condition of the hypothesis similar cases have frequently happened), what would have been the result? The reduction of the rate of discount to the bank's service, and the results therefrom as above described, are precisely what would happen if the whole business of banking should be thrown open to free competition.

Another error is the assumption that "in the last analysis the possessor of capital has acquired it by a willingness to work harder than his fellows and to sacrifice his love of spending all he produces that he may have the aid of capital to increase his power of production." This is one of the most devilish of the many infernal lies for which the economists have to answer. It is indeed true that the possessor of capital may, in rare cases, have acquired it by the method stated, though even then he could not be excused for making the capital so acquired a leech upon his fellow-men. But ninety-nine times in a hundred the modern possessor of any large amount of capital has acquired it, not "by a willingness to work harder than his fellows," but by a shrewdness in getting possession of a monopoly which makes it needless for him to do any *real work* at all; not by a willingness "to sacrifice his love of spending all he produces," but by a cleverness in procuring from the government a privilege by which he is able to spend in wanton luxury half of what a large number of other men produce. The chief privilege to which we refer is that of selling the people's credit for a price.

Again, it is an error to suppose that to confine the term *money* to coin and to call all other money *currency* would simplify matters, when in reality it is the insistence upon this false distinction that is the prevailing cause of mystification. If the idea of the royalty of gold and silver could be once knocked out of the people's heads, and they could once understand that no particular kind of merchandise is created by nature for monetary purposes, they would settle this question in a trice. Some persons seem to think that Josiah Warren based his notes on corn. Nothing of the kind. Warren simply took corn as his standard, but made *labor and all its products* his basis. His labor notes were rarely redeemed in corn. If he had made corn his exclusive basis, there would be no distinction in principle between him and the specie men. Perhaps the central point in his monetary theory was his denial of the idea that any one product of labor can properly be made the only basis of money. A charge that this system, which recognized *cost* as the only ground of price, even contemplated a promise to pay anything "for *value* received," he would deem the climax of insult to his memory.

It is a mistake, too, to think that land is not a good basis for currency. True, unimproved vacant land, not having properly a market value, cannot properly give value to anything that represents it; but permanent improvements on land, which should have a market value and carry with them a title to possession, are an excellent basis for currency. It is not the raw material of any product that fits it for a basis, but the labor that has been expended in shaping the material. As for the immovability of land unfitting it for a basis, it has just the opposite effect. We should not be misled by the idea that currency can be redeemed only in that on which it is based.

FREE MONEY FIRST

J. M. M'GREGOR, a writer for the Detroit *Labor Leaf* thinks free land the chief desideratum. And yet he acknowledges that the wage-worker can't go from any of our manufacturing centres to the western lands, because "such a move would involve a cash outlay of a thousand dollars, which he has not got, nor can he get it." It would seem, then, that free land, though greatly to be desired, is not as sorely needed here and now as free capital. And this same need of capital would be equally embarrassing if the eastern lands were free, for still more capital would be required to stock and work a farm than the wage-worker can command. Under our present money system he could not even get capital by putting up his farm as collateral, unless he would agree to pay a rate of interest that would eat him up in a few years. Therefore, free land is of little value to labor without free capital, while free capital would be of inestimable benefit to labor even if land should not be freed for some time to come. For with it labor could go into other industries on the spot and achieve its independence. Not free land, then, but free money is the chief desideratum. It is in the perception of this prime importance of the money question that the greenbackers, despite their utterly erroneous solution of it, show their marked superiority to the State Socialists and the land nationalizationists.

The craze to get people upon the land is one of the insanities that has dominated social reformers ever since social reform was first thought of. It is a great mistake. Of agriculture it is as true as of every other industry that there should be as few people engaged in it as possible,—that is, just enough to supply the world with all the agricultural products which it wants. The fewer farmers there are, after this point of necessary supply is reached, the more useful people there are to engage in other industries which have not yet reached this point, and to devise and work at new industries hitherto unthought of. It is altogether likely that we have too many farmers now. It is not best that any more of us should become farmers, even if every homestead could be made an Arcadia. The plough is very well in its way, and Arcadia was very well in its day. But the way of the plough is not as wide as the world, and the world has outgrown the day of Arcadia. Human life henceforth is to be, not a simple, but a complex thing. The wants and aspirations of mankind are daily multiplying. They can be satisfied only by the diversification of industry, which is the method of progress and the record of civilization. This is one of the great truths which Lysander Spooner has so long been shouting into unwilling ears. But the further diversification of industry in such a way as to benefit, no longer the few and the idle, but the many and the industrious, depends upon the control of capital by labor. And this, as Proudhon, Warren, Greene, and Spooner have shown, can be secured only by a free money system.

In answer to my article, "Free Money First," in which was discussed the comparative importance of the money and land questions, J. M. M'Gregor, of the Detroit *Labor Leaf*, says: "I grant free money first. I firmly believe free money will come first, too, though my critic and myself may be widely at variance in regard to what would constitute free money." I mean by free money the utter absence of restriction upon the issue of all money not fraudulent. If Mr. M'Gregor believes in this, I am heartily glad. I should like to be half as sure as he is that it really is coming first. From the present temper of the people it looks to me as if nothing *free* would come first. They seem to be bent on trying every form of compulsion. In this current Mr. M'Gregor is far to the fore with his scheme of land taxation on the Henry George plan, and although he may believe free money will be first in time, he clearly does not consider it first in importance. This last-mentioned priority he awards to land reform, and it was his position in that regard that my article was written to dispute.

The issue between us, thus confined, hangs upon the truth or falsity of Mr. M'Gregor's statement that "to-day landlordism, through rent and speculation, supports more idlers than any other system of profit-robbing known to our great commonwealth." I take it that Mr. M'Gregor, by "rent," means ground-rent exclusively, and, by the phrase "supports more idlers," means takes more from labor; otherwise, his statement has no pertinence to his position. For all rent except ground-rent would be almost entirely and directly abolished by free money, and the evil of rent to labor depends, not so much on the number of idlers it supports, as on the aggregate amount and quality of support it gives them, whether they be many or few in number. Mr. M'Gregor's statement, then, amounts to this: that ground-rent takes more from labor than any other form of usury. It needs no statistics to disprove this. The principal forms of usury are interest on money loaned or invested, profits made in buying and selling, rent of buildings of all sorts, and ground-rent. A moment's reflection will show any one that the amount of loaned or invested capital bearing interest in this country to-day far exceeds in value the amount of land yielding rent. The item of interest alone is a much more serious burden on the people than that of ground-rent. Much less, then, does ground-rent equal interest *plus* profit *plus* rent of buildings. But to make Mr. M'Gregor's argument really valid it must exceed all these combined. For a true money reform, I repeat, would abolish almost entirely and directly every one of these forms of usury except ground-rent, while a true land reform would directly abolish only ground-rent. Therefore, unless labor pays more in ground-rent than in interest, profit, and rent of buildings combined, the money question is of more importance than the land question. There are countries where this is the case, but the United States is not one of them.

It should also be borne in mind that free money, in destroying the power to accumulate large fortunes in the ordinary industries of life, will put a very powerful check upon the scramble for corner-lots and other advantageous positions, and thereby have a considerable influence upon ground-rent itself.

"How can capital be free," asks Mr. M'Gregor, "when it cannot get rid of rent?" It cannot be entirely free till it can get rid of rent; but it will be infinitely freer if it gets rid of interest, profit, and rent of buildings and still keeps ground-rent than if it gets rid of ground-rent and keeps the other forms of usury. Give us free money, the first great step to Anarchy, and we'll attend to ground-rent afterwards.

FREE BANKING

In 1889, Mr. Hugo Bilgram first published his "Involuntary Idleness," which Mr. Tucker characterized as the most important book of the generation. But, while admiring the author's examination of the relation between unemployment and interest on money, and while agreeing with his conclusion that "an expansion of the volume of money, by extending the issue of credit money, will prevent business stagnation and involuntary idleness," the editor of *Liberty* had one substantial disagreement with Mr. Bilgram, which he stated thus:

WHEN Mr. Bilgram proposes that the government shall carry on (and presumably monopolize, though this is not clearly stated) the business of issuing money, it is hardly necessary to say that *Liberty* cannot follow him. It goes with him in his economy, but not in his politics. There are at least three valid reasons, and doubtless others also, why the government should do nothing of the kind.

First the government is a tyrant living by theft, and therefore has no business to engage in any business.

Second, the government has none of the characteristics of a successful business man, being wasteful, careless, clumsy, and short-sighted in the extreme.

Third, the government is thoroughly irresponsible, having it in its power to effectively repudiate its obligations at any time.

With these qualifications *Liberty* gives Mr. Bilgram's book enthusiastic welcome. Its high price will debar many from reading it; but money cannot be expended more wisely than in learning the truth about money.

Mr. Bilgram then writes to *Liberty* in defense of his contention that State banking is preferable to mutual banking on the ground that "mutual banking cannot deprive capital of its power to bring unearned returns to its owner." Mr. Tucker proceeds to demolish that position:

Mr. Bilgram, if I understand him, prefers government banking to mutual banking, because with the former the rate of discount would simply cover risk, all banking expenses being paid out of the public treasury, while with the latter the rate of discount would cover both risk and banking expenses, which in his opinion would place the burden of banking expenses upon the borrowers instead of upon the people. The answer to this is simple and decisive: the burden of discount, no matter what elements, many or few, may constitute it, falls *ultimately*, under any system, not on the borrowers, but on the people. Broadly speaking, all the interest paid is paid by the people. Under mutual banking the expenses of the banks would, it is true, be paid directly by the borrowers, but the latter would recover this from the people in the prices placed upon their products. And it seems to me much more scientific that the people should thus pay these expenses through the borrowers in the regular channels of exchange than that they should follow the communistic method of paying them through the public treasury.

Mr. Bilgram's statement that money-lenders who, besides being compensated for risk, are compensated for their labor as bankers and for their incidental expenses "thereby obtain an income from the mere loan of money" is incomprehensible to me. He might just as well say that under government banking the officials who should receive salaries from the treasury for carrying on the business would thereby obtain an income from the mere loan of money. Under a free system the banker is as simply and truly paid only the normal wage of his labor as is the official under a government system.

But, since Mr. Bilgram does not propose to place any restriction upon private banking, I have no quarrel with him. He is welcome to his opinion that private banking could not compete with the governmental institution. I stoutly maintain the contrary, and the very existence of the financial prohibitions is the best evidence that I am right. That which can succeed by intrinsic merit never seeks a legal bolster.

Mr. Bilgram remained unconvinced that he was wrong in every respect, and still maintained that the cost of making the tokens should be defrayed by the government. To which Mr. Tucker replied that there are at least two answers:

THE first is that that factor in the rate of interest which represents the cost of making tokens is so insignificant (probably less than one-tenth of one per cent., guessing at it) that the people could well afford (if there were no alternative) to let a few individuals profit to that extent rather than suffer the enormous evils that result from transferring enterprise from private to government control. I am not so enamored of *absolute* equality that I would sacrifice both hands rather than one finger.

The second answer is that no private money-lenders could, under a free system, reap even the small profit referred to. Mr. Bilgram speaks of "those who lend money which they have acquired." Acquired how? Any money which they have acquired must have originated with issuers who paid the cost of making the tokens, and every time it has changed hands the burden of this cost has been transferred with it.

Is it likely that men who acquire money by paying this cost will lend it to others without exacting this cost? If they should, they would be working for others for nothing,—a very different thing from "receiving pay for work they had not performed." No man can lend money unless he either issues it himself and pays the cost of making the tokens, or else buys or borrows it from others to whom he must pay that cost.

Along these same lines Mr. J. K. Ingalls contributed to *Liberty* an article, and incidentally asked the editor some questions; among others, whether, if mutual money is to be made redeemable in gold or silver, it involves the principle of a legal tender, or of a tender of "common consent." Mr. Tucker answers:

YES, it does involve one of these, but between the two there is all the difference that there is between force and freedom, authority and liberty. And where the tender is one of "common consent," those who do not like it are at liberty to consent in common to use any other and better one that they can devise.

It is difficult for me to see any fraud in promising to pay a certain thing in a certain time, or on demand, and keeping the promise. That is what we do when we issue redeemable money and afterwards redeem it. The fraud in regard to money consists not in this, but in limiting by law the security for these promises to pay to a special kind of property, limited in quantity and easily monopolizable.

It is doubtful if there is anything more variable in its purchasing power than labor. The causes of this are partly natural, such as the changing conditions of production, and partly and principally artificial, such as the legal monopolies that impart fictitious values. But labor expended in certain directions is unquestionably more constant in its average results than when expended in other directions. Hence the advantage of using the commodities resulting from the former for the redemption of currency whenever redemption shall be demanded. Whether gold and silver are among these commodities is a question, not of principle, but of statistics. As a matter of fact, the holders of good redeemable money seldom ask for any other redemption than its acceptance in the market and its final cancellation by the issuer's restoration of the securities on which it was issued. But in case any other redemption is desired, it is necessary to adopt for the purpose some commodity easily transferable and most nearly invariable in value.

Does Mr. Ingalls mean that all money must be abolished? I can see no other inference from his position. For there are only two kinds of money,—commodity money and credit money. The former he certainly does not believe in, the latter he thinks fraudulent and unsafe. Are we, then, to stop exchanging the products of our labor?

It is clearly the right of every man to gamble if he chooses to, and he has as good a right to make his bets on the rise and fall of grain prices as on anything else; only he must not gamble with loaded dice, or be allowed special privileges whereby he can control the price of grain. Hence, in a free and open market, these transactions where neither equivalent is transferred are legitimate enough. But they are unwise, because, apart from the winning or losing of the bet, there is no advantage to be gained from them. Transactions, on the other hand, in which only one equivalent is immediately transferred are frequently of the greatest advantage, as they enable men to get possession of tools which they immediately need, but cannot immediately pay for. Of course the promise to pay is liable to be more or less valuable at maturity than when issued, but so is the property originally transferred. The borrower is no more exempt than the lender from the variations in value. And the interests of the holder of property who neither borrows nor lends are also just as much affected by them. There is an element of chance in all property relations. So far as this is due to monopoly and privilege, we must do our best to abolish it; so far as it is natural and inevitable, we must get along with it as best we can, but not be frightened by it into discarding credit and money, the most potent instruments of association and civilization.

Liberty is published not so much to thoroughly inform its readers regarding the ideas which it advocates as to interest them to seek this thorough information through other channels. For instance, in regard to free money, there is a book—"Mutual Banking," by William B. Greene—which sets forth the evils of money monopoly and the blessings of gratuitous credit in a perfectly plain and convincing way to all who will take the pains to study and understand it. *Liberty* can only state baldly the principles which Greene advocates and hint at some of their results. Whomsoever such statements and hints serve to interest can and will secure the book of me for a small sum. Substantially the same views, presented in different ways, are to be found in the financial writings of Lysander Spooner, Stephen Pearl Andrews, Josiah Warren, and, above all, P. J. Proudhon, whose untranslated works contain untold treasures, which I hope some day to put within the reach of English readers.

THE ABOLITION OF INTEREST

To-day, a weekly newspaper published in Boston in 1890, printed an editorial on the subject of interest which contained so many vulnerable points that the editor of *Liberty* was moved to criticize it. After pointing out the errors and fallacies in the editorial, he proceeded:

THE modern opponents of interest are perfectly willing to consider facts tending to refute their position, but no facts can have such a tendency unless they belong to one of two classes: first, facts showing that interest has generally (not sporadically) existed in a community in whose economy money was as important a factor as it is with us to-day and in whose laws there was no restriction upon its issue; or, second, facts showing that interest is sustained by causes that would still be effectively, invincibly operative after the abolition of the banking monopoly. I do not find any such facts among those cited by *To-day*. The array is formidable in appearance only. Possession of encyclopædic knowledge is a virtue which Spencer sometimes exaggerates into a vice, and a vice which some of his disciples too seldom reduce to the proportions of a virtue.

To the economic truism I will give a little more attention, its irrelevancy being less apparent. Here it is: "The existence of interest depends, of course, primarily upon the existence of private property." I call this a truism, though the word "primarily" introduces an element of error. If we are to inquire upon what interest *primarily* depends, we shall start upon an endless journey into the realm of metaphysics. But without entering that realm we certainly can go farther back in the series than private property and find that interest depends still more remotely upon the existence of human beings and even of the universe itself. However, interest undoubtedly depends upon private property, and, if this fact had any significance, I should not stop to trifle over the word "primarily." But it has no significance. It only seems to have significance because it carries, or seems to be supposed to carry, the implication that, if private property is a necessary condition of interest, interest is a necessary result of private property. The inference, of course, is wholly unwarranted by logic, but that it is intended appears from a remark almost immediately following: "Expectations have been entertained that it [interest] will eventually become zero; but this stage will probably be reached only when economic products become common free property of the human race." The word "probably" leaves the writer, to be sure, a small logical loophole of escape, but it is not expected that the reader will notice it, the emphasis being all in the other direction. The reader is expected to look upon interest as a necessary result of private property simply because without private property there could be no interest. Now, my hat sometimes hangs upon a hook, and, if there were no hook, there could be no hanging hat; but it by no means follows that because there is a hook there must be a hanging hat. Therefore, if I wanted to abolish hanging hats, it would be idle, irrelevant, and illogical to declare that I must first abolish hooks. Likewise it is idle, irrelevant, and illogical to declare that before interest can be abolished private property must be abolished. Take another illustration. If there were no winter, water-pipes would never freeze up, but it is not necessary to abolish winter to prevent this freezing. Human device has succeeded in preventing it as a general thing. Similarly, without private property there would be no borrowing of capital and therefore no interest; but it is claimed that, without abolishing private property, a human device—namely, money and banking—will, if not restricted, prevent the necessity of borrowing capital as a general thing, and therefore virtually abolish interest; though interest might still be paid in extraordinary cases, just as water-pipes still freeze up under extraordinary conditions. Is this claim true? That is the only question.

This claim is met in the single relevant sixteenth of *Today*'s article. But it is met simply by denial, which is not disproof. I give the writer's words:

"The most popular fallacy upon the subject now is that the rate of interest can be lowered by increasing the amount of currency. What men really wish to borrow usually is capital,—agencies of production,—and money is only a means for the transfer of these. The amount of currency can have no effect upon the abundance of capital, and even an increase in the abundance of capital does not always lower the rate of interest; this is partly determined by the value of capital in use."

This paragraph, though introduced with a rather *nonchalant* air, seems to have been the objective point of the entire article. All the rest was apparently written to furnish an occasion for voicing the excessively silly notion that "the amount of currency can have no effect upon the abundance of capital." As I have already said, to show how silly it is, it is only necessary to slightly change the wording of the phrase. Let it be stated thus: "The *abolition* of currency can have no effect upon the abundance of capital." Of course, if the former statement is true, the latter follows. But the latter is *manifestly* absurd, and hence the former is false. To affirm it is to affirm that currency does not facilitate the distribution of wealth; for if it does, then it increases the effective demand for wealth, and hence the production of wealth, and hence the abundance of capital. It is true that "an increase in the abundance of capital does not always lower the rate of interest." An extra horse attached to a heavy load does not always move the load. If the load is heavy enough, two extra horses will be required to move it. But it is always the tendency of the first extra horse to move it, whether he succeeds or not. In the same way, increase of capital always *tends* to lower interest up to the time when interest disappears entirely. But though increased capital lowers interest and increased currency increases capital, increased currency also acts directly in lowering interest before it has increased the amount of capital. It is here that the editor of *To-day* seems to show unfamiliarity with the position of the opponents of interest. It is true that what men really wish to get is capital,—the agencies of production. And it is precisely because money is "a means for the transfer of these" that the ability to issue money secured by their own property would make it unnecessary for them to borrow these agencies by enabling them to buy them. This raises a question which I have asked hundreds of times of defenders of interest and which has invariably proved a "poser." I will now put it to the editor of *To-day*, A is a farmer owning a farm. He mortgages his farm to a bank for $1,000, giving the bank a mortgage note for that sum and receiving in exchange the bank's notes for the same sum, which are secured by the mortgage. With the bank-notes A buys farming tools of B. The next day B uses the notes to buy of C the materials used in the manufacture of tools. The day after, C in turn pays them to D in exchange for something that he needs. At the end of a year, after a constant succession of exchanges, the notes are in the hands of Z, a dealer in farm produce. He pays them to A, who gives in return $1,000 worth of farm products which he has raised during the year. Then A carries the notes to the bank, receives in exchange for them his mortgage note, and the bank cancels the mortgage. Now, in this whole circle of transactions, has there been any lending of capital? If so, who was the lender? If not, who is entitled to any interest? I call upon the editor of *To-day* to answer this question. It is needless to assure him that it is vital.

To-day's rejoinder to my criticism of its article on interest is chiefly remarkable as an exhibition of dust-throwing. In the art of kicking up a dust the editor is an expert. Whenever he is asked an embarrassing question, he begins to show his skill in this direction. He reminds one of the clown at the circus when "stumped" by the ring-master to turn a double somersault over the elephant's back. He prances and dances, jabbers and gyrates, quotes Latin forwards and Greek backwards, declaims in the style of Dr. Johnson to the fish-wife, sings algebraical formulæ to the music of the band, makes faces, makes puns, and makes an excellent fool of himself; and when at the end of all this enormous activity he slyly slips between the elephant's legs instead of leaping over his back, the hilarious crowd, if it does not forget his failure to perform the prescribed feat, at least good-humoredly forgives it. But I am not so good-natured. I admit that, as a clown, I find the editor interesting, but his performance, appropriate enough in a Barnum circus ring, is out of place in the economic area. So I propose to ignore his three pages of antics and note only his ten-line slip between the elephant's legs, or, laying metaphor aside, his evasion of my question.

I had challenged him to point out any lending of capital in a typical banking transaction which I had described. He responds by asking me to define capital. This is the slip, the evasion, the postponement of the difficulty. He knows that, if he can draw me off into a discussion of the nature of capital, there will be an admirable opportunity for more clownishness, since there is no point in political economy that lends itself more completely to the sophist's art than this. But I am not to be turned aside. I stick to my question. In regard to the notion of capital the editor of *To-day* will find me, so far as the immediate question at issue is connected with it, the most pliable man in the world. I will take the definition, if he likes, that was given in the previous article in *To-day*. There it was said that money was one thing and capital another; that capital consists of the agencies of production, while money is only a means for the transfer of these; that what men really want is not money, but capital; that it is for the use of capital that interest is paid; and that this interest, this price for the use of capital, lowers, generally speaking, as capital becomes plentier, and probably cannot disappear unless abundance of capital shall reach the extreme of common property. Now I have shown (at least I shall so claim until my question is answered) that in the most ordinary form of transaction involving interest—namely, the discounting of notes—there is absolutely no lending of capital in the sense in which capital was used in *To-day's* first article, and the consequence, of course, is that that defence of interest which regards it as payment for the use of capital straightway falls to the ground. But if the editor of *To-day* does not like the view of capital that was given in the article criticised, he may take some other; I am perfectly willing. He may make a definition of his own. Whatever it may be, I, for the time being and for the purposes of this argument, shall say "Amen" to it. And after that I shall again press the question whether, in the transaction which I described, there was any lending of anything whatever. And if he shall then answer, as a paragraph in his latest article indicates, "Yes, the bank lent its notes to the farmer," I shall show conclusively that the bank did nothing of the kind. If I successfully maintain this contention, then it will be demonstrated that the interest paid in the transaction specified was not paid for the use of anything whatever, but was a tax levied by monopoly and *nothing else*.

Meantime it is comforting to reflect that my labor has not been entirely in vain. As a consequence of my criticism of *To-day's* article on interest, the editor has disowned it (though it appeared unsigned and in editorial type), characterized it as "trivial" (heaven knows it had the air of gravity!), and squarely contradicted its chief doctrinal assertion. This assertion was that "the amount of currency can have no effect upon the abundance of capital." It is contradicted in these terms: "Evidently money is a necessary element in the existing industrial plexus, and increase of capital is dependent upon the supply of a sufficient amount of money." After this I have hopes.

"An Enquirer" wrote to the editor of *Liberty* confessing her incapacity to understand why he advocated the abolition of rent and interest. She cited the case of a cook loaning her savings to a young man who needed some ready cash, and she wanted to know what was wrong with this. Mr. Tucker told her:

My enquiring friend is by no means stupid. Her argument is well and clearly stated and is indicative of the habit of thought. Neither is she ignorant or superficial in the sense in which those terms are usually employed for the general characterization of personality. She has simply failed to acquaint herself with the position of the Anarchistic opponents of interest, the soundness of which her native power of penetration will enable her to see when once she has become familiar with it.

Wherein consists her misapprehension? In this,—that she supposes the Anarchists to condemn the contract between the borrower and the lender, *per se*; whereas the truth is that they condemn, not the contract, but the conditions of compulsory restriction and limitation under which such contract is now necessarily made if made at all, and in the absence of which it would be prevented, not by law or by invasion of any kind, but by simple competition, from embodying the element of interest on capital.

Take the case which she cites. No Anarchist disputes that it is perfectly legitimate for the young man in question to borrow either of the cook or of the bank upon such terms as may be agreed upon in a free market. The complaint of Anarchism is that the market is not free, and that the transactions effected therein are necessarily tainted with injustice. At present, if the young man borrows, whether of the cook or of the bank, the terms of contract are dictated to his disadvantage, by means of a legal privilege or monopoly enjoyed by the bank. Neither cook nor bank will lend to the young man unless he can give a note the redemption of which is considered sure and is generally made sure by a lien upon actual property. Upon being thus secured, the lender supplies the borrower with other notes, intrinsically no stronger, but in the redemption of which not only the lender and borrower but the entire community have reason to have confidence. That is to say, the lender, either by issuing his own universally known notes or by furnishing equally well known notes previously issued by others, virtually indorses the borrower's note, or, in still other words, insures his credit. For this service what does he charge? A price as low as that for which any one else is willing and able to perform the same service. Now, the Anarchists assert that there are large numbers of people who are willing, either individually or by forming themselves into banking associations, to perform this service at something less than one per cent., and that the only reason why they are not able to do so is that they are prevented by law. The grounds upon which they base this assertion are, first, the fact that prices in a free market tend toward cost of production and performance, which, in the matter of insurance of credit, is shown by banking statistics to be about one-half of one per cent., and, second, the existence of Federal laws imposing a tax of ten per cent. on all banks of issue not complying with the provisions of the national banking act, and of State laws making it a crime to circulate as currency other notes than those specifically authorized by statute. To this it is no answer to say that all persons are equally free to comply with the provisions of the national banking act; for these provisions by their very nature, limiting the basis of currency to government bonds, limit the volume of the currency, and in any business a limitation which reduces the output is as truly a restriction of competition as a limitation specifying that only certain persons shall engage in the business. Now, if the above facts and the assertions based on them are correct, it is obvious that, but for these, the price of insuring credit would fall to less than one per cent., this small percentage paying not dividends to stockholders, but the salaries of banking officials, providing for incidental expenses, and making good any deficiencies from bad debts. Thus is justified the Anarchistic contention that interest upon capital is dependent upon the restrictions surrounding the contract between borrower and lender; for surely "An Enquirer's" young man would not be willing to pay the cook six per cent. for money when he could borrow of a bank for one per cent., or able to exact ten per cent. for his house from a homeless man when the latter could hire money at one per cent. with which to buy or build a house.

If there is a flaw in the Anarchistic argument, I wait for "An Enquirer" to point it out. For her sake I have told an old story to the readers of *Liberty;* but then, I expect to have to tell it many times again.

Mr. J. K. Ingalls, in a letter to the editor of *Liberty* arguing that interest is unescapable, asserted that there is an economic interest as well as economic rent, and that it differs from that which is captured by the stronger and more cunning from the weaker and more stupid through the enforcement of barbarous (not economic) laws and customs; and he also asserted that interest is derived from the increase of any labor over its bare support. Mr. Tucker met the issue squarely:

MR. INGALLS gives no clear definition or measure of the term "economic interest." Economic rent is measured by the difference between the poorest land in use and the grades superior thereto. But what measures economic interest? Is it the difference between the product of labor absolutely destitute of capital, and that of labor possessing capital in varying degrees? But in that case economic interest is not *entirely* "derived from the increase of any labor over its bare support," since the product of labor absolutely destitute of capital would be less than a starvation wage to a man living in the midst of our civilization. Or is it measured by the difference between the product of labor possessing the poorest capital in use, and that of labor possessing better capital? Which at once gives rise to another question: what is the poorest capital in use, and how is it to be recognized as such? In the absence of a satisfactory answer to this question, Mr. Ingalls's economic interest must be looked upon as a decidedly indeterminate economic factor. All that his theory means, so far as I can grasp it, is that interest exists because people can do more with capital than without it, and that interest actually is, in fact, this surplus obtained by the employment of capital.

Now, so defining interest, the Anarchists do not wish to abolish it. Such a wish would be absurd, for it would be a wish to lessen the world's wealth and productive power. To Anarchists the only consequence of this new definition is the necessity of finding another term to represent that which they do wish to abolish,—namely, payment by borrower to lender for the use of capital.

But, once this necessary term is found or devised, the old question recurs: will free and mutual banking make it possible to procure capital without paying for its use?

To the determination of this question three other questions lead up, and I will put them to Mr. Ingalls straightway.

1. If a thousand men engaged in different lines of business unite to form a bank of issue; and if this bank of issue unites with other similar banks for clearing purposes; and if said bank lends its naturally well-known circulating credit to its members (or to others, for that matter) against conditional titles to actual and specific values given by the borrowers,—do these loans of the bank's credit cost the bank anything beyond the salaries of manager and assistants, rent of building, expenditure for paper and printing, losses by depreciation of securities, and sundry incidentals?

2. Do not statisticians and economists agree that a discount of one-half of one per cent. covers the expenses referred to in the preceding questions?

3. If men were free to unite in the formation of such banks of issue, and subject to no penalty or tax whatsoever for so doing, would not competition between the banks thus formed force the price of the service rendered by them down to cost,—that is, one-half of one per cent.,—or to a figure closely approximating it?

Now, I insist, and I have a right to insist, that Mr. Ingalls shall answer these three fair and pertinent questions directly, without extraneous discussion, without any mingling of considerations or speculations not absolutely essential to the answers. For either these direct answers will be what I think they must be, and then the case of the Anarchists (so far as finance is concerned) is established; or else they will be something else, and then the case of the Anarchists falls.

If it falls, of course I shall have nothing more to say, and the publication of Liberty will be discontinued; but, if it is established, then I shall be ready to discuss with Mr. Ingalls those interesting but at present non-essential questions of collection of debts, enforcement of contracts, the comparative good and evil of discounting the future results of labor, etc., etc., etc.

By way of caution, let me add that the Anarchists do not look forward to a time when there will be no sporadic cases of payment for the use of capital,—such, for instance, as the example cited by Mr. Ingalls where an inducement is given to the endorser of a note. They simply claim that under freedom borrowing and lending will so generally take the shape of an exchange of credits at the mere cost of the exchange that interest—or, rather, what we used to call interest before Mr. Ingalls appropriated the term to a different purpose—will disappear as an influential economic factor.

Mr. Ingalls then offered his answers to the three questions propounded by the editor of *Liberty*, and Mr. Tucker dissected them as follows:

To MY first question Mr. Ingalls answers that the bank of my hypothesis could issue its notes at a cost not exceeding its running expenses and incidental losses. So far, then, my claim is sustained. For he answers further that such a bank could not exist in the absence of a motive for its existence. It remains for me, then, only to supply the motive. The task is easy. The thousand business men of my hypothesis would unite to form a bank of issue, and would connect this bank of issue with other similar banks for clearing purposes, because thereby they could establish a collective credit having circulating power, which each of them could obtain in exchange for his equally good but less reputable individual credit, having to pay therefor nothing but the cost of this exchange of credits. In other words, these business men would form such a bank as I describe in order to borrow money at less than one per cent. instead of paying, as they do now, from four to fifteen per cent. Is the motive sufficient?

To my second question Mr. Ingalls answers that the cost above referred to would probably be met by a discount of one-half of one per cent. Sustained again. I have not to discuss here why bank employees "should be expected to work for bare support." It suffices for the argument to know that what these employees are now willing to accept for their services can be paid to them out of funds provided by a discount of one-half of one per cent. And this Mr. Ingalls admits. When we have exhausted the present issue, then I will consider with him how many tears I can afford to shed over the sad fate of those bank presidents for whom a discount of one-half of one per cent. provides salaries of only ten, fifteen, and twenty thousand dollars.

To my third question Mr. Ingalls answers that under free conditions competition would *tend* to reduce discount to its lowest term,—ordinarily something above cost. I take it that Mr. Ingalls means by this that in banking—a business which under freedom is accompanied by no physical conditions that place a natural limit upon competition—the force of competition would have a tendency of the same strength as that which it has in other businesses similarly free from physical limitations,—in other words, that the tendency would be strong enough to cause the price to hover around the cost limit, now rising a little above it, now falling a little below it, but averaging cost, or perhaps a shade more. If this is his meaning, then I am sustained again.

The discussion now centres, therefore, upon the following question, which I put to Mr. Ingalls:

Is the desire to borrow money at less than one per cent., instead of at four per cent. or more, a sufficient consideration to induce business men to form such banks as I have described?

If Mr. Ingalls answers that it is not, he must show why it is not. If he answers that it is, then the proposition which, according to Mr. Ingalls, has never been demonstrated, will have received its demonstration,—the proposition, namely, that free and mutual banking will make it possible to procure capital without paying for its use (the discount being charged, not for the use of capital, but to meet expenses incidental to the transfer of capital).

With apology to Mr. Ingalls for my persistence, I must continue the "unilateral inquest" a little further, regretting that I have not been relieved from doing so by an unequivocal answer to my last question. The qualified answer that Mr. Ingalls gives is this: The desire to borrow at less than one per cent. is a sufficient motive to business men as borrowers to induce them to embark in mutual banking, but the desire to lend at more than four per cent. is a sufficient motive to business men as lenders to keep them from embarking in mutual banking. Now I must ask for answers to the following questions:

(1) Does the business man who has capital but lacks cash—that is, the business man who wishes to borrow—sacrifice, by engaging with others in mutual banking, any

opportunity of lending (at four per cent. or any other rate) which he enjoys before so engaging?

(2) If so, what?

(3) If not; if the business man in question, by embarking with others in mutual banking, does not thereby damage himself as lender,—is not the desire to borrow at less than one per cent. a sufficient consideration to induce him to so embark?

I respectfully insist on answers to these questions. Mr. Ingalls is a very able and sincere writer on economic problems. He deservedly exercises an influence on the class of people to whom Liberty appeals. Repeatedly during its publication he has come forward with a denial of the position that mutual banking will make it possible to borrow money without interest. I have now determined to force him, once and for all, to make good this denial by proof, or else to retract it.

Mr. Ingalls seems to imagine that the answers which he now gives to my last series of questions are as equivocal as his answer to my previous question. Not so. The terms in which he answered my previous question implied two opposite motives influencing at the same time a business man fulfilling a double capacity,—a borrower and lender,—and cancelling each other. As my question did not concern men, who, as individuals, were in the market as lenders, but only those who were in the market as borrowers, this answer was equivocal. But the answers now given to my last questions distinctly recognize the borrowing business man and the lending business man as two individuals, and this recognition removes all the equivocation; for the desire of a lender to lend at a high rate cannot cancel the desire of a borrower to borrow at a low rate, provided the borrower, by association with other borrowers, can provide himself with a source from which to borrow at a low rate,—a condition not as paradoxical as it seems, since the fact of association creates a credit that before had no existence.

The present answers, then, being straight-forward and satisfactory, let us review the admissions which I have secured. Mr. Ingalls has admitted that business men desiring to borrow have an adequate motive for embarking in mutual banking; he has admitted that the loans of a mutual bank's credit would cost the bank nothing but running expenses and incidental outlays and losses; he has admitted that this cost would probably be covered by a discount of one-half of one per cent.; and he has admitted that, "in the absence of State or collective meddling, competition would tend unquestionably to reduce discount to its lowest term, which would ordinarily be something above cost." I have interpreted this last admission as meaning that in banking the force of competition would have a tendency of the same strength as that which it has in other businesses similarly free from physical limitations,—in other words, that the tendency would be strong enough to cause the price to hover around the cost limit, now rising a little above it, now falling a little below it, but averaging cost, or perhaps a shade more. In neither of the two articles which Mr. Ingalls has written since this interpretation appeared has he taken any exception to it. I am justified therefore in assuming that he admits this also.

Now, this series of admissions constitutes the entire case for mutual banking. Whether or not it was ever demonstrated before that mutual banking would abolish the payment of interest for the use of borrowed money, I have now led Mr. Ingalls to demonstrate this himself. His declarations show that under freedom the rate of discount would fall to nearly one-half of one per cent. This is equivalent to the abolition of the payment of interest, for in such a money market an individual case of interest payment would cut no figure economically, any more than one's occasional payment of a quarter to an urchin for delivering a letter cuts a figure now that letter-postage has fallen to two cents. Mr. Ingalls has formally allowed that mutual banking will do all that it claims for itself, and he is forever debarred from repeating that denial or doubt of its claims which has been heard from him at intervals for many years. I began this little campaign of question and answer for the purpose of silencing this gun, and I have effectually done it.

At present Mr. Ingalls finds but one course open to him,—viz., to deny that he ever denied. The plea comes at a suspiciously late hour. Strange that he did not advance it in response to my first questions four months ago, and thus save much time, trouble and ink. But never mind; late or not, is it true?

Mr. Ingalls denied,—or, if he did not deny, he expressed a doubt equivalent to a denial and equally calling for proof—that mutual banking can eradicate usury, and the phraseology shows that he meant by this to deny that mutual banking can eradicate the payment of a premium for the use of money. And, if I had his entire writings for the last fifteen years before me, I could point out equally conclusive instances. As I have not, I can only say that I remember such.

Thus ends this matter. Now Mr. Ingalls desires me to discuss with him the question of the existence of what he calls economic interest,—that is, the question whether people can do more with capital than without it. He asks me to retract my "denial of the existence of economic interest." I pledge him my word that I will retract it as soon as he shall quote to me the passage in which the denial occurred. *There exists no such passage.* To have denied so trite a truth would have been no less remarkable than Mr. Ingalls' grave persistence in affirming it. I do not approve the new use that Mr. Ingalls makes of the word, interest, but I have nothing to say in dispute of the entirely undisputed idea which he expresses by the phrase, "economic interest." When he denied my position, I had a right to expect him to answer my questions. When he shall show that I have denied his position, he will have a similar right to expect me to answer his questions. And, if he drives me into a corner, I swear that he shall hear no complaint from me that he is trying to "force answers."

NECESSITY FOR A STANDARD OF VALUE

In the early 90's, the Galveston *News* had on its staff an exceptionally able and clear-thinking editorial writer. *Liberty* frequently reprinted his editorials. Concerning one on "The Functions of Money" Mr. Tucker wrote the following article for the *News:*

I ENTIRELY sympathize with your disposal of the *Evening Post's* attempt to belittle the function of money as a medium of exchange; but do you go far enough when you content yourself with saying that a standard of value is highly desirable? Is it not absolutely necessary? Is money possible without it? If no standard is definitely adopted, and then if paper money is issued, does not the first commodity that the first note is exchanged for immediately become a standard of value? Is not the second holder of the note governed in making his next purchase by what he parted with in his previous sale? Of course it is a very poor standard that is thus arrived at, and one that must come in conflict with other standards adopted in the same indefinite way by other exchanges occurring independently but almost simultaneously with the first one above supposed. But so do gold and silver come in conflict now. Doesn't it all show that the idea of a standard is inseparable from money? Moreover, there is no danger in a standard. The whole trouble disappears with the abolition of the basis privilege.

The *News* printed the article, but followed it with a rejoinder in which it attempted to maintain its previous position. In the columns of *Liberty*, then, Mr. Tucker proceeded with the discussion:

First, I question the *News'* admission that a measure of value differs from a measure of length in that the former is empirical. True, value is a relation; but then, what is extension? Is not that a relation also,—the relation of an object to space? If so, then the yardstick does not possess the quality of extension in itself, being as dependent for it upon space as gold is dependent for its value upon other commodities. But this is metaphysical and may lead us far; therefore I do not insist, and pass on to a more important consideration.

Second, I question whether the *News's* "countervailing difference between a standard of length and a standard of value" establishes all that it claims. In the supposed case of a bank loan secured by mortgage, the margin between the valuation and the obligation practically secures the noteholder against loss from a decline in the value of the security, but it does not secure him against loss from a decline in the value of the standard, or make it impossible for him to profit by a rise in the value of the standard. Suppose that a farmer, having a farm worth $5000 in gold, mortgages it to a bank as security for a loan of $2500 in notes newly issued by the bank against this farm. With these notes he purchases implements from a manufacturer. When the mortgage expires a year later, the borrower fails to lift it. Meanwhile gold has declined in value. The farm is sold under the hammer, and brings instead of $5000 in gold, $6000 in gold. Of this sum $2500 is used to meet the notes held by the manufacturer who took them a year before in payment for the implements sold to the farmer. Now, can the manufacturer buy back his implements with $2500 in gold? Manifestly not, for by the hypothesis gold has gone down. Why, then, is not this manufacturer a sufferer from the variation in the standard of value, precisely as the man who buys cloth with a short yardstick and sells it with a long one is a sufferer from the variation in the standard of length? The claim that a standard of value varies, and inflicts damage by its variations, is perfectly sound; but the same is true, not only of the standard of value, but of every valuable commodity as well. Even if there were no standard of value and therefore no money, still nothing could prevent a partial failure of the wheat crop from enhancing the value of every bushel of wheat. Such evils, so far as they arise from natural causes, are in the nature of inevitable disasters and must be borne. But they are of no force whatever as an argument against the adoption of a standard of value. If every yardstick in existence, instead of constantly remaining thirty-six inches long, were to vary from day to day within the limits of thirty-five and thirty-seven inches, we should still be better off than with no yardstick at all. But it would be no more foolish to abolish the yardstick because of such a defect than it would be to abolish the standard of value, and therefore money, simply because no commodity can be found for a standard which is not subject to the law of supply and demand.

At this point Mr. Alfred B. Westrup, who believed that to talk of a standard of value was not only a delusion but a misuse of language and whose ideas had been refered to in the controversy, took a hand in the discussion. Mr. Tucker then turned his attention to him:

MR. WESTRUP'S article sustains in the clearest manner my contention that money is impossible without a standard of value. Starting out to show that such a standard is a delusion, he does not succeed in writing four sentences descriptive of his proposed bank before he adopts that "delusion." He tells us that "one of the conditions in obtaining the notes (paper money) of the Mutual Bank is that they will be taken *in lieu of current money*." What does this mean? Why, simply that the patrons of the bank agree to take its notes as the equivalent of gold coin of the same face value. In other words, they agree to adopt gold as a standard of value. They will part with as much property in return for the notes as they would part with in return for gold. And if there were no such standard, the notes would not pass at all, because nobody would have any idea of the amount of property that he ought to exchange for them. The *naïveté* with which Mr. Westrup gives away his case shows triumphantly the puerility of his raillery at the idea of a standard of value.

Indeed, Comrade Westrup, I ask nothing better than to discuss the practicability of mutual banks. All the work that I have been doing for liberty these nineteen years has been directed steadily to the establishment of the conditions that alone will make them practicable. I have no occasion to show the necessity for a standard of value. Such necessity is already recognized by the people whom we are trying to convince of the truth of mutual banking. It is for you, who deny this necessity, to give your reasons. And in the very moment in which you undertake to tell us why you deny it, you admit it without knowing it. It would never have occurred to me to discuss the abstract theory of a standard of value. I regard it as too well settled. But when you, one of the most conspicuous and faithful apostles of mutual banking, begin to bring the theory into discredit and ridicule by basing your arguments in its favor on a childish attack against one of the simplest of financial truths, I am as much bound to repudiate your heresy as an engineer would be to disavow the calculations of a man who should begin an attempt to solve a difficult problem in engineering by denying the multiplication table.

I fully recognize Mr. Westrup's faithful work for freedom in finance and the ability with which he often defends it. In fact, it is my appreciation of him that has prevented me from criticising his error earlier. But when I see Individualists holding Anarchism responsible for these absurdities and on the strength of them making effective attacks upon a financial theory which, when properly defended, is invulnerable,—it seems high time to declare that the free and mutual banking advocated by Proudhon, Greene, and Spooner never contemplated for a moment the desirability or the possibility of dispensing with a standard of value. If others think that a standard of value is a delusion, let them say so by all means; but let them not say so in the name of the financial theories and projects which the original advocates of mutual banking gave to the world.

Another phase of the standard of value problem, concerning currency and its convertibility, was thus treated by the editor of *Liberty*:

To AVOID misunderstanding, it should be stated that, when Mr. Yarros urges the substitution of convertibility into products for convertibility into gold as a quality of the circulating medium, he does not refer at all to that convertibility in point of right which is guaranteed by the issuer of a note, but simply to that convertibility in point of fact which exists when a note finds ready circulation. He means to say that the currency of a mutual bank, while not redeemable in gold on demand at the bank, will be to all intents and purposes redeemable in products on demand at the store of every dealer. His position is correct, but his new use of the words "convertibility" and "redeemability" will lead to much misunderstanding when not accompanied by such an explanation as that which I have just given.

A similar use of these terms in a previous article by Mr. Yarros led a Philadelphia correspondent to ask me what, even supposing that gold were retained as a standard of value, would maintain the equality of a paper dollar with a gold dollar if the paper dollar were redeemable, not in gold, but in commodities. The gentleman evidently supposed Mr. Yarros to mean that mutual currency would be redeemed in commodities by the bank. If such were the case, then, to be sure, the value of the mutual money would be measured, not by gold, but by the commodities in which the bank agreed to redeem it. Gold in that case would no longer be the standard of value, its function as such being performed instead by the commodity chosen by the bank for redemption purposes. My correspondent was guilty of an absurdity in supposing gold to be still the standard in such a case, but he was led into this absurdity by Mr. Yarros's use of the term "convertibility," which was not easily intelligible to one not perfectly familiar with the mutual-banking idea.

Mutual money will be expressed in terms of some chosen standard of value; if gold be chosen, then in terms of gold. It will be based, not necessarily or probably on gold, but on notes given by the borrowers and secured by mortgage on the borrower's property. It will not be redeemable in gold on demand at the bank. It will circulate readily, and without depreciation, if the bank has a good standing with the community and with the clearinghouse. It will be redeemed, in the vast majority of cases, by a re-exchange of it for the borrowers' notes against which it was originally issued. That is, the borrower himself will present at the bank notes equivalent to those which he received from the bank, and will get in exchange the notes which he gave to the bank and a cancellation of the mortgage on his property. If he does not do this, the mortgage on his property will be foreclosed, and the property will be sold at auction. It will be sold for gold, if gold is what the holders of the bank's notes desire. And it is this fact—that such a sale of the property insures an ultimate redemption in gold if demanded—which will maintain the equality of mutual money with gold.

The liability to misinterpretation is increased by Mr. Yarros's statement that "the government could not issue currency redeemable in products, since it hasn't any products." The indication here is that a mutual bank issuing currency redeemable in products must have products. But this is contrary to the mutual banking idea, and equally contrary, I am sure, to the meaning that Mr. Yarros intended to convey, —namely, that the government could not issue currency that would circulate, to borrowers mortgaging no property for its security. The Anarchists maintain that government should not engage in the business of issuing money, but there is nothing in the nature of mutual banking that makes it impossible for the government to carry it on; and, if it decided to carry it on, it would not need products (beyond those mortgaged by borrowers) in order to issue a circulating currency any more than a private banking enterprise would need them. The statement of Mr. Yarros tends to confirm the reader in the mistaken idea that under mutual banking the bank notes will be redeemed in products at and by the bank.

In a letter to the editor of *Liberty*, Mr. Steven T. Byington reported a discussion which he had had with a professor of political economy and in which he had taken the position that, in order to maintain the value of mutual money and to keep the notes of a mutual bank at par, all property pledged to the bank as security should be appraised in terms of the standard of value, and that the loans offered should never exceed a certain ratio to this appraisal. He also contended that the steady supply and demand would keep the value of the notes at a steady ratio to the standard in which the property was appraised. Mr. Tucker then analyzed and criticised those ideas:

IN COMMENT on Mr. Byington's letter, I can say at once that with him I should oppose any legal restriction of the denominations of the notes issued by mutual banks. It is probable that Colonel Greene himself would oppose such restriction, were he alive today. It must be remembered that his "Mutual Banking" is an economic rather than a political treatise, and was written at a time when the philosophy of Anarchy had been scarcely heard of in this country. Nevertheless I consider it an exaggeration to say that Greene, to keep mutual bank notes at par, "would depend *wholly*" on this restriction, or even on the customers' contract to take the notes at par with the standard. I have not a copy of "Mutual Banking" at hand, and do not remember whether there is any sentence in it which warrants Mr. Byington's statement; but, even if there is, it is none the less an exaggeration (by the author himself) of his real position. For the customers' willingness to make this contract depends in turn upon their knowledge that the notes will ultimately command their face value at the bank. As soon as the general public, through time and experience, becomes possessed of this knowledge, the customers' contract may be dispensed with without the least impairment of the value of the notes. The restriction and the contract were, in Greene's mind, only devices for making plain to the public the truth upon which he placed his *real* dependence,—*viz.*, that, if the original borrower of the notes should fail to meet his obligations to the bank, the security for the notes would be converted into the actual commodity adopted as standard, and this commodity used in redemption of the notes. It is this great fact that will always keep mutual bank notes at par. And it will do this whether the standard is actually coined and in circulation, or not. Nothing is needed but the standard's presence in the market as a commodity. The market quotations of the price of gold per grain serve the purpose as well as the actual circulation of coined dollars.

Mr. Byington's plan for keeping the notes at par doesn't make as great an impression upon me as it did upon his professor of political economy. He seems to think he has made a discovery. But all that is true in his plan is old and has long been accepted as a matter of course, while all that is new in it is in flat contradiction with the cardinal truth about mutual money which distinguishes it vitally and eternally from all forms of fiat money. Outside of those who deny the possibility of a standard of value (a quantity which may safely be neglected), no believer in mutual banking within my knowledge ever dreamed of appraising the property pledged as security in anything but the standard. It is largely for this purpose that a standard is necessary. A safe ratio of notes issued to standard valuation of security is another point that the defenders of mutual banking regularly insist upon. Greene urges two dollars of security for each dollar-note. Competition between the banks will fix this ratio. Those banks adopting a ratio which unduly sacrifices neither safety or enterprise will get the business. These two points of Mr. Byington's plan—appraisal in terms of standard and ratio of issue to appraisal—are very good, and they have grown gray in their goodness. But, when he assumes that the value of the notes issued will be regulated by their supply and demand, he becomes a financial heretic of the worst description.

There is nothing more certain (and oftener denied) in finance than the statement which Colonel Greene, in "Mutual Banking," prints in small capitals,—that mutual money differs from merchandise money (and, I may add, from fiat money also) in that it is absolutely exempt from the operation of the law of supply and demand. Be there more of it, or be there less, the value of each note remains the same. The hypothesis of free and mutual banking excludes on the one hand any legal limitation of the supply of currency whereby each note would acquire an extra value due to the enforced scarcity of the tool of exchange, and, on the other hand, any inflation of the currency to a volume exceeding the basis or sufficiently aproaching the limit of the basis to inspire an appreciable fear that the notes are in danger from a possible depreciation of the security. Now, within these limits no change in the volume of the currency can by any possibility affect the value of the individual paper dollar. The value of the paper dollar depends not at all upon the demand and supply of paper dollars, but altogether upon the demand and supply of the kinds of property upon which the paper dollars rest. And, unless these kinds of property themselves depreciate sufficiently to endanger the notes, each paper dollar is worth a standard dollar, neither more or less. Mr. Byington's plan for maintaining this parity by providing steadiness in the demand and supply of notes is worthless, then, for two reasons: first, of itself it could do nothing toward accomplishing its purpose; second, without it its purpose is otherwise accomplished. I do not know how to respond to Mr. Byington's request that I describe more fully the method of this accomplishment. If he will try to point out just what it is that he does not understand, I will try to make him understand it.

Mr. Byington, in his letter in another column, asks me what would maintain the par value of mutual bank notes in a community where every borrower promptly meets his obligations to the bank as they mature, in the absence of any contract binding the individual parties thereto to receive the bank notes at par. Mr. Byington's hypothetical community is one in which every man in it is as certain as of the daily rising of the sun that every other man in it is thoroughly honest, absolutely capable, infallible in judgment, and entirely exempt from liability to accident. Such must be the case in any community where there is and can be absolutely no failure to meet financial obligations. In this ideal community the necessity for collateral as security for mutual money vanishes. But so also vanishes the necessity of any agreement to take the notes at par, for it is perfectly certain that then the notes will be so taken whether such an agreement exists or not. And the knowledge of this fact, arising out of the absolute certainty prevailing on every hand, would be more potent in maintaining the par value of the notes than any confidence based on contract. The supposed community, however, is, if not an absurd impossibility, at least too remote a possibility to be considered. During the pre-millennial period it will be necessary to count on the element of risk in considering banking problems. While risk remains, collateral will be a necessity. Now, this collateral, instead of being a subsidiary security, is the final dependence of all who use the money. Even those who contract to receive the money make this contract mainly because they know the collateral to have been deposited or pledged. All the other devices for security are merely props to this main bulwark. Abandon this bulwark, and, until risk disappears from the world, bank notes will depreciate. Maintain it, and, though all the props be removed, the notes will remain at par. People who live by buying and selling merchandise will always take in lieu of a gold dollar that which they know, and which other dealers know, to be convertible into a gold dollar if the occasion for such conversion shall arise. In answer to the closing paragraph of Mr. Byington's letter, I need only point out that to use the fact that mutual money will be at par with the standard as a reason for dispensing with the cause that maintains it at par with the standard is to reason in a circle.

Mr. Byington was still not quite satisfied, and, in order that Mr. Tucker's meaning might be made a little more clear to him, he asked for answers to the following questions: "In the ideal community of perfect men, what would make it certain that mutual-bank notes would be taken at par, if there were no contract to take them at par?" and "In the present world, what will maintain the value of a mutual-bank note which has good collateral, if 'all the props be removed', or if that particular prop be removed which consists in the contract to take the money at par?" To which the editor of *Liberty* replied:

In an ideal community of perfect men, from which, by the hypothesis, failure to meet financial obligations is absolutely eliminated, mutual-bank notes would circulate, even if unsecured, because this very hypothesis implies a demand for these notes, after their issue; borrowers must regain possession of them in order to make the hypothesis a reality, and those from whom the borrowers buy will accept the notes from them in the first place because they know—again by the hypothesis—that the borrowers must in some way recover them. They will circulate at par because, being issued in terms of a commodity standard, and redemption by cancellation being assured, there is no reason why they should circulate at a figure below their face. Or, at least, if there is such a reason, it is incumbent upon Mr. Byington to point it out.

In the existing unideal world the collateral securing a mutual-bank note would guarantee its holder that, unless the original borower buys back the note in order to cancel therewith his own note held by the bank, the bank itself will ultimately convert the collateral into the commodity agreed upon for redemption purposes and with the proceeds buy back the note. Therefore it is precisely this convertibility, even though conversion is not to be had on demand, that will maintain the value of the mutual-bank note.

The mutual bank will never show anybody that paper money which is never convertible can ever be made steadily useful in an unideal world, either with or without a government fiat. For such is not the truth, and neither the mutual bank or anything else can establish an error.

Mutual banking, it is true, is not a cardinal doctrine of Anarchism. But free banking *is*. Now, free banking will lead to mutual banking, and mutual banking is the greatest single step that can possibly be taken in the direction of emancipating labor from poverty. Mutual banking, then, is as intimately connected with Anarchism as though it were one of its cardinal doctrines. Liberty is valuable only as it contributes to happiness, and to this end no single liberty is as necessary at present as the liberty of banking.

Because the editor of *Liberty* considered it important to demolish "the most specious plea" that had yet appeared for "the notion that a monetary system is possible without a standard of value," he asked Mr. Hugo Bilgram to review Mr. Arthur Kitson's "A Scientific Solution of the Money Question." Mr. Bilgram performed the task in a masterly manner, and Mr. Tucker added the following caustic criticism of Mr. Kitson's book:

IT OFTEN happens that some of the most active men in a movement are not its most rational exponents. The movement for freedom in finance is an instance of this truth. Two or three of its most enthusiastic propagandists are basing their advocacy upon propositions regarding value and its measurement which are so absurd that I have to blush for the rational utterances which I find in their company. If I were interested in some great discovery in mechanics, and if others interested with me were to persist in bringing it into ridicule by associating it with, and even basing it upon, a professed solution of the perpetual motion problem, I could not feel a deeper sense of humiliation for my cause than I feel when I receive a new book, written by an earnest comrade, in which the social ends that I seek are defended on grounds so laughably untenable that they give rational men a warrant for entertaining a suspicion of our sanity. Such a book is Mr. Kitson's, which, in asking for freedom in finance for the purpose of creating a monetary system professing to estimate concrete values in the terms of a value-less abstraction, is liable to do more harm to the cause of financial freedom than all the writings of the orthodox economists. It may seem that, in calling upon one of the ablest living writers on finance to expose an error so childish, I have trained a columbiad upon an egg-shell. Yet, after all, one is seldom set a more difficult task than that of dealing with those forms of error which fly in one's face with a flat and fatuous denial of truths so nearly axiomatic that they do not admit of much elucidation. Of this task Mr. Bilgram has acquitted himself triumphantly. Mr. Kitson's theory of an invariable monetary unit is riddled completely. If Mr. Kitson will set himself to answer the question asked him by Mr. Bilgram regarding the value, in terms of the invariable unit, of several commodities assumed to have certain exchange relations on the day following the adoption of this unit, he will begin to appreciate the difficulties of his situation. I would like him to deal also with a problem of somewhat similar character which I will set him. Suppose that today, April 20, 1895, Mr. Kitson's monetary system goes into operation. Suppose, further, that, in his preliminary tabulation of the exchange relations of commodities as existing on April 20, he finds that 48 ounces of silver = 1 ounce of gold = 200 ounces of copper; and that he takes 1 ounce of gold, at its valuation of April 20, as his invariable unit. A year elapses. On April 20, 1896, the exchange relations of silver, gold, and copper, in consequence of variations in the supply and demand of these commodities, are found, we will suppose, to be as follows: 48 ounces of silver = 3 ounces of gold = 300 ounces of copper. Now let us leave copper out of consideration for a moment. If on April 20, 1895, when 48 ounces of silver were worth 1 ounce of gold, 1 ounce of gold was worth 1 unit, then on April 20, 1896, when 48 ounces of silver are worth 3 ounces of gold, 1 ounce of gold is worth 1/3 of a unit. So far, so good. Now let us take copper into consideration once more, but leave out silver. If on April 20, 1895, when 200 ounces of copper were worth 1 ounce of gold, 1 ounce of gold was worth 1 unit, then on April 20, 1896, when 200 ounces of copper are worth 2 ounces of gold, 1 ounce of gold is worth ½ of a unit. But we have just proved it to be worth 1/3 of a unit. That is to say, starting with the same data and following two parallel and irrefutable lines of argument, we arrive at contradictory conclusions. And by taking other commodities into account and applying the same argument in each case, it could be shown that, with Mr. Kitson's "invariable" unit, an ounce of gold at any given moment would have a thousand and one different values, all expressed in terms of the same unit or denominator. In dealing thus severely with Mr. Kitson's book, I am moved by no unfriendly spirit, and I have no inclination to deny that it contains much valuable truth,—truth that would be of great service to liberty were it not "queered" by pages of intolerable balderdash. I would like the work to be read by every person who has previously familiarized himself with the literature of free and mutual banking. But no work could be better calculated to fill the mind of a beginner with confusion and that of a keen opponent with contempt. For this reason I cannot include it—much to my regret—in the literature of Liberty's propaganda.

Concerning Mr. Tucker's criticism of Mr. Kitson's book, Mr. Victor Yarros submitted some quotations from Proudhon which seemed to indicate that that great economist did not believe in the necessity for a standard of value. The editor of *Liberty* thus analyzed the quotations and discussed them:

I DO NOT consider the question thus raised of very great importance. However momentous the standard-of-value question may be in itself, it is of very little consequence on which side of it any given writer stands, unless, first, he takes his position so clearly and unmistakably that those who read him most attentively can agree, at least broadly, as to what his position is, and, second, brings arguments to bear in support of his position sufficiently weighty, and sufficiently different from the arguments adduced by others, to exercise an influence where other arguments have failed to induce agreement.

I do not accept Proudhon or any one else as a financial authority beyond question. There is more than one important point in his banking plan to which I cannot give assent. Proudhon has made a signal and a revolutionary contribution to economic science by his overpowering demonstration that the chief hope of labor lies in the power of monetization of all its products,—a power now allowed only to one or two of them. For this he has my lasting gratitude and honor, but not my worship. I grant him no infallibility, and I reserve my right to differ when his declarations do not commend themselves to my reason. On the matter now at issue his works do not throw much light. In his numerous volumes of financial writings references to the standard-of-value question are casual, incidental, and rare. Even if they were clearly against the standard-of-value theory, they would call for little attention or opposition from me, because they are inconspicuous, because they are assertions rather than arguments, and because they are not basic in his financial plan. With Mr. Kitson it is different. He places his opposition to a standard of value at the very foundation of his theory, he pretends that it is basic, and he even declares that with a standard of value the free-money theory becomes ridiculous. It is necessary therefore, to attack him in a way in which it would not be necessary to attack Proudhon, even could it be shown that the latter's references to a standard of value are clearly antagonistic to it. But, were it necessary to attack Proudhon, I should not hesitate to do so. I have no gods.

But now to the merits. I claim that Proudhon acknowledged the necessity of a standard of value; that the passages cited from his writings in Mr. Yarros's letter are not clearly and conclusively against the theory of a standard, but are capable of another explanation; that one or two other passages can be cited which are so clearly in favor of the theory of a standard as to exclude any other explanation; and that—most important of all—a standard of value is adopted both in his Bank of Exchange and his Bank of the People.

Let us examine first the quotations cited by Mr. Yarros,—four in number. The first, which speaks of Law, Ricardo, and the economists as "always taking metal as a standard of value," does not thereby antagonize the theory of a standard of value. The most that can be gathered from it is a hint that Proudhon considered that, when all values should be "constituted," to use his phrase, perhaps a better standard than metal might be found. It is fair to presume that, if he had been opposed to a standard, he would have said "always taking a standard of value." The phrase actually used implies opposition to metal rather than opposition to a standard.

The proposal, in the second quotation, to destroy the royalty of gold and to republicanize specie by making each product of labor current money does not necessarily mean anything more than an intention to strip specie of its exclusive privilege as a *basis of currency* and to give each product of labor the liberty of representation in the currency. In fact, *Liberty* and the free-money advocates who believe in a standard have always been in the habit of using these phrases from Proudhon to express exactly that idea. The concluding portion of the second quotation obviously refers to paper *based* upon metal and not simply expressed in terms of metal; and its language, like the language of the first quotation, implies opposition to metal rather than to a standard.

The third quotation simply establishes the undisputed point that Proudhon did not believe in a currency redeemable in specie. This is an entirely separate question from that of the necessity of a standard of value. It is perfectly possible, theoretically, for a bank to issue currency on an understanding that its members are pledged to receive it in lieu of a definite quantity of a definite commodity, without any promise or intention on the part of the bank to redeem it in the said commodity or in any other commodity. True, I do not think that such a currency is practicable; that is to say, I do not think that, the world being what it is, such a currency would circulate. This is one of the important points, already referred to by me, on which I disagree with Proudhon. But it in no way concerns the standard-of-value problem.

A greater stumbling-block is the fourth quotation. I do not pretend to know the thought that lay in Proudhon's mind when he wrote it. But I do know that he could not have intended to exclude the idea of the necessity of a standard, for this is proved by the sentence immediately preceding it, —a sentence which Mr. Yarros's correspondent could not have understood, since, if he had understood it, honesty would have forbidden him to omit it. Here it is: "Each subscriber [to the Bank] binds himself to receive in every payment, from any person whomsoever, and at par, the paper of the Bank of Exchange." *At par*, mind you. At par with what; if you please? Evidently at par with some chosen standard; and, no other standard being specified, evidently at par with the ordinary specie standard. In the absence of a standard of value, to talk of any currency as receivable at par is to use a nonsensical phrase.

So much for the passages cited. It may be said of them, as it may be said with truth of many other passages in Proudhon's writings on many other subjects, that it is to be regretted that they are not more explicit. But it cannot be truthfully said of them that they establish Proudhon's opposition to the adoption of a standard of value.

Look now at the evidence on the other side. First of all, there is the passage which I have cited in the last paragraph but one. As I have pointed out, the words "at par" absolutely necessitate a standard of value, and exclude any other explanation. *This is sufficient in itself.* Even if a passage were to be discovered indisputably denying the necessity of a standard, it would prove only that Proudhon had flatly contradicted himself.

But this is not all. In the chapter on value in the "Contradictions" these words occur: "In geometry the point of comparison is extent, and the unit of measure is now the division of the circle into three hundred and sixty parts, now the circumference of the terrestrial globe, now the average dimension of the human arm, hand, thumb, or foot. In economic science, we have said after Adam Smith, the point of view from which all values are compared is labor; as for the unit of measure, that adopted in France is the FRANC." The small capitals here are Proudhon's own. Now, a franc, like a dollar, is a definite quantity commodity,— four and one-half grammes of silver alloyed with half a gramme of copper,—and any one who will read this passage carefully, and especially in connection with its several pages of context, will see that the author means to point out a precise analogy between the adoption of a definite amount of extension embodied in a material object as a standard of length, and the adoption of a definite quantity of labor embodied in a definite commodity as a standard of value; yet it is this very analogy which the opponents of a standard deny and attempt to ridicule. This passage also is conclusive; it excludes any other interpretation.

Above all, however, and finally disposing of the subject, are the provisions contained in the constitutions of the Bank of Exchange and the Bank of the People. No note was to be issued by the former for any sum less than twenty francs (four dollars), and it was specified in Article 18 that the Bank would make change in coin. This is unintelligible except on the hypothesis that a franc in the Bank's paper was to be kept at par with a silver franc. For, if the silver franc were worth more than the paper franc, it would be ridiculous for the Bank to pay out a silver franc when it owed only a paper franc; and, if the silver franc were worth less, it would be equally ridiculous to suppose that any one would take it from the Bank in lieu of a paper franc. Again, in Article 21 of the act incorporating the Bank of the People, we find this: "Every producer or merchant adhering to the Bank of the People binds himself to deliver to the other adherents, at a reduced price, the articles which he manufactures or offers for sale." At a price reduced from what? The phrase can mean only that the merchant agrees to put a premium on the Bank's paper. Now, a premium implies a standard. More conclusive still, if possible, is Article 24, which says: "All consumers, whether associated or not, who desire to profit by the low prices guaranteed by the producers adhering to the Bank of the People will turn over to the Bank the coin intended for their purchases and will receive an equal sum in the Bank's paper." That is to say, Proudhon's Bank was to issue its notes against coined gold and silver among other things, *franc for franc*. Need more be said?

Besides this direct evidence there are circumstantial considerations of much force. One of these is that a thinker like Proudhon, writing many volumes on finance with the intent of revolutionizing it,—of making the sun rise in the west instead of in the east, as he once expressed it,—would unquestionably have argued at great length the standard-of-value question, if he had dreamed of denying for a moment the current view that money is an impossibility without a standard. But the fact is that he said very little about the question, and in the little that he did say, instead of always taking pains to make his language clear and unmistakable, sometimes expressed himself carelessly, as one is apt to do when speaking upon a matter where he does not fear misinterpretation.

A second telling circumstance is that Colonel William B. Greene, a disciple of Proudhon who enjoyed with him for years in Paris a personal acquaintance and a considerable intimacy, did not, when noting in his "Mutual Banking" certain points of difference between Proudhon's plan and his own, even hint at any difference regarding the necessity of a standard of value, although Colonel Greene himself, who saw the importance of a clear position on this matter, treated the question at some length in another part of his pamphlet. There can be little doubt that, if there had been any difference between them on this point, Colonel Greene would have alluded to it either in "Mutual Banking" or in his later writings on finance. It is further significant that in the many conversations regarding Proudhon and regarding finance which I have had with Colonel Greene, he never signified in the remotest way that Proudhon rejected the standard-of-value theory.

Believing that it has cleared Proudhon of the charge that he entertained the Kitsonian absurdity, the defence rests, and awaits the plaintiff's rebuttal. I hope no one will suspect Mr. Yarros of being the plaintiff's attorney. He is not. It is simply as a juror that he makes his request for information.

THE REDEMPTION OF PAPER MONEY

In a paper entitled "Banking and the State," read before the Single Tax Club of Chicago, Mr. A. W. Wright took the position, which he considered of the greatest importance, that paper money must always be subject to immediate redemption, the sole reason assigned for that contention being that nothing but public confidence can make paper money possible. The editor of *Liberty* took issue with him on that point:

IT remains to be proved that immediate redemption is essential to public confidence. It is, of course, true that *certainty* of *ultimate* redemption is such an essential. But this is the most that can be claimed. A run on a bank of issue is caused by the fear of the note-holders that the notes will *never* be redeemed, and not because they desire them redeemed at once. On the contrary, if they felt sure of ultimate redemption, and felt sure that other people felt equally sure, they would go precisely contrary to their desire in presenting the notes for immediate redemption, for they are in need of the money for actual monetary use and in this respect find solvent paper preferable to gold. The pledge of immediate redemption, far from being essential to the usefulness of paper money, is one of the two things that in the past have done most to cripple it (the other being the restriction of its basis to one or two forms of wealth). Paper money, to attain its highest usefulness, must be issued in the form of notes either maturing at a definite date or else redeemable within a certain period following demand. There would be no lack of confidence in such money, if issued against specific and good security and under a system of banking furnishing all known means of safeguarding and informing the public. Mr. Wright's mistake probably arises from adherence to the old notion that a bank of issue needs capital of its own, and that this capital constitutes the security of the note-holders. The real fact is that the security and all the needful capital is that which the borrowers themselves furnish. There is no *special* reason why the State should not do a banking business, but only those *general* reasons which make it improper for the State to undertake any business. The fact that it has nothing of its own is no bar, for it is in the very essence of money-issuing that it is done on other people's property.

When banks cease promising to pay on demand, it will no longer be possible to precipitate a panic by cornering gold. But as long as demand notes alone are issued, banks will have to keep large quantities of coin in their vaults, and there will be a constant effort on the part of speculators to gain control of specie, success in which will cause a run on the banks and a general lack of confidence. The true way to maintain confidence is to refrain from making promises that cannot be kept. The fact that less than half the gold is coined proves nothing. Gold has other than monetary uses. It is needed in the arts; and in the worst panics, when money is so scarce that business men will pay enormous prices for it, but little of the uncoined gold finds its way into the market. The pressure upon the rich in times of panic is never great enough to cause them to melt their jewelry, carry their watch-cases to the mint, or have the fillings extracted from their own teeth and those of their dead ancestors to be turned into coin. To induce such a result money would have to command a much higher price than it ever does. And yet the high price of money proves its scarcity.

Mr. Wright further errs, it seems to me, in saying that "banks should be permitted to issue paper money equal to their unimpaired capital," implying thereby that they should not be permitted to issue more than this amount. This would be a virtual prohibition of mutual banks, which do not profess to have any capital and claim to need none. As Colonel Greene has pointed out, banks serve simply as clearing-houses for their customers' business paper running to maturity, and no more need capital than does the central clearing-house which serves them in the same way. By what right does Mr. Wright pretend to say how many notes a bank shall issue to people who are willing to receive them? I ask him in his own words: Must the State afford holders of bank paper protection that is denied to holders of individual notes? "Can a note of issue justly be held more sacred than other promises to pay?" In putting a limit to paper issues Mr. Wright violates his principle of liberty in finance. And he does so again when he insists on unlimited liability. To deny the right of two parties to contract on a basis of limited liability is to abridge the freedom of contract. If unlimited liability is a better arrangement, those banks which offer it will survive, while the others will go down. Trust more to liberty, Mr. Wright, and less to law.

Erroneous also is the statement that "bills of issue should be a first lien upon the assets of the bank." But this I have no need to discuss, for I have received a letter from Mr. Wright in which he says that he has changed his opinion. I am convinced that further reflection will show him that prohibition of other than demand notes, restrictions upon the amount of issue, and invalidation of contracts specifying limited liability are, equally with his "first-lien" privilege, unwarrantable invasions of individual and associative liberty, and, as such, entirely at variance with the great doctrine of which his essay is, in the main, so excellent an exposition.

In a letter to the editor of *Liberty* Mr. Wright attempted to defend himself, and from his statements it became evident that he had not considered the use of anything but gold as a basis for banking. Mr. Tucker then went more deeply into that phase of the problem, as well as into other related aspects of mutual banking:

It now appears that the possibility of anything else than gold as adequate security for paper money is a conception which Mr. Wright's mind never before entertained. When I speak of paper money based upon adequate security and yet not upon gold, he opens wide his eyes and asks: What can you mean? Why, my dear Mr. Wright, the very keystone of Anarchistic economics, so far as finance is concerned, is the proposition to extend from gold to all other commodities that right of direct representation in the currency which gold now enjoys exclusively. The prohibition, or ruinous taxation, of money issued directly against miscellaneous securities is the chief denial of freedom of which the banking monopoly is guilty, and the right to so issue money is the chief liberty which freedom in banking will bestow upon us. How this right may be utilized and the tremendous changes that would follow its exercise are things not explained in "Social Statics." To understand them Mr. Wright must lay down his Spencer and pick up Colonel Greene, whose "Mutual Banking," though temporarily out of print, will probably be republished soon. If Mr. Wright will then read it carefully, our discussion will proceed more profitably. Meanwhile I will briefly examine the facts and arguments which he now offers.

For proof of the possibility of a solvent demand currency without a dollar-for-dollar coin reserve he advances the solvency of the Suffolk Bank and the Scotch banks. I answer that the case of the Suffolk Bank must be considered in connection with the history of the whole State banking system then prevailing. That history is one long succession of failures of banks intrinsically solvent but unable to meet sudden demands for gold. During such an experience everything does not fall; something has to stand, and people naturally reserve their confidence for the institution which has the greatest reputation. The Suffolk Bank stood, not because it was solvent while other banks were insolvent, but because the noteholders knew that the men at the back of it were men of great reputation and wealth who could and would supply it with coin in case of need. The illustration is really an unfortunate one for Mr. Wright, since by it he cites an entire banking system in which institution after institution, with assets far exceeding liabilities, were forced to suspend for lack of ready coin.

The solvency of the Scotch banks is due mainly to the following facts: first, that the stockholders in every bank except the three oldest of these institutions are liable to the whole exent of their personal fortunes for the bank's debts; secondly, that Scotch law enables property, both real and personal, to be attached with exceptional ease; third, that every note issued by a bank in excess of its average circulation for the year ending May 1, 1845, must be represented by an equal amount of coin in its coffers; and, fourth, that all new banks of issue have been forbidden since 1845. I do not deny that under such conditions demand notes can hold their solvency without a full coin reserve; but certainly Mr.

Wright must withdraw his assertion that free banking prevails in Scotland. It is surely an invasion to prohibit banks run on the plan of limited liability. But where these are not prohibited and where there is otherwise perfect freedom in banking, there will be no banks on the plan of unlimited liability, for they could get no business. Wealthy men will not jeopardize their entire fortunes without being roundly rewarded in the shape of dividends, and borrowers will not pay four, five, or six per cent. for the notes of an unlimited-liability bank when they can get *adequately-secured* notes from a limited-liability bank for less than one per cent.

It should be added here that, however true the statement may have been when "Social Statics" was written, it is not true now that no Scotch bill has ever been discredited. Two of the largest Scotch banks suspended in 1857, and one of them, the Western Bank, went entirely to pieces; and, if my memory is correct, Scotland has known one or two serious bank failures within the last twenty years.

Mr. Wright is mistaken as to the necessary conditions of a "corner." A commodity may be cornered whether there are any promises to deliver it in existence or not. It can be cornered to induce a scarcity and consequent rise in price. Now, this rise in price would surely be much greater, and therefore also the incentive to create a corner, if the corner would give rise to a panic and thus cause a tremendous artificial demand. And it is precisely this that happens when gold is cornered and demand notes are in circulation. There is just as much incentive for the speculator when he knows that he can frighten people into calling for ten millions on a certain day as when he knows that some one has promised to pay ten millions on a certain day. Furthermore, the incentive in the former case would be very much greater than in the latter if the obligation to pay the ten millions were in the latter case contingent upon the happening of a very improbable thing. Now with mutual banking such would be the case. If the banks of New York held notes of borrowers to the amount of a million dollars and all maturing on the same day, and if the million dollars (or slightly less) which the banks had issued in their own notes to these borrowers were redeemable in gold at a later day if not presented on the earlier day for redemption by a re-exchange of notes, the borrowers, by turning in the bank-notes in fulfilment of their own obligations to the banks, would wipe out the banks' indebtedness of a million, with the exception of perhaps two or three thousand dollars, the percentage of bad debts being very small. Thus gold would be needed only to settle this trivial balance, and so slight a demand would furnish very little incentive for a corner.

I have now examined all the evidence adduced by Mr. Wright to show that demand notes can surely stand against a run (the only question that I am now discussing with him), and I claim, on the strength of this examination, that the evidence leads to precisely the opposite conclusion.

Mr. A. W. Wright has an interesting article in *Electrical Engineering* on "Governmentalism versus Individualism in Relation to Banking." It is thoroughly and avowedly Anarchistic, and is written in answer to criticism directed against Mr. Wright's financial views by the so-called Professor Gunton.

Mr. Wright's paper is admirably brave and earnest, and presents the case for liberty in banking with great force. Nevertheless, there are grave heresies in it,—among them the assertions that it is impossible to get bank-bills into circulation without agreeing to redeem them on demand, and that "an I O U cannot be made secure without totally destroying the economic reason for its existence." The reasons for the existence of an I O U are two in number: first, the desire of the giver of the I O U for an advance of capital; second, the generally-felt necessity of a circulating medium. Practically these two reasons are but one, since the desire of the giver of the I O U for an advance of capital is almost always a demand for that form of capital which will most readily buy all other forms,—that is, currency.

Now, to say that a man who needs more capital than he has, but who already has an amount of capital sufficient to enable him to secure his I O U by giving a mortgage, has therefore no reason to issue an I O U, or to say that such an I O U, when issued, will not be received by others in exchange for goods because it is secured, is to go to the extreme length of possible economic absurdity. Yet it is precisely what Mr. Wright has said. He should have said, on the contrary, that, unless liberty in banking will result in the issue of I O U's as secure as the best financial mechanism can make them, this liberty itself will lose much the weightier part of its reason for existence, becoming merely one of many petty liberties,—good enough in themselves, but not screaming necessities, or pregnant with great results. If financial liberty will not result in a secure currency, it will do nothing to lessen the exploitation of labor. But in Anarchistic eyes the destructive effect of liberty upon human exploitation constitutes ninety-nine per cent. of its value, and, if it will not have such effect, Mr. Wright is wasting his time in writing sixteen-page articles in its favor.

In all polemical writing there frequently occurs the necessity of interpreting the language or statements of an author. Such an occasion arose concerning a sentence in Col. William B. Greene's work on "Mutual Banking," which made necessary the following analysis by the editor of *Liberty*:

SOME months ago Comrade Henry Cohen wrote a letter to the *Conservator* in which he declared that the ultimate of the mutual bank note is not redemption, but cancellation. He may not have used exactly these words, but they do not misrepresent the position that he took. The object of his letter was to show that the mutual bank note is not redeemable in specie by its issuer. In a later issue of the *Conservator* I undertook to correct Comrade Cohen, showing that, while cancellation by re-exchange for the borrower's note would be the usual mode of disposing of bank notes at maturity, their ultimate, properly speaking, is redemption in specie by the bank, since that would be the course adopted in case of a borrower's insolvency and consequent failure to take up his own note given to the bank; and I intimated that the author of "Mutual Banking" would not have died a peaceful death, could he have foreseen that some of his disciples would represent him as favoring an irredeemable currency. When I said this, I was unaware that a single sentence could be quoted from "Mutual Banking" in support of Comrade Cohen's view. But Hugo Bilgram, seeing the letters in the *Conservator*, promptly wrote to me, calling my attention to the fact that, of the seven provisions constituting Greene's plan for a mutual bank, the seventh is that "the bank shall never redeem any of its notes in specie." Mr. Bilgram added that this sentence from "Mutual Banking" is obviously inconsistent with the rest of the work and seriously impairs its value, and, finally, he endorsed my position that a currency, to be reliable, must be ultimately redeemable in a fixed amount of a specific commodity. Soon came also a letter from Cohen, in which, fresh from his editing of "Mutual Banking," he desired to know how I explain the very sentence cited by Mr. Bilgram. I now answer unequivocally that I do not attempt to explain it, and that Cohen would have been justified in pointing to it with an air of triumph, instead of asking me his modest question. When I wrote to the *Conservator*, I had forgotten that this sentence occurs in "Mutual Banking." In fact, I never at any time could have been thoroughly aware of it. I first read the pamphlet in 1872. Possibly I read it again a year or two later. During the last twenty years or more, though I have often re-read single pages, I have not read it from end to end. In 1872 the subject was new to me. I was greatly interested in it, and the pamphlet made a deep impresion on me, suggesting to me a thousand thoughts; but my boyish unfamiliarity with discussions of finance made it impossible for me to subject each and every one of its statements to that searching criticism which such a book would now receive at my hands. The subsequent clarification of my thought was effected largely by personal intercourse with Colonel Greene himself. During the five years following 1872 which constituted the closing period of his life (he died at Tunbridge Wells, England, in 1877 or 1878) I had the privilege of his acquaintance, and enjoyed many a long talk with him on the subjects in which we were most interested. It should be remembered that even then "Mutual Banking" had been published almost a quarter of a century, and that in the meantime its author's thought, while not fundamentally changing, had undoubtedly matured, and his methods of presenting it had become more careful and precise. Now, in all our talks on finance, never once did he give expression to the doctrine laid down in the sentence cited by Bilgram and Cohen; on the contrary, all our arguments proceeded on the assumption that a mutual bank note would be a claim (though not a demand claim) on its issuer for specie to the amount of its face.

In determining, then, whether Cohen's interpretation of Greene or my own is the correct one, my testimony as to the conception of mutual banking which I derived from Greene personally must be considered, as well as the inconsistency between the sentence cited and Greene's proposal to have the notes secured by property salable under the hammer. This inconsistency is seen as soon as we ask ourselves in what form payment would be made for property sold under the hammer. It would have to be made either in specie or in bank notes. Now, we cannot assume that it would be made in bank notes, unless we also assume, first, that it is possible to float a large volume of mutual bank currency merely on the strength of members' agreement to receive it in trade in lieu of its face in specie, so that no one would ever present a note to the bank, even after maturity, for redemption in specie, and, second, that the insolvent borrower or his assignee would always consent to receive in bank notes so much of the proceeds of the sale as might remain to his credit after satisfaction of the bank's claim,—both of which, in my view, are assumptions of unwarrantable violence. The payment, then, would be made in specie, and this specie would have to be used partly in paying the balance due to the insolvent borrower and partly in calling in the bank notes which the insolvent borrower had failed to pay in at the maturity of his obligation. But such calling in would be specie redemption, which is forbidden in the sentence cited by Cohen.

It seems to me, then, that we are forced to the conclusion that this sentence was written carelessly by Colonel Greene, and that he really intended to say only that the bank shall never agree to redeem any of its notes in specie *on demand*.

This conclusion is further justified by Greene's provision for the acceptance of specie by the bank, at a slight discount, in payment of debts due the bank, and his failure to provide any means of disposing of the specie so accepted. The presumption is that he expected it to be used in redemption of notes. (Let me say, parenthetically, that I dissent from Greene's proposal to receive specie at a discount. Such dis-

crimination might properly be made against bank bills redeemable on demand, but it would be absurd for a bank to
discriminate against, and thus discredit, its own chosen standard of value.)

Another fact of significance in this connection is that,
of the seven provisions laid down in the fourth chapter of
"Mutual Banking" as constituting the author's plan for a
mutual bank, *every one except this questionable seventh*
is carefully embodied, almost word for word, in the petition
for a general mutual-banking act which constitutes the fifth
chapter, while this questionable seventh, though of the greatest importance if it means what Cohen thinks, is omitted
altogether.

I maintain, then, for the various reasons urged, that Colonel
Greene did not believe in an irredeemable currency, and I sug-
gest that, in subsequent editions of "Mutual Banking," an
editorial foot-note should adequately qualify the misleading
sentence that has occasioned this discussion. Nevertheless,
it clearly becomes me to apologize to Comrade Cohen for
"calling him down" so abruptly, when he really had at his
back evidence of seemingly considerable strength.

The question of the redemption of mutual bank notes
in specie was still engaging the attenion of some of the
students of the problem, Mr. Cohen still contending that
the author of "Mutual Banking" did not expect the
mutual banks to handle specie at all; and Mr. Francis D.
Tandy arguing that, even with definite maturity dates,
a great many of the notes of the mutual bank would
become payable in specie on demand, or else the bank
would be compelled to accept from borrowers, in cancellation of loans, nothing but notes that have reached
maturity, in which case the borrower might be obliged
to pay a premium to obtain such notes. Mr. Tucker
argued the matter still further with both his critics:

AT the time when Colonel Greene wrote "Mutual Banking," the banks of issue in vogue were the old State banks

professing to redeem their notes in specie on demand. It was this system which he had to combat, and the entire assault of "Mutual Banking" is upon a demand-note currency. There being no other currency in the people's mind, he had not to guard against other ideas. Consequently he declared the mutual bank-notes' independence of hard money in language so absolute and unqualified as to give some color to the latter-day claim made by Henry Cohen that his plan excludes specie-redemption at any time and under all circumstances. If the passages which Mr. Cohen quotes in another column are to be construed with all the rigor that he seems to desire, they absolutely exclude the use of the specie dollar; but that Colonel Greene contemplated no such exclusion is undoubtedly shown by his declaration that no paper bill of less than five dollars should be issued, in which case disuse of the specie dollar would mean disuse of all dollars, for the specie dollar would be the only dollar in existence. The alternative, then, is to construe these passages liberally rather than literally, and in the light of the fact that an essential feature of the Mutual Banking plan is the provision of a collateral to serve for the redemption of notes not cancelled in the ordinary fashion. Despite the keen intellectual quality shown in "Mutual Banking" as a whole, it contains here and there obviously inexact statements that will not bear analysis. There is, for instance, the declaration that the mutual bank is by its nature incapable of owing anything, —a clear absurdity if vigorously insisted upon instead of being interpreted by the context; for Colonel Greene elsewhere defines the issue of mutual money as an exchange of credits,—an exchange inconceivable between two parties one of whom is by nature incapable of indebtedness. I might take up the cited passages *seriatim*, but it is needless, for my general answer covers the ground.

Possibly Mr. Cohen's suggestion that the security for uncancelled notes would be converted by sale partly into banknotes and partly into gold, the former to satisfy the bank's claim and the latter to satisfy the borrower's equity, meets my argument that the collateral would have to be converted into gold because of the rights of the borrower,—though I have some doubts as to the practicability of the plan,—but my argument that the collateral could not be converted into bank-notes unless these bank-notes had first shown a greater power of general circulation than they would be likely to acquire by a mere agreement of members to receive them in trade regardless of redeemability in specie remains untouched. To be sure, Mr. Cohen urges that the notes will float if enough members join to insure their immediate convertibility into all marketable products; but to assume that a membership of this size and variety can be obtained, and that the non-enforcible agreement of the members to receive the notes in trade would inspire the same confidence in them that would be inspired by an enforcible agreement of the issuer to redeem them in specie, is to beg the question. It is this consideration—the necessity of inspiring confidence in the notes—that makes it desirable that the notes should mature,—that is, be made redeemable by the issuer under definitely-prescribed conditions.

Which brings me to Mr. Tandy's criticism. His error lies not in his logic, which is sound, but in his false premise,—namely, that the tendency of the matured note to flow back to the bank is no greater, and perhaps less, than the tendency of the unmatured note to so flow back. If this were true, then the conditions ultimately resulting would not differ materially from those obtaining under a demand-note currency. But it is not true. Most of the mutual banks would probably be banks of deposit as well as of issue, and large sums of circulating currency would be constantly passing through their hands, as a result of which they would be able, not only by their individual efforts, but by their associative efforts taking effect through the clearing-house, to call in matured notes, paying out in their stead unmatured notes previously paid in by borrowers in cancellation of loans. Mr. Tandy hints, to be sure, that there would be a counter-effort on the outside to corner matured notes in the hope of their going to a premium. I do not think this in the least likely, for people seldom execute movements which may be so simply and easily thwarted. It would not take a very expert financier to knock such a corner in the head. Suppose the bank notes were promises to pay in gold, dollar for dollar, thirty days after presentation at maturity or later, but subject to a proviso that all notes presented later than, say, ninety days after maturity should be liable, at the option of the bank, to a discount from the face value at a percentage rising in the ratio of the period of delay. How long, in Mr. Tandy's opinion, would a corner in matured notes last under such circumstances? He has discovered a mare's-nest.

GOVERNMENT AND VALUE

IN a letter to the London *Herald of Anarchy*, Mr. J. Greevz Fisher asserts that "government does not, and never can, fix the value of gold or any other commodity," and cannot even affect such value except by the slight additional demand which it creates as a consumer. It is true that government cannot *fix* the value of a commodity, because its influence is but one of several factors that combine to govern value. But its power to *affect* value is out of all proportion to the extent of its consumption. Government's consumption of commodities is an almost infinitesimal influence upon value in comparison with its prohibitory power. One of the chief factors in the constitution of value is, as Mr. Fisher himself states, utility; and as long as governments exist, utility is largely dependent upon their arbitrary decrees. When government prohibits the manufacture and sale of liquor, does it not thereby reduce the value of everything that is used in such manufacture and sale? If government were to allow theatrical performances on Sundays, would not the value of every building that contains a theatre rise? Have not we, here in America, just seen the McKinley bill change the value of nearly every article that the people use? If government were to decree that all plates shall be made of tin, would not the value of tin rise and the value of china fall? Unquestionably. Well, a precisely parallel thing occurs when government decrees that all money shall be made of or issued against gold or silver; these metals immediately take on an artificial, government-created value, because of the *new use* which arbitrary power enables them to monopolize, and all other commodities, which are at the same time forbidden to be put to this use, correspondingly lose value. How absurd, then, in view of these indisputable facts, to assert that government can affect values only in ratio of its consumption! And yet Mr. Fisher makes this assertion the starting-point of a lecture to the editor of the *Herald of Anarchy* delivered in that dogmatic, know-it-all style which only those are justified in assuming who can sustain their statements by facts and logic.

Mr. Fisher replied, in a letter to *Liberty*, so Mr. Tucker continued:

THE central position taken by Mr. Fisher at the start that government cannot affect the value of gold or any other commodity except by the slight additional demand which it creates as a consumer he has been forced to abandon at the first onslaught. If government were to allow the opening of theatres on Sunday, it would not thereby become a consumer of theatres itself (at least not in the economic sense; for, in the United States, at any rate, our governors always go to the theatre as "dead-heads"), and yet Mr. Fisher admits that in such a case the value of theatres would immediately rise very greatly. This admission is an abandonment of the position taken at first so confidently, and no other consideration can make it anything else. The fact that competition would soon arise to reduce the value does not alter the fact that for a time this action of government would materially raise it, which Mr. Fisher originally declared an impossibility. But even if such a plea had any pertinence, it could be promptly destroyed by a slight extension of the hypothesis. Suppose government, in addition to allowing the theatres now existing to open on Sunday, were to prohibit the establishment of any additional theatres. Then the value would not only go up, but stay up. It is hardly necessary to argue the matter further; Mr. Fisher undoubtedly sees that he is wrong. The facts are too palpable and numerous. Why, since my comment of a month ago on Mr. Fisher's position, it has transpired that the cost of making twist drills in the United States has been increased *five hundred and twenty per cent.* by the McKinley bill. Government cannot affect value, indeed!

In the paragraph to which Mr. Fisher's letter is a rejoinder I said that "when government decrees that all money shall be made of or issued against gold or silver, these metals immediately take on an artificial, government-created value, because of the *new use* which arbitrary power enables them to monopolize." Mr. Fisher meets this by attempting to belittle the restrictions placed upon the issue of paper money, as if all vitally necessary liberty to compete with the gold-bugs were even now allowed. Let me ask my opponent one question. Does the law of England allow citizens to form a bank for the issue of paper money against any property that they may see fit to accept as security; said bank perhaps owning no specie whatever; the paper money not redeemable in specie except at the option of the bank; the customers of the bank mutually pledging themselves to accept the bank's paper in lieu of gold or silver coin of the same face value; the paper being redeemable only at the maturity of the mortgage notes, and then simply by a return of said notes and a release of the mortgaged property,—is such an institution, I ask, allowed by the law of England? If it is, then I have only to say that the working people of England are very great fools not to take advantage of this inestimable liberty, that the editor of the *Herald of Anarchy* and his comrades have indeed nothing to complain of in the matter of finance, and that they had better turn their attention at once to the organization of such banks as that which I have just described. But I am convinced that Mr. Fisher will have to answer that these banks are illegal in England; and in that case I tell him again that the present value of gold is a monopoly value sustained by the exclusive monetary privilege given it by government. It may be true, as Mr. Fisher says, that just as much gold would be used if it did not possess this monopoly. But that has nothing to do with the question. Take the illustration that I have already used in this discussion when I said: "If government were to decree that all plates shall be made of tin, would not the value of tin rise and the value of china fall?" Now, if the supply of tin were limited, and if nearly all the tin were used in making plates, and if tin had no other use of great significance, it is quite conceivable that, if the decree prohibiting the use of china in making plates should be withdrawn, the same amount of tin might continue to be used for the same purpose as before, and yet the value of tin would fall tremendously in consequence of the admitted competition of china. And similarly, if all property were to be admitted to competition with gold in the matter of representation in the currency, it is possible that the same amount of gold would still be used as money, but its value would decrease notably,—would fall, that is to say, from its abnormal, artificial, government-created value, to its normal, natural, open market value.

Mr. Fisher then came back with another contribution to *Liberty*—in fact, several of them—in which he attacked the editor and also Mr. Alfred B. Westrup, whose "Citizens' Money" and "The Financial Problem" he had just read. Mr. Tucker's reply, therefore, is a defense of his own position and of that of Mr. Westrup as well, and the controversy develops into a discussion of free trade in banking, of currency and government, and of the equalization of wage and product:

I KNOW of no friend of liberty who regards it as a panacea for every ill, or claims that it will make fools successful, or believes that it will make all men equal, rich, and perfectly happy. The Anarchists, it is true, believe that under liberty the laborer's wages will buy back his product, and that this will make men more nearly equal, will insure the industrious and the prudent against poverty, and will add to human happiness. But between the fictitious claims which Mr. Fisher scouts and the real claims which the Anarchists assert it is easy to see the vast difference.

I do not understand how "the unvarying failure of unsound currency enactments" makes the interference of government with finance seem less pernicious. In fact, it drives me to precisely the opposite conclusion. In the phrase, "concomitant dwindling of monetary law into a mere specification of truisms," Mr. Fisher repeats his attempt, of which I complained in the last issue of *Liberty,* to belittle the restrictions placed upon the issue of paper money. When he has answered the question which I have asked him regarding the English banking laws, we can discuss the matter more intelligently. Meanwhile it is futile to try to make a monopoly seem less than a monopoly by resorting to such a circumlocution as "system of licensing individuals to carry on certain kinds of trades," or to claim that the monopoly of a tool not only common but indispensable to all trades is not more injurious than the monopoly of a tool used by only one trade or a few trades.

It is true that if the mass of capital competing for investment were increased, the rate of interest would fall. But it is not true that scarcity of capital is the only factor that keeps up the rate of interest? If I were free to use my capital directly as a basis of credit or currency, the relief from the necessity of borrowing additional capital from others would decrease the borrowing demand, and therefore the rate of interest. And if, as the Anarchists claim, this freedom to use capital as a basis of credit should give an immense impetus to business, and consequently cause an immense demand for labor, and consequently increase productive power, and consequently augment the amount of capital, here another force would be exercised to lower the rate of interest and cause it to gradually vanish. Free trade in banking does not mean *only* unlimited liberty to create debt; it means also vastly increased ability to meet debt: and, so accompanied, the liberty to create debt is one of the greatest blessings. It is not erroneous to label evidence of debt as money. As Col. Wm. B. Greene well said: "That is money which does the work of the tool money." When evidence of debt circulates as a medium of exchange, to all intents and purposes it is money. But this is of small consequence. The Anarchists do not insist on the word "money." Suppose we call such evidence of debt *currency* (and surely it is currency), what then? How does this change of name affect the conclusions of the "currency-faddists"? Not in the least, as far as I can see. By the way, it is not becoming in a man who has, not simply one bee in his bonnet, but a whole swarm of them, to talk flippantly of the "fads" of men whose lives afford unquestionable evidence of their earnestness.

Mr. Fisher seems to think it inherently impossible to use one's property and at the same time pledge it. But what else happens when a man, after mortgaging his house, continues to live in it? This is an actual every-day occurrence, and mutual banking only seeks to make it possible on easier terms, —the terms that will prevail under competition instead of the terms that do prevail under monopoly. The man who calls this reality an *ignis fatuus* must be either impudent or ignorant.

Mr. Fisher, in his remark that "no attempt is made to show how displacing gold from currency would reduce the price as long as its cost and utility remain what they now are," is no less absurd than he would be if he were to say that no attempt is made to show how displacing flour as an ingredient of bread would reduce the price of flour as long as its cost and utility remain what they now are. The utility of flour consists in the fact that it is an ingredient of bread, and the main utility of gold consists in the fact that it is used as currency. To talk of displacing these utilities and at the same time keeping them what they now are is a contradiction in terms, of which Mr. Fisher is guilty. But Mr. Westrup is guilty of no contradiction at all in claiming that money can be made very much more plentiful and yet maintain its value at the same time that he contends that the present value of money is due to its monopoly or scarcity. For to quote Colonel Greene again:

"All money is not the same money. There is one money of gold, another of brass, another of leather, and another of paper; and there is a difference in the glory of these different kinds of money. There is one money that is a commodity, having its exchangeable value determined by the law of supply and demand, which money may be called (though somewhat barbarously) *merchandise-money;* as, for instance, gold, silver, brass, bank-bills, etc.: there is another money, which is not a commodity, whose exchangeable value is altogether independent of the law of supply and demand, and which may be called *mutual money.* . . . If ordinary bank-bills represented specie actually existing in the vaults of the bank, no mere issue or withdrawal of them could affect a fall or rise in the value of money: for every issue of a dollar-bill would correspond to the locking-up of a specie dollar in the banks' vaults; and every cancelling of a dollar-bill would correspond to the issue by the banks of a specie dollar. It is by the exercise of *banking privileges*—that is, by the issue of bills purporting to be, but which are not, convertible—that the banks effect a depreciation in the price of the silver dollar. It is this *fiction* (by which legal value is assimilated to, and becomes, to all business intents and purposes, actual value) that enables bank-notes to depreciate the silver dollar. *Substitute* VERITY *in the place of fiction,* either by permitting the banks to issue no more paper than they have specie in their vaults, or by effecting an entire divorce between bank-paper and its pretended specie basis, and the power of paper to depreciate specie is at an end. So long as the fiction is kept up, the silver dollar is depreciated, and tends to emigrate for the purpose of travelling in foreign parts; but, the moment the fiction is destroyed, the power of paper over metal ceases. By its intrinsic nature specie is merchandise, having its value determined, as such, by supply and demand; but on the contrary, paper money is, by its intrinsic nature, *not* merchandise, but the means whereby merchandise is exchanged, and, as such, ought always to be commensurate in quality with the amount of merchandise to be exchanged, be that amount great or small. *Mutual money is measured by specie, but is in no way assimilated to it; and therefore its issue can have no effect whatever to cause a rise or fall in the price of the precious metals.*"

This is one of the most important truths in finance, and perfectly accounts for Mr. Westrup's position. When he says that money can be made very much more plentiful and yet maintain its value, he is speaking of *mutual money;* when he says that the present value of money depends upon monoply or scarcity, he is speaking of *merchandise money.*

As sensibly might one say to Mr. Fisher, who is a stanch opponent of government postal service, that "the immediate effect of the total abstention of government from its protection of the public from the roguery of private mail-carriers would be that a great crop of fresh schemes would offer themselves to those desirous of intrusting any of their letters to others to carry. A very large proportion of these schemes— possibly the majority—would be unsound." Well, what of it? Are we on this account to give up freedom? No, says Mr. Fisher. But, then, what is the force of the consideration?

Mr. Westrup's money not only shows that A has given B a conditional title to certain wealth, but guarantees that this wealth has been preserved. That is, it affords a guarantee so nearly perfect that it is acceptable. If you take a mortgage on a house and the owner insures it in your favor, the guarantee against loss by fire is not perfect, since the insurance company may fail, but it is good enough for practical purposes. Similarly, if B, the bank, advances money to A against a mortgage on the latter's stock of goods, it is within the bounds of possibility that A will sell the goods and disappear forever, but he will thus run the risk of severe penalties; and these penalties, coupled with B's caution, make a guarantee that practically serves. To be sure, Mr. Westrup's money does not assure the holder that the bank will deliver the borrowed articles on demand, but it does assure him that he can get similar articles or their equivalents on demand from any customers of the bank that have them for sale, because all these customers are pledged to take the bank's notes; to say nothing of the fact that the bank, though not bound to redeem on demand, is bound to redeem as fast as the mortgage notes mature.

The truisms which Mr. Fisher enunciates so solemnly do not establish the absence of any necessity for enabling all wealth to be represented by money. This necessity is shown by the fact that, when the monetary privilege is conferred upon one form of wealth exclusively, the people have to obtain this form of wealth at rates that sooner or later send them into bankruptcy.

The value of gold would be reduced by mutual banking, because it would thereby be stripped of that exclusive monetary utility conferred upon it by the State. The percentage of this reduction no one can tell in advance, any more than he can tell how much whiskey would fall in price if there were unrestricted competition in the sale of it.

Neither gold nor any other commodity is bought by people who don't want to consume it or in some way cause others to consume it. Gold is in process of consumption when it is in use as currency.

Mutual banking might or might not cause gold to lose its pre-eminence as the most thoroughly constituted value. If it should do so, then some other commodity more constantly demanded and uniformly supplied would take the place of gold as a standard of value. It certainly is unscientific to impart a factitious monopoly value to a commodity in order to make its value steady.

Other things being equal, the rate of interest is inversely proportional to the residual increment of wealth, for the reason that a low rate of interest (except when offered to an already bankrupted people) makes business active, causes a more universal employment of labor, and thereby adds to productive capacity. The residual increment is less in the United Kingdom, where interest is low, than in the United States, where interest is high, because other things are not equal. But in either country this increment would be greater than it now is if the rate of interest were to fall.

If gold became as abundant as copper, legislation, if it chose, could maintain its value by decreeing that we should drink only from gold goblets. If the value were maintained, the volume of money would be greater on account of the abundance of gold. This increase of volume would lower the rate of interest.

A *voluntary* custom of selling preferentially for gold would not be a monoply, but there is no such voluntary custom. Where cattle are used voluntarily as a medium of exchange, they are not a monopoly; but where there is a law that *only* cattle shall be so used, they are a monopoly.

It is not incumbent on Anarchists to show an analogy between a law to require the exclusive consumption of hand-made bricks and any law specifying that the word Dollar in a bond shall imply a certain quantity of gold. But they are bound and ready to show an analogy between the first-named law and any laws prohibiting or taxing the issue of notes, of whatever description, intended for circulation as currency. Governments force people to consume gold, in the sense that they give people no alternative but that of abandoning the use of money. When government swaps off gold for other commodities, it thereby consumes it in the economic sense. The United States government purchases its gold and silver. It can hardly be said, however, that it purchases silver in an open market, because, being obliged by law to buy so many millions each month, it thereby creates an artificial market.

Again Mr. Fisher came back, in his characteristic style, to which Mr. Tucker replied in the following manner:

Mr. Fisher's article is nothing but a string of assertions,

most of which, as matters of fact, are untrue. The chief of
these untruths is the statement that in exchanging gold we
do not consume it. What is consumption? It is the act of
destroying by use or waste. One of the uses of gold—and
under the existing financial system its chief use—is to act
as a medium of exchange, or else as the basis of such a medium.
In performing this function it wears out; in other words, it is
consumed. Being given a monopoly of this use or function, it
has an artificial value,—a value which it would not have if
other articles, normally capable of this function, were not
forbidden to compete with it. And these articles suffer from
this restriction of competition in very much the same way
that a theatre forbidden to give Sunday performances suffers
if its rival is allowed the privilege. Mr. Fisher may deny the
analogy as stoutly as he chooses; it is none the less established.
This analogy established, Mr. Fisher's position falls,—falls as
surely as his other position has fallen: the position that government cannot affect values, which he at first laid down
with as much contemptuous assurance as if no one could deny
it without thereby proving himself a born fool. So there
is no need to refute the rest of the assertions. I will simply
enter a specific denial of some of them. It is untrue that gold
is not withdrawn from the market to raise its price. It is
untrue that the gold mines are kept open *principally* to supply the arts. It is untrue that, if gold were twice as dear or
twice as cheap, bankers would not lose or gain; the chief
business of the banker is not to buy and sell gold, but to lend
it. And I believe it to be untrue—though here I do not
speak of what I positively know—that English law permits
the establishment of such banks as Proudhon, Greene, and
Spooner proposed. Mr. Fisher certainly should know more
about this than I, but I doubt his statement, first, because
I have found him in error so often; second, because nine out
of ten Massachusetts lawyers will tell you with supreme confidence that there is no law in Massachusetts prohibiting the
use of notes and checks as currency (yet there is one of many
years' standing, framed in plain terms, and often have I
astonished lawyers of learning and ability by showing it to
them); and, third, because I am sure that, if such banks were
legal in England, they would have been started long ago.

Another long letter from Mr. Fisher here intervened and the editor of *Liberty* took up each point and carefully replied to it:

A laborer's product is such portion of the value of that which he delivers to the consumer as his own labor has contributed. To expect the laborer's wages to buy this value back is to expect no more than simple equity. If some other laborer has contributed to the total value of the delivered article by making a tool which has been used in its manufacture by the laborer who delivers it, then the wages of the laborer who makes the tool should also buy back *his* product or due proportion of value, and would do so under liberty. But his portion of the value and therefore his wage would be measured by the wear and tear which the tool had suffered in this single act of manufacture, and not by any supposed benefit conferred by the use of the tool over and above its wear and tear. In other words, the tool-maker would simply sell that portion of the tool destroyed in the act of manufacture instead of lending the tool and receiving it again accompanied by a value which would more than restore it to its original condition. Mr. Fisher's interpretation rests, furthermore, on a misconception of the term wages. When a farmer hires a day-laborer for a dollar a day and his board, the board is as truly a part of the wages as is the dollar; and when I say that the laborer's wages should buy back his product, I mean that the total amount which he receives for his labor, whether in advance or subsequently, and whether consumed before or after the performance of his labor, should be equal in market value to his total contribution to the product upon which he bestows his labor. Is this expecting too much? If so, might I ask to whom the excess of product over wage should equitably go?

Every man who postpones consumption takes a risk. If he keeps commodities which he does not wish to consume, they may perish on his hands. If he exchanges them for gold, the gold may decline in value. If he exchanges them for government paper promising gold on demand, the paper may decline in value. And if he exchanges them for mutual money, this transaction, like the others (though in a smaller degree, we claim), has its element of risk. But, as long as merchants seem to think that they run less risk by temporarily placing their valuables at the disposal of others than by retaining possession of them, the advocates of mutual money will no more concern themselves about giving them recompense beyond the bare return of their valuables unimpaired than the advocates of gold and government paper will concern themselves to insure the constancy of the one or the solvency of the other. As for the "something out of nothing" fallacy, that is shared between God and the Shylocks, and, far from being entertained by the friends of free banking, is their special abomination. "Credit without remuneration!" shrieks Mr. Fisher in horror. But, if credit is reciprocal, why should there be remuneration? "Debt without cost!" But, if debt is reciprocal, why should there be cost? "Unlimited or very plentiful money without depreciation!" But if the contemplated addition to the volume of currency contemplates in turn a broadening of the basis of currency, why should there be depreciation? Free and mutual banking means simply reciprocity of credit, reciprocity of debt, and an extension of the currency basis.

It is the especial claim of free banking that it will increase production. To make capital fluent is to make business active and to keep labor steadily employed at wages which will cause a tremendous effective demand for goods. If free banking were only a picayunish attempt to distribute more equitably the small amount of wealth now produced, I would not waste a moment's energy on it.

I am interested in securing the greatest possible liberty for banking so that I may profit by the greater competition that would then be carried on between those born with a genius for finance. But what about Proudhon, Mr. Fisher? He was no amateur. He could value, not only a horse, but a railroad, the money kings utilized his business brains, his Manual for a Bourse Speculator served them as a guide, and, when he started his Banque du Peuple, it immediately assumed such proportions that Napoleon had to construct a crime for which to clap him into jail in order to save the Bank of France from this dangerous competitor. The suppression of Proudhon's bank was a coercion of the market. And in this country attempt after attempt has been made to introduce credit money outside of government and national bank channels, and the promptness of suppression has always been proportional to the success of the attempt.

I tell Mr. Fisher again that it is a crime to issue and circulate as currency a note promising to deliver iron at a certain time. I know that it is a crime in this country, and I believe that the laws of England contain restrictions that occomplish virtually the same result.

There is no contradiction between my position and Greene's. Greene held, as I hold, that the existing monopoly imparts an artificial value to gold, and that the abolition of the monopoly would take away this artificial value. But he also held, as I hold, that, after this reduction of value had been effected, the variations in the volume of mutual money would be independent of the price of specie. In other words, this reduction of the value of gold from the artificial to the normal point will be effected by the equal liberty given to other commodities to serve as a basis of currency; but, this liberty having been granted and having taken effect, the issue of mutual money against these commodities, each note being based on a specific portion of them, cannot affect the value of any of these commodities, of which gold is one. It is no answer to the charge of monopoly to say that any one can buy and sell gold coin. No one denies that. The monopoly complained of is this,—that only holders of gold (and, in this country, of government bonds) can use their property as currency or as a basis of currency. Such a monopoly has even more effect in enhancing the price of gold than would a monopoly that should allow only certain persons to deal in gold. The price of gold is determined less by the number of persons dealing in it than by the ratio of the total supply to the total demand. The monopoly that the Anarchists complain of is monopoly that increases the demand for gold by giving it the currency function to the exclusion of other commodities. If my whiskey illustration isn't satisfactory, I will change it. If whiskey were the only alchoholic drink allowed to be used as a beverage, it would command a higher price than it commands now. I should then tell Mr. Fisher that the value of whiskey was artificial and that free rum would reduce it to its normal point. If he should then ask me what the normal point was,

I should answer that I had no means of knowing. If he should respond that the fall in whiskey resulting from free rum "would be limited to such relinquishment of profit as would be forced upon the dealers by competition," I should acquiesce with the remark that the distance from London to Liverpool is equal to the distance from Liverpool to London.

It is Mr. Fisher's analogy, not mine, that is false and inapplicable. The proper analogy is not between gold and the commodities carried, but between gold and the vehicle in which they are carried. The cargo of peaches that rots on its way from California to New England may not be economically consumed (though for my life I can't see why such consumption isn't as economic as the tipping of silver into the Atlantic by the United States government, which Mr. Fisher considers purely economic), but at any rate the wear of the car that carries the cargo is an instance of economic consumption. Now the gold that goes to California to pay for those peaches and comes back to New England to pay for cotton cloth, and thus goes back and forth as constantly as the railway car and facilitates exchange equally with the railway car and wears out in the process just as the railway car wears out, is in my judgment consumed precisely as the railway car is consumed. That only is a complete product, Mr. Fisher tells us, which is in the hands of a person who applies it to the direct gratification of some personal craving. I suppose Mr. Fisher will not deny that a railway car is a complete product. But if it can be said to be in the hands of a person who applies it to the direct gratification of some personal craving, then the same can be said of gold.

HENRY GEORGE AND INTEREST

When Henry George was conducting his *Standard* some of his correspondents inveigled him into a discussion of the question of interest, in which he attempted to prove that interest is a vital reality apart from the money monopoly. The editor of *Liberty* at once took issue with him there:

THE STANDARD now acknowledges that "the theory of interest as propounded by Mr. George has been more severely and plausibly criticized than any other phase of the economic problem as he presents it." When we consider that George regards it as an economic law that interest varies inversely with so important a thing as rent, we see that he cannot consistently treat as unimportant any "plausible" argument urged in support of the theory that interest varies principally, not with rent, but with the economic conditions arising from a monopoly of the currency.

It appears that all the trouble of the enemies of interest grows out of their view of it as exclusively incidental to borrowing and lending, whereas interest on borrowed capital is itself "incidental to real interest," which is "the increase that capital yields irrespective of borrowing and lending." This increase, Mr. George claims, is the work of time, and from this premise he reasons as follows:

"The laborer who has capital ready when it is wanted, and thus, by saving time in making it, increases production, will get and ought to get some consideration,—higher wages, if you choose, or interest, as we call it,—just as the skilful printer who sets fifteen hundred ems an hour will get more for an hour's work than the less skilful printer who sets only a thousand. In the one case greater power due to skill, and in the other greater power due to capital, produce greater results in a given time; and in neither case is the increased compensation a deduction from the earnings of other men."

To make this analogy a fair one it must be assumed that skill is a product of labor, that it can be bought and sold, and that its price is subject to the influence of competition; otherwise it furnishes no parallel to capital. With these assumptions the opponent of interest eagerly seizes upon the analogy as entirely favorable to his own position and destructive of Mr. George's. If the skilful printer produced his skill and can sell it, and if other men can produce similar skill and sell it, the price that will be paid for it will be limited, under free competition, by the cost of production, and will bear no relation to the extra five hundred ems an hour. The case is precisely the same with capital. Where there is free competition in the manufacture and sale of spades, the price of a spade will be governed by the cost of its production, and not by the value of the extra potatoes which the spade will enable its purchaser to dig. Suppose, however, that the skilful printer enjoyed a monopoly of skill. In that case, its price would no longer be governed by the cost of production, but by its utility to the purchaser, and the monopolist would exact nearly the whole of the extra five hundred ems, receiving which hourly he would be able to live for the rest of his life without ever picking up a type. Such a monopoly as this is now enjoyed by the holders of capital in consequence of the currency monopoly, and this is the reason, and the only reason, why they are able to tax borrowers nearly up to the limit of the advantage which the latter derive from having the capital. In other words, increase which is purely the work of time bears a price only because of monopoly. Abolish the monopoly, then, and what becomes of Mr. George's "real interest" except as a benefit enjoyed by all consumers in proportion to their consumption? As far as the owner of the capital is concerned, it vanishes at once, and Mr. George's wonderful distinction with it.

He tells us, nevertheless, that the capitalist's share of the results of the increased power which capital gives the laborer is "not a deduction from the earnings of other men." Indeed! What are the normal earnings of other men? Evidently what they can produce with all the tools and advantages which they can procure *in a free market* without force or fraud. If, then, the capitalist, by abolishing the free market, compels other men to procure their tools and advantages of him on less favorable terms than they could get before, while it may be better for them to come to his terms than to go without the capital, does he not deduct from their earnings?

But let us hear Mr. George further in regard to the great value of time to the idler.

"Suppose a natural spring free to all, and that Hodge carries a pail of water from it to a place where he can build a fire and boil the water. Having hung a kettle and poured the water into it, and arranged the fuel and started the fire, he has by his labor set natural forces at work in a certain direction; and they are at work for him alone, because without his previous labor they would not be at work in that direction at all. Now he may go to sleep, or run off and play, or amuse himself in any way that he pleases; and when an hour—a period of time—shall have elapsed, he will have, instead of a pail of cold water, a pot of boiling water. Is there no difference in value between that boiling water and the cold water of an hour before? Would he exchange the pot of boiling water for a pail of cold water, even though the cold water were in the pot and the fire started? Of course not, and no one would expect him to. And yet between the time when the fire is started and the time when the water boils he does no work. To what, then, is that difference in value due? Is it not clearly due to the element of time? Why does Hodge demand more than a pail of cold water for the pot of boiling water if it is not that the ultimate object of his original labor—the making of tea, for example—is nearer complete than it was an hour before, and that an even exchange of boiling water for cold water would delay him an hour, to which he will not submit unless he is paid for it? And why is Podge willing to give more than a pail of cold water for the pot of boiling water, if it is not that it gives him the benefit of an hour's time in production, and thus increases his productive power very much as greater skill would? And if Podge gives to Hodge more than a pail of cold water for the pot of boiling water, does Podge lose anything that he had, or Hodge gain anything that he had not? No. The effect of the transaction is a transfer for a consideration of the advantage in point of time that Hodge had, to Podge who had not, as if a skilful compositor should, if he could, sell his skill to a less skilful member of the craft."

We will look a little into this economic Hodge-Podge.

The illustration is vitiated from beginning to end by the neglect of the most important question involved in it,—namely, whether Hodge's idleness during the hour required for the boiling of the water is a matter of choice or of necessity. It was necessary to leave this out in order to give time the credit of boiling the water. Let us not leave it out, and see what will come of it. If Hodge's idleness is a matter of necessity, it is equivalent, from the economic standpoint, to labor, and counts as labor in the price of the boiling water. A storekeeper may spend only five hours in waiting *on* his customers, but, as he has to spend another five hours in waiting *for* them, he gets paid by them for ten hours' labor. His five hours' idleness counts as labor, because, to accommodate his customers, he has to give up what he could produce in those five hours if he could labor in them. Likewise, if Hodge, when boiling water for Podge, is obliged to spend an hour in idleness, he will charge Podge for the hour in the price which he sets on the boiling water. But it is Hodge himself, this disposition of himself, and not the abstraction, time, that gives the water its exchangeable value. The abstraction, time, is as truly at work when Hodge is bringing the water from the spring and starting the fire as when he is asleep waiting for the water to boil; yet Mr. George would not dream of attributing the value of the water after it had been brought from the spring to the element of time. He would say that it was due entirely to the labor of Hodge. Properly speaking, time does not work at all, but, if the phrase is to be insisted on in economic discussion, it can be admitted only with some such qualification as the following: The services of time are venal only when rendered through human forces; when rendered exclusively through the forces of nature, they are gratuitous.

That time does not give the boiling water any exchangeable value becomes still more evident when we start from the hypothesis that Hodge's idleness, instead of being a matter of necessity, is a matter of choice. In that case, if Hodge chooses to be idle, and still tries, in selling the boiling water to Podge, to charge him for this unnecessary idleness, the enterprising Dodge will step up and offer boiling water to Podge at a price lower than Hodge's, knowing that he can afford to do so by performing some productive labor while waiting for the water to boil, instead of loafing like Hodge. The effect of this will be that Hodge himself will go to work productively, and then will offer Podge a better bargain than Dodge has proposed, and so competition between Hodge and Dodge will go on until the price of the boiling water to Podge shall fall to the value of the labor expended by either Hodge or Dodge in bringing the water from the spring and starting the fire. Here, then, the exchangeable value of the boiling water which was said to be due to time has disappeared, and yet it takes just as much time to boil the water as it did in the first place.

Mr. George gets into difficulty in discussing this question of the increase of capital simply because he continually loses sight of the fact that competition lowers prices to the cost of production and thereby distributes this so-called product of capital among the whole people. He does not see that capital in the hands of labor is but the utilization of a natural force or opportunity, just as land is in the hands of labor, and that it is as proper in the one case as in the other that the benefits of such utilization of natural forces should be enjoyed by the whole body of consumers.

Mr. George truly says that rent is the price of monopoly. Suppose, now, that some one should answer him thus: You misconceive; you clearly have leasing exclusively in mind, and suppose an unearned bonus for a lease, whereas rent of leased land is merely incidental to real rent, which is the superiority in location or fertility of one piece of land over another, irrespective of leasing. Mr. George would laugh at such an argument if offered in justification of the receipt and enjoyment of unearned increment or economic rent by the landlord. But he himself makes an equally ridiculous and precisely parallel argument in defence of the usurer when he says, in answer to those who assert that interest is the price of monopoly: "You misconceive; you clearly have borrowing and lending exclusively in mind, and suppose an unearned bonus for a loan, whereas interest on borrowed capital is merely incidental to real interest, which is the increase that capital yields, irrespective of borrowing and lending."

The truth in both cases is just this,—that nature furnishes man immense forces with which to work in the shape of land and capital, that in a state of freedom these forces benefit each individual to the extent that he avails himself of them, and that any man or class getting a monopoly of either or both will put all other men in subjection and live in luxury on the products of their labor. But to justify a monopoly of either of these forces by the existence of the force itself, or to argue that without a monopoly of it any individual could get an income by lending it instead of by working with it, is equally absurd whether the argument be resorted to in the case of land or in the case of capital, in the case of rent or in the case of interest. If any one chooses to call the advantages of these forces to mankind rent in one case and interest in the other, I do not know that there is any serious objection to his doing so, provided he will remember that in practical economic discussion rent stands for the absorption of the advantages of land by the landlord, and interest for the absorption of the advantages of capital by the usurer.

The remainder of Mr. George's article rests entirely upon the time argument. Several new Hodge-Podge combinations are supposed by way of illustration, but in none of them is there any attempt to justify interest except as a reward of time. The inherent absurdity of this justification having been demonstrated above, all that is based upon it falls with it. The superstructure is a logical ruin; it remains only to clear away the *débris*.

Hodge's boiling water is made a type of all those products of labor which afterwards increase in utility purely by natural forces, such as cattle, corn, etc.; and it may be admitted that, if time would add exchangeable value to the water while boiling, it would do the same to corn while growing, and cattle while multiplying. But that it would do so under freedom has already been disproved. Starting from this, however, an attempt is made to find in it an excuse for interest on products which do not improve except as labor is applied to them, and even on money itself. Hodge's grain, after it has been growing for a month, is worth more than when it was first sown; therefore Podge, the shovel-maker, who supplies a market which it takes a month to reach, is entitled to more pay for his shovels at the end of that month than he would have been had he sold them on the spot immediately after production; and therefore the banker who discounts at the time of production the note of Podge's distant customer maturing a month later, thereby advancing ready money to Podge, will be entitled, at the end of the month, from Podge's customer, to the extra value which the month's time is supposed to have added to the shovels.

Here Mr. George not only builds on a rotten foundation, but he mistakes foundation for superstructure. Instead of reasoning from Hodge to the banker he should have reasoned from the banker to Hodge. His first inquiry should have been how much, in the absence of a monopoly in the banking business, the banker could get for discounting for Podge the note of his customer; from which he could then have ascertained how much extra payment Podge could get for his month's delay in the shovel transaction, or Hodge for the services of time in ripening his grain. He would then have discovered that the banker, who invests little or no capital of his own, and, therefore, lends none to his customers, since the security which they furnish him constitutes the capital upon which he operates, is forced, in the absence of money monopoly, to reduce the price of his services to labor cost, which the statistics of the banking business show to be much less than one per cent. As this fraction of one per cent. represents simply the banker's wages and incidental expenses, and is not payment for the use of capital, the element of interest disappears from his transactions. But, if Podge can borrow money from the banker without interest, so can Podge's customer; therefore, should Podge attempt to exact from his customer remuneration for the month's delay, the latter would at once borrow the money and pay Podge spot cash. Furthermore Podge, knowing this, and being able to get ready money easily himself, and desiring, as a good man of business, to suit his customer's convenience, would make no such attempt. So Podge's interest is gone as well as the banker's. Hodge, then, is the only usurer left. But is any one so innocent as to suppose that Dodge, or Lodge, or Modge will long continue to pay Hodge more for his grown grain than his sown grain, after any or all of them can get land free of rent and money free of interest, and thereby force time to work for them as well as for Hodge. Nobody who can get the services of time for nothing will be such a fool as to pay Hodge for them. Hodge, too, must say farewell to his interest as soon as the two great monopolies of land and money are abolished. *The rate of interest on money fixes the rate of interest on all other capital the production of which is subject to competition, and when the former disappears the latter disappears with it.*

Presumably to make his readers think that he has given due consideration to the important principle just elucidated, Mr. George adds, just after his hypothesis of the banker's transaction with Podge:

"Of course there is discount *and* discount. I am speaking of a legitimate economic banking transaction. But frequently bank discounts are nothing more than taxation, due to the choking up of free exchange, in consequence of which an institution that controls the common medium of exchange can impose arbitrary conditions upon producers who must immediately use that common medium."

The evident purpose of the word "frequently" here is to carry the idea that, when a bank discount is a tax imposed by monopoly of the medium of exchange, it is simply a somewhat common exception to the general rule of "legitimate economic banking transactions." For it is necessary to have such a general rule in order to sustain the theory of interest on capital as a reward of time. The exact contrary, however, is the truth. Where money monopoly exists, it is the rule that bank discounts are taxes imposed by it, and when, in consequence of peculiar and abnormal circumstances, discount is not in the nature of a tax, it is a rare exception. The abolition of money monopoly would wipe out discount as a tax and, by adding to the steadiness of the market, make the cases where it is not a tax even fewer than now. Instead of legitimate, therefore, the banker's transaction with Podge, being exceptional in a free money market and a tax of the ordinary discount type in a restricted money market, is illegitimate if cited in defence of interest as a normal economic factor.

In the conclusion of his article Mr. George strives to show that interest would not enable its beneficiaries to live by the labor of others. But he only succeeds in showing, though in a very obscure, indefinite, and intangible fashion,—seemingly afraid to squarely enunciate it as a proposition,—that where there is no monopoly there will be little or no interest. Which is precisely our contention. But why, then, his long article? If interest will disappear with monopoly, what will become of Hodge's reward for his time? If, on the other hand, Hodge is to be rewarded for his mere time, what will reward him save Podge's labor? There is no escape from this dilemma. The proposition that the man who for time spent in idleness receives the product of time employed in labor is a parasite upon the body industrial is one which an expert necromancer like Mr. George may juggle with before an audience of gaping Hodges and Podges, but can never successfully dispute with men who understand the rudiments of political economy.

VARIOUS MONEY SCHEMES

The Greenbackers were always a fair target for *Liberty*'s shafts of satire and ridicule, but there were many other money schemes, both fiat and other, that drew its fire—and not infrequently its commendation. Several of these are here subjected to analysis and criticism by *Liberty*'s editor:

THE persistent way in which Greenbackers dodge argument on the money question is very tiresome to a reasoning mortal. Let an Anarchist give a Greenbacker his idea of a good currency in the issue of which no government has any part, and it is ten to one that he will answer: "Oh, that's not money. It isn't legal tender. Money is that thing which the supreme law of the land declares to be legal tender for debts in the country where that law is supreme."

Brick Pomeroy made such an answer to Stephen Pearl Andrews recently, and appeared to think that he had said something final. Now, in the first place, this definition is not correct, for that is money which performs the functions of money, no matter who issues it. But even if it were correct, of what earthly consequence could it be? Names are nothing. Who cares whether the Anarchistic currency be called money or something else? Would it make exchange easy? Would it make production active? Would it measure prices accurately? Would it distribute wealth honestly? Those are the questions to be asked concerning it; not whether it meets the arbitrary definition adopted by a given school. A system of finance capable of supplying a currency satisfying the above requirements is a solution of what is generally known as the money question; and Greenbackers may as well quit now as later trying to bind people to this fact by paltry quibbling with words.

But after thus rebuking Brick Pomeroy's evasion of Mr. Andrews, something needs to be said in amendment of Mr. Andrew's position as stated by him in an admirable article on "The Nature of Money," published in the New York

Truth Seeker of March 8, 1884. Mr. Andrews divides the properties of money into essentials, incidentals, and accidentals. The essential properties of money, he says,—those in the absence of which it is not money whatever else it may have, and in the possession of which it is money whatever else it may lack,—are those of measuring mutual estimates in an exchange, recording a commercial transaction, and inspiring confidence in a promise which it makes. All other properties of money Mr. Andrews considers either incidental or accidental, and among the accidental properties he mentions the security or "collateral" which may back up and guarantee money.

Now as an analysis made for the purpose of arriving at a definition, this is entirely right. No exception can be taken to it. But it is seriously to be feared that nearly every person who reads it will infer that, because security or "collateral" is an accidental feature of money, it is an unimportant and well-nigh useless one. And that is where the reader will make a great mistake. It is true that money is money, with or without security, but it cannot be a perfect or reliable money in the absence of security; nay, it cannot be a money worth considering in this age. The advance from barter to unsecured money is a much shorter and less important step logically than that from unsecured money to secured money. The rude vessel in which primitive men first managed to float upon the water very likely had all the essentials of a boat, but it was much nearer to no boat at all than it was to the stanch, swift, and sumptuous Cunarder that now speeds its way across the Atlantic in a week. It was a boat, sure enough; but not a boat in which a very timid or even moderately cautious man would care to risk his life in more than five feet of water beyond swimming distance from the shore. It had all the essentials, but it lacked a great many accidentals. Among them, for instance, a compass. A compass is not an essential of a boat, but it is an essential of satisfactory navigation. So security is not an essential of money, but it is an essential of steady production and stable commerce. A boat without a compass is almost sure to strike upon the rocks. Likewise money without security is almost sure to precipitate the people using it into general bankruptcy. When products can be had for the writing of promises and the idea gets abroad that such promises are good money whether kept or not, the promisors are very likely to stop producing; and, if the process goes on long enough, it will be found at the end that there are plenty of promises with which to buy, but that there is nothing left to be bought, and that it will require an infinite number of promises to buy an infinitesimal amount of nothing. If, however, people find that their promises will not be accepted unless accompanied by evidence of an intention and ability to keep them, and if this evidence is kept definitely before all through some system of organized credit, the promisors will actively bestir themselves to create the means of keeping their promises; and the free circulation of these promises, far from checking production, will vastly stimulate it, the result being, not bankruptcy, but universal wealth. A money thus secured is fit for civilized people. Any other money, though it have all the essentials, belongs to barbarians, and is hardly fit to buy the Indian's dug-out.

The introduction in congress by Leland Stanford of a bill proposing to issue one hundred millions or more of United States notes to holders of agricultural land, said notes to be secured by first mortgages on such land and to bear two per cent. interest, is one of the most notable events of this time, and its significance is increased by the statement of Stanford, in his speech supporting the bill, that its provisions will probably be extended ultimately to other kinds of property. This bill is pregnant with the economics (not the politics) of Anarchism. It contains the germ of the social revolution. It provides a system of governmental mutual banking. If it were possible to honestly and efficiently execute its provisions, it would have only to be extended to other kinds of property and to gradually lower its rate of interest from two per cent. (an eminently safe figure to begin with) to one per cent., or one half of one per cent., or whatever figure might be found sufficient to cover the cost of operating the system, in order to steadily and surely transfer a good three-fourths of the income of idle capitalists to the pockets of the wage-workers of the country. The author of this bill is so many times a millionaire that, even if every cent of his income were to be cut off, his principal would still be sufficient to support his family for generations to come, but it is none the less true that he has proposed a measure which, with the qualifications already specified, would ultimately make his descendants either paupers or toilers instead of gigantic parasites like himself. In short, Leland Stanford has indicated the only blow (considered solely in its economic aspect) that can ever reach capitalism's heart. From his seat in the United States Senate he has told the people of this country, in effect, that the fundamental economic teaching reiterated by *Liberty* from the day of its first publication is vitally true and sound.

Unhappily his bill is vitiated by the serious defect of governmentalism. If it had simply abolished all the restrictions and taxes on banking, and had empowered all individuals and associations to do just what its passage would empower the government to do, it would not only have been significant, but, adopted by congress, it would have been the most tremendously and beneficially effective legislative measure ever recorded on a statute book. But, as it is, it is made powerless for good by the virus of political corruption that lurks within it. The bill, if passed, would be entrusted for execution either to the existing financial cabal or to some other that would become just as bad. All the beneficent results that, as an economic measure, it is calculated to achieve would be nearly counteracted, perhaps far more than counteracted, by the cumulative evils *inherent* in State administration. It deprives itself, in advance, of the vitalizing power of free competition. If the experiment should be tried, the net result would probably be evil. It would fail, disastrously fail, and *the failure and disaster would be falsely and stupidly attributed to its real virtue, its economic character.* For perhaps another century free banking would have to bear the odium of the evils generated by a form of governmental banking more or less similar to it economically. Some bad name would be affixed to the Stanford notes, and this would replace the *assignat,* the "wild cat," and the "rag baby," as a more effective scarecrow.

While hoping, then, that it may never pass, let us nevertheless make the most of its introduction by using it as a text in our educational work. This may be done in one way by showing its economic similarity to Anarchistic finance and by disputing the astounding claim of originality put forward by Stanford. In his Senate speech of May 23, he said: "There is no analogy between this scheme for a government of 65,000,000 people, with its boundless resources, issuing its money, secured directly by at least $2 for $1, on the best possible security that could be desired, and any other financial proposition that has ever been suggested." If Stanford said this honestly, his words show him to be both an intellectual pioneer and a literary laggard. More familiarity with the literature of the subject would show him that he has had several predecessors in this path. Col. William B. Greene used to say of Lysander Spooner's financial proposals that their only originality lay in the fact that he had taken out a patent on them. The only originality of Stanford's lies in the fact that it is made for a government of 65,000,000 of people. For governments of other sizes the same proposal has been made before. Parallel to it in all essentials, both economically and politically, are Proudhon's Bank of Exchange and the proposal of Hugo Bilgram. Parallel to it economically are Proudhon's Bank of the People, Greene's Mutual Banks, and Spooner's real estate mortgage banks. And the financial thought that underlies it is closely paralleled in the writings of Josiah Warren, Stephen Pearl Andrews, and John Ruskin. If Stanford will sit at the feet of any of these men for a time, he will rise a wiser and more modest man.

Like most serious matters, this affair has its amusing side. It is seen in the idolization of Stanford by the Greenbackers. This shows how ignorant these men are of their own principles. Misled by the resemblance of the proposed measure to Greenbackism in some incidental respects, they hurrah themselves hoarse over the California senator, blissfully unaware that his bill is utterly subversive to the sole essential of Greenbackism, —namely, the fiat idea. The Greenbacker is distinguished from all other men in this and only in this,—that in his eyes a dollar is a dollar because the government stamps it as such. Now in Stanford's eyes a dollar is a dollar because it is based upon and secured by a specific piece of property that will sell in the market for at least a certain number of grains of gold. Two views more antagonistic than these it would be impossible to cite. And yet the leading organs of Greenbackism apparently regard them as identical.

The great central principle of Anarchistic economics—

namely, the dethronement of gold and silver from their position of command over all other wealth by the destruction of their monopoly currency privilege—is rapidly forging to the front. The Farmers' Alliance sub-treasury scheme, unscientific and clumsy as it is, is a glance in this direction. The importance of Senator Stanford's land bill, more scientific and workable, but incomplete, and vicious because governmental, has already been emphasized in these columns. But most notable of all is the recent revolution in the financial attitude of Edward Atkinson, the most orthodox and cocksure of American economists, who now swells with his voice the growing demand for a direct representation of all wealth in the currency.

The proposal is briefly this: that the national banks of the country shall be divided into several districts, each district having a certain city as a banking centre; that any bank may deposit with the clearing-house securities satisfactory to the clearing-house committee, and receive from the clearing-house certificates in the form of bank-notes of small denominations, to the extent of seventy-five per cent. of the value of the securities; that these notes shall bear the bank's promise to pay on the back, and shall be redeemable on demand at the bank in legal-tender money, and, in case of failure on the bank's part to so redeem them, they shall be redeemable at the clearing-house; and that this new circulating medium shall be exempt from the ten per cent. tax imposed upon State bank circulation.

Of course a scheme like this would not work the economic revolution which Anarchism expects from free banking. It does not destroy the monopoly of the right to bank; it retains the control of the currency in the hands of a cabal; it undertakes the redemption of the currency in legal-tender money, regardless of the fact that, if any large proportion of the country's wealth should become directly represented in the currency, there would not be sufficient legal-tender money to redeem it. It is dangerous in its feature of centralizing responsibility instead of localizing it, and it is defective in less important respects. I call attention to it, and welcome it, because here for the first time Proudhon's doctrine of the republicanization of specie is soberly championed by a recognized economist. This fact alone makes it an important sign of the times.

Still another Greenbacker, Mr. E. H. Benton, stepped forward to plead for his favorite doctrine, the unlimited issue of government fiat money, a "full legal tender," which, he maintained, needed no other security than "its inherent function and non-discountableness," making a non-interest-bearing currency. Mr. Tucker tried to make him see the light:

Let me suppose a case for Mr. Benton. A is a farmer, and owns a farm worth five thousand dollars. B keeps a bank of issue, and is known far and wide as a cautious and honest business man. C, D, E, etc., down to Z are each engaged in some one of the various pursuits of civilized life. A needs ready money. He mortgages his farm to B, and receives in return B's notes, in various denominations, to the amount of five thousand dollars, for which B charges A this transaction's just proportion of the expenses of running the bank, which would be a little less than one-half of one per cent. With these notes A buys various products which he needs of C, D, E, etc., down to Z, who in turn with the same notes buy products of each other, and in course of time come back to A with them to buy his farm produce. A, thus regaining possession of B's notes, returns them to B, who then cancels his mortgage on A's farm. All these parties, from A to Z, have been using for the performance of innumerable transactions B's notes based on A's farm,— that is, a currency based on some security "other than its inherent function and non-discountableness." They were able to perform them only because they all knew that the notes were thus secured. A knew it because he gave the mortgage; B knew it because he took the mortgage; C, D, E, etc., down to Z knew it because they knew that B never issued notes unless they were secured in this or some similar way. Now, *Liberty* is ready to see, as Mr. Benton says it *ought* to see, that any or all of these parties have been robbed by the use of this money when Mr. Benton shall demonstrate it by valid fact and argument. Until then he must stay in his corner.

A word as to the phrase "legal tender." That only is legal tender which the government prescribes as valid for the discharge of debt. Any currency not so prescribed is not legal tender, no matter how universal its use or how unlimited its issue, and to label it so is a confusion of terms.

Another word as to the term "Greenbacker." He is a Greenbacker who subscribes to the platform of the Greenback party. The cardinal principle of that platform is that the government shall monopolize the manufacture of money, and that any one who, in rebellion against that sacred prerogative, may presume to issue currency on his own account shall therefore be taxed, or fined, or imprisoned, or hanged, or drawn and quartered, or submitted to any other punishment or torture which the government, in pursuit and exercise of its good pleasure, may see fit to impose upon him. Unless Mr. Benton believes in that, he is not a Greenbacker, and I am sure I am not, although, with Mr. Benton, I believe in a non-interest-bearing currency.

Mr. Frank A. Matthews, an Anarchist and believing in the "Cost" principle, expressed a feeling that there was something arbitrary about that principle, and at the same time confessed that his mind was unable to reconcile "Cost" and competition. The editor of *Liberty* revealed the cause of his difficulty and explained the operation of the Cost principle:

THE Cost principle cannot fail to seem arbitrary to one who does not see that it can only be realized through economic processes that go into operation the moment liberty is allowed in finance. To see this it is necessary to understand the principles of mutual banking, which Mr. Matthews has not attentively studied. If he had, he would know that the establishment of a mutual bank does not require the investment of capital, inasmuch as the customers of the bank furnish all the capital upon which the bank's notes are based, and that therefore the rate of discount charged by the bank for the service of exchanging its notes for those of its customers is governed, under competition, by the cost of that service, and not by the rate of interest that capital commands. The relation is just the contrary of Mr. Matthews's supposition. It is the rate of interest on capital that is governed by the bank's rate of discount, for capitalists will not be able to lend their capital at interest when people can get money at the bank *without interest* with which to buy capital outright. It is this effect of free and mutual banking upon the rate of interest on capital that insures, or rather constitutes, the realization of the Cost principle by economic processes. For the moment interest and rent are eliminated as elements of price, and brisk competition is assured by the ease of getting capital, profits fall to the level of the manufacturer's or merchant's proper wage. It is well, as Mr. Matthews says, to have the Cost principle in view; for it is doubtless true that the ease with which society travels the path of progress is largely governed by the clearness with which it foresees it. But, foresight or no foresight, it "gets there just the same." The only foresight absolutely necessary to progress is foresight of the fact that liberty is its single *essential* condition.

"Edgeworth," writing to *Liberty*, expressed doubt about how some phases of Proudhon's Exchange Bank would work out in practice. Mr. Tucker patiently explained the various points criticised:

PROUDHON was accustomed to present his views of the way in which credit may be organized in two forms,—his Bank of Exchange and his Bank of the People. The latter was his real ideal; the former he advocated whenever he wished to avoid the necessity of combating the objections of the governmentalists. The Bank of Exchange was to be simply the Bank of France transformed on the mutual principle. It is easy to see that the precautions against forgery and overissue now used by the Bank of France would be equally valid after the transformation. But in the case of the Bank of the People, which involves the introduction of free competition into the banking business, these evils will have to be otherwise guarded against. The various ways of doing this are secondary considerations, having nothing to do with the principles of finance; and human ingenuity, which has heretofore conquered much greater obstacles, will undoubtedly prove equal to the emergency. The more reputable banks would soon become distinguished from the others by some sort of voluntary organization and mutual inspection necessary to their own protection. The credit of all such as declined to submit to thorough examination by experts at any moment or to keep their books open for public inspection would be ruined, and these would receive no patronage. Probably also the better banks would combine in the use of a uniform bank-note paper difficult to counterfeit, which would be guarded most carefully and distributed to the various banks only so far as they could furnish security for it. In fact, any number of checks can be devised by experts that would secure the currency against all attempts at adulteration. There is little doubt that the first essays will be, as "Edgeworth" hopes, "local and limited." But I do not think the money so produced will be nearly as safe as that which will result when the system has become widespread and its various branches organized in such a way that the best means of protection may be utilized at small expense.

Frequently the editor of *Liberty* found it necessary to attack the delusions and sophistries of writers in other periodicals, and the following is a case in point. (In this article Mr. Tucker used the term "Socialist" in its generic sense, and of course did not mean "state" Socialist.)

VAN BUREN DENSLOW, discussing in the *Truth Seeker* the comparative rewards of labor and capital, points out that the present wage system divides profits almost evenly between the two, instancing the railways of Illinois, which pay annually in salaries and wages $81,936,170, and to capital, which Mr. Denslow defines as the "labor previously done in constructing and equipping the roads," $81,720,265. Then he remarks:

"No system of intentional profit-sharing is more equal than this, provided we assent to the principle that a day's work already done and embodied in the form of capital is as well entitled to compensation for its use as a day's work not yet done, which we call labor." Exactly. But the principle referred to is the very thing which we Socialists deny, and until Mr. Denslow can meet and vanquish us on that point, he will in vain attempt to defend the existing or any other form of profit-sharing. The Socialists assert that "a day's work embodied in the form of capital" has already been fully rewarded by the ownership of that capital; that, if the owner lends it to another to use and the user damages it, destroys it, or consumes any part of it, the owner is entitled to have this damage, destruction, or consumption made good; and that, if the owner receives from the user any surplus beyond the return of his capital intact, his day's work is paid for a second time.

Perhaps Mr. Denslow will tell us, as we have so often been told before, that this day's work should be paid for a second and a third and a hundredth and a millionth time, because the capital which it produced and in which it is embodied increased the productivity of future labor. The fact that it did cause such an increase we grant; but that labor, where there is freedom, is or should be paid in proportion to its usefulness we deny. All useful qualities exist in nature, either actively or potentially, and their benefits, under freedom, are distributed by the natural law of free exchange among mankind. The laborer who brings any particular useful quality into action is paid according to the labor he has expended, but gets only his share, in common with all mankind, of the special usefulness of this product. It is true that the usefulness of his product has a tendency to enhance its price; but this tendency is immediately offset, wherever competition is possible,—and as long as there is a money monopoly there is no freedom of competition in any industry requiring capital,—by the rush of other laborers to create this product, which lasts until the price falls back to the normal wages of labor. Hence it is evident that the owner of the capital embodying the day's work above referred to cannot get his work paid for even a second time by selling his capital. Why, then, should he be able to get it paid for a second time and

an infinite number of times by repeatedly lending his capital?
Unless Mr. Denslow can give us some reason, he will have to
admit that all profit-sharing is a humbug, and that the entire
net product of industry should fall into the hands of labor
not previously embodied in the form of capital,—in other
words, that wages should entirely absorb profits.

Some nincompoop, writing to the Detroit *Spectator* in opposition to cheap money, says: "If low interest insured high
wages, during times of business depression wages would be
high, for then interest reaches its minimum." Another man
unable to see below the surface of things and distinguish association from causation! The friends of cheap money do
not claim that low interest insures high wages. What they
claim is that free competition in currency-issuing and the consequent activity of capital insure both low interest and high
wages. They do not deny that low interest sometimes results
from other causes and unaccompanied by any increase in
wages. When the money monopolists through their privilege
have bled the producers nearly all they can, hard times set in,
business becomes very insecure, no one dares to venture in
new directions or proceed much further in old directions,
there is no demand for capital, and therefore interest falls;
but, there being a decrease in the volume of business, wages
fall also. Suppose, now, that great leveller, bankruptcy, steps
in to wipe out all existing claims, and economic life begins
over again under a system of free banking. What happens
then? All capital is at once made available by the abundance
of the currency, and the supply is so great that interest is
kept very low; but confidence being restored and the way
being clear for all sorts of new enterprises, there is also a
great demand for capital, and the consequent increase in the
volume of business causes wages to rise to a very high point.
When people are afraid to borrow, interest is low and wages
are low; when people are anxious to borrow, but can find only
a very little available capital in the market, interest is high
and wages are low; when people are both anxious to borrow
and can readily do so, interest is low and wages are high, the
only exception being that, when from some special cause labor
is extraordinarily productive (as was the case in the early
days of California), interest temporarily is high also.

II—LAND AND RENT

LAND FOR THE PEOPLE

Although secondary in the study of economics, in the view of the Anarchists, the land question nevertheless ranks high with a large number of persons, hence it was always coming to the front in the columns of *Liberty*. During the period covered by the matter in this volume the Single Tax was very prominent in most discussions of this subject, and Henry George was very active in his propaganda, hence, in the following pages, there will be many references to his pet theory. The Irish land question also was very much in the public eye, and the Liverpool speech, referred to here, is that in which Michael Davitt, in 1882, first publicly endorsed the doctrine of land nationalization. The term "rent," as here used by Mr. Tucker, means monopolistic rent, paid by the tenant to the landlord, and not economic rent, the advantage enjoyed by the occupant of superior land. This distinction is maintained generally throughout these discussions.

THE Liverpool speech, it seems, was delivered by Davitt in response to a challenge from the English press to explain the meaning of the phrase, "the land for the people." We hope they understand it now.

"The land for the people," according to Parnell, appears to mean a change of the present tenants into proprietors of the estates by allowing them to purchase on easy terms fixed by the State and perhaps with the State's aid, and a maintenance thereafter of the present landlord system, involving the collection of rents by law.

"The land for the people," according to Davitt, as explained at Liverpool, appears to mean a change of the whole agricultural population into tenants of the State, which is to become the sole proprietor by purchase from the present proprietors, and the maintenance thereafter of the present landlord system involving the collection of rents in the form of taxes.

"The land for the people," according to George, appears to be the same as according to Davitt, except that the State is to acquire the land by confiscation instead of by purchase, and that the amount of rental is to be fixed by a different method of valuation.

"The land for the people," according to *Liberty*, means the protection (by the State while it exists, and afterwards by such voluntary association for the maintenance of justice as may be destined to succeed it) of all people who desire to cultivate land in the possession of whatever land they personally cultivate, without distinction between the existing classes of landlords, tenants, and laborers, and the positive refusal of the protecting power to lend its aid to the collection of any rent whatsoever; this state of things to be brought about by inducing the people to steadily refuse the payment of rent and taxes, and thereby, as well as by all other means of passive and moral resistance, compel the State to repeal all the so-called land titles now existing.

Thus "the land for the people" according to *Liberty* is the only "land for the people" that means the abolition of landlordism and the annihilation of rent; and all of Henry George's talk about "peasant proprietorship necessarily meaning nothing more than an extension of the landlord class" is the veriest rot, which should be thrown back upon him by the charge that land nationalization means nothing more than a diminution of the landlord class and a concentration and hundred-fold multiplication of the landlord's power.

RENT

"Edgeworth," a frequent contributor to *Liberty*, had read a couple of Proudhon's books, treating of the rent question, which Mr. Tucker had recommended to him, and he seemed to be muddled about the "fiction of the productivity of capital," and some other things. And so the editor enlightened him:

THE two works which I recommended to Edgeworth are among Proudhon's best; but they are very far from all that he has written, and it is very natural for the reader of a very small portion of his writings to draw inferences which he will find unwarranted when he reads more. This is due principally to Proudhon's habit of using words in different senses at different times, which I regard as unfortunate. Now, in the article which gave rise to this discussion, Edgeworth inferred (or seemed to infer), from the fact that some of Proudhon's transitional proposals allowed a share to capital for a time, that he contemplated as a permanent arrangement a division of labor's earnings between labor and capital as two distinct things. Lest this might mislead, I took the liberty to correct it, and to state that Proudhon thought labor the only legitimate title to wealth.

Now comes Edgeworth, and says that he meant by capital only the result of preparatory labor, which is as much entitled to reward as any other. Very good, say I; no one denies that. But this is not what is ordinarily meant by the "productivity of capital"; and Edgeworth, by his own rule, is bound to use words in their usual sense. The usual sense of this phrase, and the sense in which the economists use it, is that capital has such an independent share in all production that the owner of it may rightfully farm out the privilege of using it, receive a steady income from it, have it restored to him *intact* at the expiration of the lease, farm it out again to somebody else, and go on in this way, he and his heirs forever, living in a permanent state of idleness and luxury simply from having performed a certain amount of "preparatory labor." That is what Proudhon denounced as "the fiction of the productivity of capital"; and Edgeworth, in interpreting the phrase otherwise, gives it a very unusual sense, in violation of his own rule.

Moreover, what Edgeworth goes on to say about the proportional profits of landlord and tenant indicates that he has very loose ideas about the proper reward of labor, whether present or preparatory. The scientific reward (and under absolutely free competition the actual reward is, in the long run, almost identical with it) of labor is the product of an equal amount of equally arduous labor. The product of an hour of Edgeworth's labor in preparing a field for cotton culture, and the product of an hour of his tenant's labor in sowing and harvesting the crop, ought each to exchange for the product of an hour's labor of their neighbor the shoemaker, or their neighbor the tailor, or their neighbor the grocer, or their neighbor the doctor, provided the labor of all these parties is equally exhausting and implies equal amounts of acquired skill and equal outlays for tools and facilities. Now, supposing the cases of Edgeworth and his tenant to be representative and not isolated; and supposing them to produce, not for their own consumption, but for the purpose of sale, which is the purpose of practically all production, it then makes no difference to either of them whether their hour's labor yields five pounds of cotton or fifteen. In the one case they can get no more shoes or clothes or groceries or medical services for the fifteen pounds than they can in the other for the five. The great body of landlords and tenants, like the great body of producers in any other industry, does not profit by an increased productivity in its special field of work, except to the extent that it consumes or repurchases its own product. The profit of this increase goes to the people at large, the consumers. So it is not true (assuming always a *régime* of free competition) that Edgeworth's tenant "profits three times as much" as Edgeworth because of the latter's preparatory labors. Neither of them profit thereby, but each gets an hour of some other man's labor for an hour of his own.

So much for the reward of labor in general. Now to get back to the question of rent.

If Edgeworth performs preparatory labor on a cotton field, the result of which would remain intact if the field lay idle, and that result is damaged by a tenant, the tenant ought to pay him for it on the basis of reward above defined. This does not bring a right of ownership to the tenant, to be sure, for the property has been destroyed and cannot be purchased. But the transaction, nevertheless, is in the nature of a sale, and not a payment for a loan. Every sale is an exchange of labor, and the tenant simply pays money representing his own labor for the result of Edgeworth's labor which he (the tenant) has destroyed in appropriating it to his own use. If the tenant does not damage the result of Edgeworth's preparatory labor, then, as Edgeworth admits, whatever money the tenant pays justly entitles him to that amount of ownership in the cotton field. Now, this money, paid over and above all damage, if it does not bring equivalent ownership, is payment for use, usury, and, in my terminology, rent. If Edgeworth prefers to use the word rent to signify all money paid to landlords as such by tenants as such for whatever reason, I shall think his use of the word inaccurate; but I shall not quarrel with him, and shall only protest when he interprets other men's thought by his own definitions, as he seemed to me to have done in Proudhon's case. If he will be similarly peaceful towards me in my use of the word, there will be no logomachy.

The difference between us is just this. Edgeworth says that from tenant to landlord there is payment for damage, and this is just rent; and there is payment for use, and that is unjust rent. I say there is payment for damage, and this is indemnification or sale, and is just; and there is payment for use, and that is rent, and is unjust. My use of the word is in accordance with the dictionary, and is more definite and discriminating than the other; moreover, I find it more effective in argument. Many a time has some small proprietor, troubled with qualms of conscience and anxious to justify the source of his income, exclaimed, on learning that I believe in payment for wear and tear: "Oh! well, you believe in rent, after all; it's only a question of how much rent;" after which he would settle back, satisfied. I have always found that the only way to give such a man's conscience a chance to get a hold upon his thought and conduct was to insist on the narrower use of the word rent. It calls the attention much more vividly to the distinction between justice and injustice.

More from "Edgeworth" about "unearned increment," "judgment and skill," "employer the appraiser of work," etc. Then a few more remarks from Mr. Tucker:

This smacks of Henry George. If the municipality is an organization to which every person residing within a given territory must belong and pay tribute, it is not a bit more defensible than the State itself,—in fact, is nothing but a small State; and to vest in it a title to any part of the value of real estate is simply land nationalization on a small scale, which no Anarchist can look upon with favor. If the municipality is a voluntary organization, it can have no titles except what it gets from the individuals composing it. If they choose to transfer their "unearned increments" to the municipality, well and good; but any individual not choosing to do so ought to be able to hold his "unearned increment" against the world. If it is unearned, certainly his neighbors did not earn it. The advent of Liberty will reduce all unearned increments to a harmless minimum.

I have never maintained that judgment and skill are less important than labor; I have only maintained that neither judgment nor skill can be charged for in equity except so far as they have been acquired. Even then the payment is not for the judgment or skill, but for the labor of acquiring; and, in estimating the price, one hour of labor in acquiring judgment is to be considered equal,—not, as now, to one day, or week, or perhaps year of manual toil,—but to one hour of manual toil. The claim for judgment and skill is usually a mere pretext made to deceive the people into paying exorbitant prices, and will not bear analysis for a moment.

On the contrary, the employee, the one who does the work, is naturally and ethically the appraiser of work, and all that the employer has to say is whether he will pay the price or not. Into his answer enters the estimate of the value of the result. Under the present system he offers less than cost, and the employee is forced to accept. But Liberty and competition will create such an enormous market for labor that no workman will be forced by his incompetency to work for less than cost, as he will always be in a position to resort to some simpler work for which he is competent and can obtain adequate pay.

ECONOMIC RENT

Mr. Steven T. Byington, who at that time was a supporter of the Single Tax, asked the editor of *Liberty* to explain some phases of economic rent, especially as to the hope for its disappearance under Anarchism. Mr. Tucker gave him this answer:

LIBERTY has never stood with those who profess to show on strictly economic grounds that economic rent *must* disappear or even decrease as a result of the application of the Anarchistic principle. It sees no chance for that factor in the human constitution which makes competition such a powerful influence—namely, the disposition to buy in the cheapest market—to act directly upon *economic* rent in a way to reduce it. This disposition to buy cheap, which in a free market is fatal to all other forms of usury, is on the contrary the mainstay of economic rent, whether the market be free or restricted, when, through freedom of banking, it shall become possible to furnish money at cost, no one will pay for money more than cost; and hence interest on money, as well as on all capital consisting of commodities which money will buy and to the production of which there is no natural limit, will necessarily disappear. But the occupant of land who is enabled, by its superiority, to undersell his neighbor and at the same time to reap, through his greater volume of business, more profit than his neighbor, enjoys this economic rent precisely because of his opportunity to exploit the consumer's disposition to buy cheap. The effect of freedom is not felt here in the same way and with the same directness that it is felt elsewhere.

There are other grounds, however, some of them indirectly economic, some of them purely sentimental, which justify the belief of the Anarchist that a condition of freedom will gradually modify to a very appreciable extent the advantage enjoyed by the occupant of superior land. Take first one that is indirectly economic. I agree with my correspondent that great cities are not destined to disappear. But I believe also that they will be able to maintain their existence only by offering their advantages at a lower price than they now exact. When the laborer, in consequence of his increased wages and greater welfare resulting from the abolition of interest, shall enjoy a larger freedom of locomotion, shall be tied down less firmly to a particular employment, and shall be able to remove to the country with greater facility and in possession of more capital than he can now command, and when the country, partly because of this mobility of labor and partly because of the advances in science, shall continually offer a nearer approach to the undoubted privileges of city life, the representatives of commercial and other interests in the great cities will be able to hold their patrons about them only by lowering their prices and contenting themselves with smaller gains. In other words, economic rent will lessen. Here the disposition to buy cheap, not any special commodity, but an easy life, does exert an indirect and general influence upon economic rent. And, under this influence and yielding to it, the city may increase in prosperity simultaneously with the decline of economic rent. Nay, the increase in prosperity may accelerate this decline; for under liberty increased prosperity means also well-distributed prosperity, which means in turn a lowering of the barriers between classes and a consequent tendency to equalize the different localities of the city one with another.

Upon the sentimental grounds for believing in the evanescence of economic rent it is perhaps not worth while to dwell. I have an aversion to definite speculations based on hypothetical transformations in human nature. Yet I cannot doubt that the disappearance of interest will result in an attitude of hostility to usury in any form, which will ultimately cause any person who charges more than cost for any product to be regarded very much as we now regard a pickpocket. In this way, too, economic rent will suffer diminution.

I think my correspondent fails to understand what is meant by the freeing of vacant land. It does not mean simply the freeing of unoccupied land. It means the freeing of all land not occupied *by the owner*. In other words, it means land ownership limited by occupancy and use. This would destroy not only speculative but monopolistic rent, leaving no rent except the economic form, which will be received, while it lasts, not as a sum paid by occupant to owner, but as an extra and usurious reward for labor performed under special advantages.

But even if economic rent had to be considered a permanency; if the considerations which I have urged should prove of no avail against it,—it would be useless, tyrannical, and productive of further tyranny to confiscate it. In the first place, if I have a right to a share of the advantages that accrue from the possession of superior land, then that share is mine; it is my property; it is like any other property of mine; no man, no body of men, is entitled to decide how this property shall be used; and any man or body of men attempting so to decide deprives me of my property just as truly as the owner of the superior land deprives me of it if allowed to retain the economic rent. In fact, still assuming that this property is mine, I prefer, if I must be robbed of it, to be robbed by the land-owner, who is likely to spend it in some useful way, rather than by an institution called government, which probably will spend it for fireworks or something else which I equally disapprove. If the property is mine, I claim it, to do as I please with; if it is not mine, it is impertinent, dishonest, and tyrannical for anybody to forcibly take it from the land-occupant on the pretense that it is mine and to spend it in my name. It is precisely this, however, that the Single-Taxers propose, and it is this that makes the Single-Tax a State Socialistic measure. There was never anything more absurd than the supposition of some Single-Taxers that this tax can be harmonized with Anarchism.

But I now and then meet a Single-Taxer who allows that the government, after confiscating this economic rent, has no right to devote it to any so-called public purposes, but should distribute it to the people. Supposing the people to be entitled to the economic rent, this certainly looks on its face like a much saner and more honest proposition than that of the ordinary Single-Taxer. But the question at once arises: Who is to pay the government officials for their services in confiscating the economic rent and handing me my share of it? And how much is to be paid them? And who is to decide these matters? When I reflect that under such a Single-Tax system the occupants of superior land are likely to become the politicians and to tax back from the people to pay their salaries what the people have taxed out of them as economic rent, again I say that, even if a part of the economic rent is rightly mine, I prefer to leave it in the pocket of the land-owner, since it is bound to ultimately get back there. As M. Schneider, the Carnegie of France, said in a recent interview with a *Figaro* reporter: "Even if we were to have a collectivist system or society and my property should be confiscated, I believe that I am shrewd enough to find a way to feather my nest just the same." M. Schneider evidently understands State Socialism better than the State Socialists themselves. The Socialists and Single-Taxers will have attained their paradise when they are robbed by officials instead of by landlords and capitalists.

In my view it is idle to discuss what shall be done with the economic rent after it has been confiscated, for I distinctly deny the propriety of confiscating it at all. There are two ways, and only two, of affecting the distribution of wealth. One is to let it distribute itself in a free market in accordance with the natural operation of economic law; the other is to distribute it arbitrarily by authority in accordance with statute law. One is Anarchism; the other is State Socialism. The latter, in its worst and most probable form, is the exploitation of labor by officialdom, and at its best is a *régime* of spiritless equality secured at the expense of liberty and progress; the former is a *régime* of liberty and progress, with as close an approximation to equality as is compatible therewith. And this is all the equality that we ought to have. A greater equality than is compatible with liberty is undesirable. The moment we invade liberty to secure equality we enter upon a road which knows no stopping-place short of the annihilation of all that is best in the human race. If absolute equality is the ideal; if no man must have the slightest advantage over another,—then the man who achieves greater results through superiority of muscle or skill or brain must not be allowed to enjoy them. All that he produces in excess of that which the weakest and stupidest produce must be taken from him and distributed among his fellows. The economic rent, not of land only, but of strength and skill and intellect and superiority of every kind, must be confiscated. And a beautiful world it would be when absolute equality had been thus achieved! Who would live in it? Certainly no freeman.

Liberty will abolish interest; it will abolish profit; it will abolish monopolistic rent; it will abolish taxation; it will abolish the exploitation of labor; it will abolish all means whereby any laborer can be deprived of any of his product; but it will not abolish the limited inequality between one laborer's product and another s. Now, because it has not this power last named, there are people who say: We will have no liberty, for we must have absolute equality. I am not of them. If I go through life free and rich, I shall not cry because my neighbor, equally free, is richer. Liberty will ultimately make all men rich; it will not make all men equally rich. Authority may (and may not) make all men equally rich in purse; it certainly will make them equally poor in all that makes life best worth living.

Mr. Byington's erroneous conclusions regarding the confiscation of economic rent are due, as I view it, to his confusion of liberties with rights, or, perhaps I might better say, to his foundation of equality of liberty upon a supposed equality of rights. I take issue with him at the very start by denying the dogma of equality of rights,—in fact, by denying rights altogether except those acquired by contract. In times past, when, though already an Egoist and knowing then as now that every man acts and always will act solely from an interest in self, I had not considered the bearing of Egoism upon the question of obligation, it was my habit to talk glibly and loosely of the right of man to the land. It was a bad habit, and I long ago sloughed it off. Man's only right over the land is his might over it. If his neighbor is mightier than he and takes the land from him, then the land is his neighbor's until the latter is dispossessed in turn by one mightier still. But while the danger of such dispossession continues there is no society, no security, no comfort. Hence men contract. They agree upon certain conditions of land ownership, and will protect no title in the absence of the conditions fixed upon. The object of this contract is *not to enable all to benefit equally from the land,* but to enable each to hold securely at his own disposal the results of his efforts expended upon such portion of the earth as he may possess under the conditions agreed upon. It is principally to secure this absolute control of the results of one's efforts that equality of liberty is instituted, not as a matter of right, but as a social convenience. I have always maintained that liberty is of greater importance than wealth,—in other words, that man derives more happines from freedom than from luxury,—and this is true; but there is another sense in which wealth, or, rather, property, is of greater importance than liberty. Man has but little to gain from liberty unless that liberty includes the liberty to control what he produces. One of the chief purposes of equal liberty is to secure this fundamental necessity of property, and, if property is not thereby secured, the temptation is to abandon the *régime* of contract and return to the reign of the strongest.

Now the difference between the equal liberty of the Anarchists and the system which Mr. Byington and the Single-Taxers consider equal liberty is this: the former secures property, while the latter violates it.

The Anarchists say to the individual: "Occupancy and use is the only title to land in which we will protect you; if you attempt to use land which another is occupying and using, we will protect him against you; if another attempts to use land to which you lay claim, but which you are not occupying and using, we will not interfere with him; but of such land as you occupy and use you are the sole master, and we will not ourselves take from you, or allow anyone else to take from you, whatever you may get out of such land."

The Single-Taxers, on the other hand, say to the individual: "You may hold all the land you have inherited or bought, or may inherit or buy, and we will protect you in such holding; but, if you produce more from your land than your neighbors produce from theirs, we will take from you the excess of your product over theirs and distribute it among them, or we will spend it in taking a free ride whenever we want to go anywhere, or we will make any use of it, wise or foolish, that may come into our heads."

The reader who compares these two positions will need no comment of mine to enable him to decide "on which side the maximum of liberty lies," and on which side property, or the individual control of product is respected.

If Mr. Byington does not accept my view thus outlined, it is incumbent upon him to overthrow it by proving to me that man has a right to land; if he does accept it, he must see that it completely disposes of his assertion that "when another man takes a piece of land for his own and warns me off it, he exceeds the limits of equal liberty toward me with respect to that land," upon which assertion all his argument rests.

LIBERTY, LAND, AND LABOR

While the Single Tax is now rarely spoken of, at one time, during Henry George's activity, it was very much in the public eye. But George was inclined to belittle or ignore all other factors of the economic problem, so he frequently received caustic criticism from the editor of *Liberty*:

HERE is a delicious bit of logic from Mr. George: "If capital, a mere creature of labor, is such an *oppressive* thing, its creator, *when free,* can strangle it by refusing to reproduce it." The italics are mine. If capital is oppressive, it must be oppressive of labor. What difference does it make, then, what labor can do when free? The question is what it can do when oppressed by capital. Mr. George's next sentence, to be sure, indicates that the freedom he refers to is freedom from land monopoly. But this does not improve his situation. He is enough of an economist to be very well aware that, whether it has land or not, labor which can get no capital—that is, which is oppressed by capital—cannot, without accepting the alternative of starvation, refuse to reproduce capital for the capitalists.

It is one thing for Mr. George to sit in his sanctum and write of the ease with which a man whose sole possession is a bit of land can build a home and scratch a living; for the man to do it is wholly another thing. The truth is that this man can do nothing of the sort until you devise some means of raising his wages above the cost of living. And you can only do this by increasing the demand for his labor by enabling more men to go into business. And you can only enable more men to go into business by enabling them to get capital without interest, which, in Mr. George's opinion, would be very wrong. And you can only enable them to get capital without interest by abolishing the money monopoly, which, by limiting the supply of money, enables its holders to exact interest. And when you have abolished the money monopoly, and when, in consequence, the wages of the man with the bit of land have begun to rise above the cost of living, the labor question will be nine-tenths solved. For then either this man will live better and better, or he will steadily lay up money, with which he can buy tools to compete with his employer or to till his bit of land with comfort and advantage. In short, he will be an independent man, receiving all that he produces or an equivalent thereof. How to make this the lot of all men is the labor question. Free land will not solve it. Free money, supplemented by free land, will.

In trying to answer the argument that land is practically useless to labor unprovided with capital, Henry George declares that "labor and land, even in the absence of secondary factors obtained from their produce, have in their union to-day, as they had in the beginning, the potentiality of all that man ever has brought, or ever can bring, into being."

This is perfectly true; in fact, none know it better than the men whom Mr. George thus attempts to meet.

But, as Cap'n Cuttle was in the habit of remarking, "the bearin' o' this 'ere hobserwation lies in the application on't," and in its application it has no force whatever. Mr. George uses it to prove that, if land were free, labor would settle on it, thus raising wages by relieving the labor market.

But labor would do no such thing.

The fact that a laborer, given a piece of land, can build a hut of mud, strike fire with flint and steel, scratch a living with his finger-nails, and thus begin life as a barbarian, even with the hope that in the course of a lifetime he may slightly improve his condition in consequence of having fashioned a few of the ruder of those implements which Mr. George styles "secondary factors" (and he could do no more than this without producing for exchange, which implies, not only better machinery, but an entrance into that capitalistic maelstrom which would sooner or later swallow him up),—this fact, I say, will never prove a temptation to the operative of the city, who, despite his wretchedness, knows something of the advantages of civilization and to some extent inevitably shares them.

Man does not live by bread alone.

The city laborer may live in a crowded tenement and breathe a tainted air; he may sleep cold, dress in rags, and feed on crumbs; but now and then he gets a glimpse at the morning paper, or if not that, then at the bulletin-board; he meets his fellow-men face to face; he knows by contact with the world more or less of what is going on in it; he spends a few pennies occasionally for a gallery-ticket to the theatre or for some other luxury, even though he knows he "can't afford it"; he hears the music of the street bands; he sees the pictures in the shop windows; he goes to church if he is pious, or if not, perhaps attends the meetings of the Anti-Poverty Society and listens to stump speeches by Henry George; and, when all these fail him, he is indeed unfortunate if some fellow-laborer does not invite him to join him in a social glass over the nearest bar.

Not an ideal life, surely; but he will shiver in his garret and slowly waste away from inanition ere he will exchange it for the semi-barbarous condition of the backwoodsman without an axe. And, were he to do otherwise, I would be the first to cry: The more fool he!

Mr. George's remedy is similar—at least for a part of mankind—to that which is attributed to the Nihilists, but which few of them ever believed in,—namely, the total destruction of the existing social order and the creation of a new one on its ruins.

Mr. George may as well understand first as last that labor will refuse to begin this world anew. It never will abandon even its present meagre enjoyment of the wealth and the means of wealth which have grown out of its ages of sorrow, suffering, and slavery. If Mr. George offers it land alone, it will turn its back upon him. It insists upon both land and tools. These it will get, either by the State Socialistic method of concentrating the titles to them in the hands of one vast monopoly, or by the Anarchistic method of abolishing all monopolies, and thereby distributing these titles gradually among laborers through the natural channels of free production and exchange.

Mr. T. W. Curtis thought he discovered inconsistency and exaggeration in the foregoing, and upbraided Mr. Tucker. The latter then went into the matter more deeply:

HENRY GEORGE and his co-workers are of that class who "speak in the name of liberty, but do not know the meaning of the word." Mr. George has no conception of liberty as a universal social law. He happens to see that in some things it would lead to good results, and therefore in those things favors it. But it has never dawned upon his mind that disorder is the inevitable fruit of every plant which has authority for its root. As John F. Kelly says of him, "he is inclined to look with favor on the principle of *laissez faire*, yet he will abandon it at any moment, whenever regulation seems more likely to produce immediate benefits, regardless of the evil thereby produced by making the people less jealous of State interference." The nature of his belief in liberty is well illustrated by his attitude on the tariff question. One would suppose from his generalization that he has the utmost faith in freedom of competition; but one does not realize how little this faith amounts to until he hears him, after making loud free-trade professions, propose to substitute a system of bounties for the tariff system. If such political and economic empiricism is not rubbish beside the coherent proposals of either Anarchism or State Socialism, then I don't know chaff from wheat.

Liberty, of course, had something to do with the writing of "Progress and Poverty." It also had something to do with the framing of divorce laws as relief from indissoluble marriage. But the divorce laws, instead of being libertarian, are an express recognition of the rightfulness of authority over the sexual relations. Similarly "Progress and Poverty" expressly recognizes the rightfulness of authority over the cultivation and use of land. For some centuries now evolution has been little else than the history of liberty; nevertheless all its factors have not been children of liberty.

Mr. Curtis turns his attention to the editorial on "Secondary Factors." He thinks that my assertion that George asks labor to "begin this world anew" ought to be backed by some show of argument. Gracious heavens! I backed it at the beginning of my article by a quotation from George himself. Dislodged by his critics from one point after another, George had declared that "labor and land, even in the absence of secondary factors obtained from their produce, have in their union today, as they had in the beginning, the potentiality of all that man ever has brought, or ever can bring, into being." When such words as these are used to prove that, if land were free, labor would settle on it, even without secondary factors, —that is, without tools,—what do they mean except that the laborer is expected to "begin this world anew"? But if this is not enough for Mr. Curtis, may I refer him to the debate between George and Shewitch, in which the former, being asked by the latter what would have become of Friday if Crusoe had fenced off half the island and turned him loose upon it without any tools, answered that Friday would have made some fish-hooks out of bones and gone fishing? Isn't that sufficiently primitive to substantiate my assertion, Mr. Curtis? Tell Mr. George that the laborer can do nothing without capital, and he will answer you substantially as follows: Originally there was nothing but a naked man and the naked land; free the land, and then, if the laborer has no tools, he will again be a naked man on naked land and can do all that Adam did. When I point out that such a return to barbarism is on a par with the remedy attributed to the Nihilists, the total destruction of the existing social order, Mr. Curtis asserts that "this is wild talk;" but his assertion, it seems to me, "ought to be backed by some show of argument."

He is sure, however, that there is no need of going to the backwoods. There is enough vacant land in the neighborhood of cities, he thinks, to employ the surplus workers, and thus relieve the labor market. But this land will not employ any workers that have no capital, and those that have capital can get the land now. Thus the old question comes back again. Make capital free by organizing credit on a mutual plan, and then these vacant lands will come into use, and then industry will be stimulated, and then operatives will be able to buy axes and rakes and hoes, and then they will be independent of their employers, and then the labor problem will be solved.

My worst offense Mr. Curtis reserves till the last. It consists in telling the workingman that he would be a fool not to prefer the street bands, the shop windows, the theatres, and the churches to a renewal of barbaric life. Mr. Curtis again misapprehends me in thinking that I commend the bands, the windows, etc. I said explicitly that there is nothing ideal about them. But society has come to be man's dearest possession, and the advantages and privileges which I cited, crude and vulgar and base as some of them are, represent society to the operative. He will not give them up, and I think he is wise. Pure air is good, but no one wants to breathe it long alone. Independence is good, but isolation is too heavy a price to pay for it. Both pure air and independence must be reconciled with society, or not many laborers will ever enjoy them. Luckily they can be and will be, though not by taxing land values. As for the idea that persons can be induced to become barbarians from altruistic motives in sufficient numbers to affect the labor market, it is one that I have no time to discuss. In one respect at least Mr. George is preferable to Mr. Curtis as an opponent: he usually deals in economic argument rather than sentimentalism.

Next came "Egoist," who was pained at the frequent attacks on Henry George, and it required a discussion that continued through several numbers of *Liberty* to thresh out all the points at issue:

My correspondent, who, by the way, is a highly intelligent man, and has a most clear understanding of the money question, should point out the truths that I have derided before accusing me of deriding any. I certainly never have derided the truth contained in Ricardo's theory of rent. What I have derided is Henry George's proposal that a majority of the people shall seize this rent by force and expend it for their own benefit, or perhaps for what they are pleased to consider the benefit of the minority. I have also derided many of the arguments by which Mr. George has attempted to justify this proposal, many of which he has used in favor of interest and other forms of robbery, and his ridiculous pretense that he is a champion of liberty. But I have never disputed that, under the system of land monopoly, certain individuals get, in the form of rent, a great deal that they never earned by their labor, or that it would be a great blessing if some plan should be devised and adopted whereby this could be prevented without violating the liberty of the individual. I am convinced, however, that the abolition of the money monopoly, and the refusal of protection to all land titles except those of occupiers, would, by the emancipation of the workingman from his present slavery to capital, reduce this evil to a very small fraction of its present proportions, especially in cities, and that the remaining fraction would be the cause of no more inequality than arises from the unearned increment derived by almost every industry from the aggregation of people or from that unearned increment of superior natural ability which, even under the operation of the cost principle, will probably always enable some individuals to get higher wages than the average rate. In all these cases the margin of difference will tend steadily to decrease, but it is not likely in any of them to disappear altogether. Whether, after the abolition of the State, voluntary coöperators will resort to communistic methods in the hope of banishing even these vestiges of inequality is a question for their own future consideration, and has nothing whatever to do with the scheme of Henry George. For my part, I should be inclined to regard such a course as a leap not from the frying-pan into the fire, but from a Turkish bath into the nethermost hell. I take no pleasure in attacking Mr. George, but shall probably pursue my present policy until he condescends to answer and refute my arguments, if he can, or gives some satisfactory reason for declining to do so.

Egoist's acquaintance with *Liberty* is of comparatively recent date, but it is hard to understand how he could have failed to find out from it that, in opposing all government, it so defines the word as to exclude the very thing which Egoist considers ideal government. It has been stated in these columns I know not how many times that government, Archism, invasion, are used here as equivalent terms; that whoever invades, individual or State, governs and is an Archist; and that whoever defends against invasion, individual or voluntary association, opposes government and is an Anarchist. Now, a voluntary association doing equity would not be an invader, but a defender against invasion, and might include in its defensive operations the protection of the occupiers of land. With this explanation, does Egoist perceive any lack of harmony in my statements? Assuming, then, protection by such a method, occupiers would be sure, no matter how covetous others might be. But now the question recurs: What is equity in the matter of land occupancy? I admit at once that the enjoyment by individuals of increment which they do not earn is not equity. On the other hand, I insist that the confiscation of such increment by the State (not a voluntary association) and its expenditure for public purposes, while it might be a little nearer equity practically in that the benefits would be enjoyed (after a fashion) by a larger number of persons, would be exactly as far from it theoretically, inasmuch as the increment no more belongs equally to the public at large than to the individual land-holder, and would still be a long way from it even practically, for the minority, not being allowed to spend its share of the increment in its own way, would be just as truly robbed as if not allowed to spend it at all. A voluntary association in which the land-holders should consent to contribute the increment to the association's treasury, and in which all the members should agree to settle the method of its disposition by ballot, would be equitable enough, but would be a short-sighted, wasteful, and useless complication. A system of occupying ownership, however, accompanied by no legal power to collect rent, but coupled with the abolition of the State-guaranteed monopoly of money, thus making capital readily available, would distribute the increment naturally and quietly among its rightful owners. If it should not work perfect equity, it would at least effect a sufficiently close approximation to it, and without trespassing at all upon the individualities of any. Spots are "choice" now very largely because of monopoly, and those which, under a system of free land and free money, should still remain choice for other reasons would shed their benefits upon all, just in the same way that choice countries under free trade will, as Henry George shows, make other countries more prosperous. When people see that such would be the result of this system, it is hardly likely that many of them will have to be coerced into agreeing to it. I see no point to Egoist's analogy in the first sentence of his last paragraph, unless he means to deny the right of the individual to become a banker. A more pertinent analogy would be a comparison of the George scheme for the confiscation of rent with a system of individual banking of which the State should confiscate the profits.

Under the influence of competition the best and cheapest protector, like the best and cheapest tailor, would doubtless get the greater part of the business. It is conceivable even that he might get the whole of it. But if he should, it would be by his virtue as a protector, not by his power as a tyrant.

He would be kept at his best by the possibility of competition and the fear of it; and the source of power would always remain, not with him, but with his patrons, who would exercise it, not by voting him down or by forcibly putting another in his place, but by withdrawing their patronage. Such a state of things, far from showing the impossibility of Anarchy, would be Anarchy itself, and would have little or nothing in common with what now goes by the name "equitable democratic government."

If "it can be shown that the value of the protection to the possession of land equals its economic rent," the demonstration will be interesting. To me it seems that the measure of such value must often include many other factors than economic rent. A man may own a home the economic rent of which is zero, but to which he is deeply attached by many tender memories. Is the value of protection in his possession of that home zero? But perhaps Egoist means the exchange value of protection. If so, I answer that, under free competition, the exchange value of protection, like the exchange value of everything else, would be its cost, which might in any given case be more or less than the economic rent. The condition of receiving protection would be the same as the condition of receiving beefsteak,—namely, ability and willingness to pay the cost thereof.

If I am right, the payment of rent, then, would not be an *essential* feature in the contract between the land-holder and the protector. It is conceivable, however, though in my judgment unlikely, that it might be found an *advantageous* feature. If so, protectors adopting that form of contract would distance their competitors. But if one of these protectors should ever say to land-holders "Sign this contract; if you do not, I not only will refuse you protection, but I will myself invade you and annually confiscate a portion of your earnings equal to the economic rent of your land," I incline to the opinion that "intelligent people" would sooner or later, "by the process of natural selection," evolve into Anarchy by rallying around these land-holders for the formation of a new social and protective system, which would subordinate the pooling of economic rents to the security of each individual in the possession of the raw materials which he uses and the disposition of the wealth which he thereby produces.

If government should be abruptly and entirely abolished to-morrow, there would probably ensue a series of physical conflicts about land and many other things, ending in re-action and a revival of the old tyranny. But if the abolition of government shall take place gradually, beginning with the downfall of the money and land monopolies and extending thence into one field after another, it will be accompanied by such a constant acquisition and steady spreading of social truth that, when the time shall come to apply the voluntary principle in the supply of police protection, the people will rally as promptly and universally to the support of the pro-tector who acts most nearly in accordance with the prin-ciples of social science as they now rally to the side of the assaulted man against his would-be murderer. In that case no serious conflict can arise.

Egoist neglects to consider my statement in reply to him in the last issue of *Liberty*, to the effect that the source of the protector's power lies precisely in the patronage. The pro-tector who is most patronized will, therefore, be the strongest; and the people will endow with their power the protector who is best fitted to use it in the administration of justice.

If the masses, or any large section of them, after having come to an understanding and acceptance of Anarchism, should then be induced by the sophistry of tyrants to reject it again, despotism would result. This is perfectly true. No Anarchist ever dreamed of denying it. Indeed, the Anarchist's only hope lies in his confidence that people who have once intelligently accepted his principle will "stay put."

The present State cannot be an outgrowth of Anarchy, because Anarchy, in the philosophic sense of the word, has never existed. For Anarchy, after all, means something more than the possession of liberty. Just as Ruskin defines wealth as "the possession of the valuable by the valiant," so Anarchy may be defined as the possession of liberty by libertarians,— that is by those who know what liberty means. The barbaric liberty out of which the present State developed was not Anarchy in this sense at all, for those who possessed it had not the slightest conception of its blessings or of the line that divides it from tyranny.

Nothing can have value in the absence of demand for it. Therefore the basis of the demand cannot be irrelevant in considering value. Now, it is manifest that the demand for protection in the possession of land does not rest solely upon excess of fertility or commercial advantage of situation. On the contrary, it rests, in an ever-rising degree and among an ever-increasing proportion of the people, upon the love of security and peace, the love of home, the love of beautiful scenery, and many other wholly sentimental motives. Inasmuch, then, as the strength of some of the motives for the demand of protection bears often no relation to economic rent, the value of such protection is not necessarily equal to economic rent. Which is the contrary of Egoist's proposition.

Egoist's definition of the right of possession of land rests on an assumption which Anarchists deny,—namely, that there is an entity known as the community which is the rightful owner of all land. Here we touch the central point of the discussion. Here I take issue with Egoist, and maintain that "the community" is a nonentity, that it has no existence, and that what is called the community is simply a combination of individuals having no prerogatives beyond those of the individuals themselves. This combination of individuals has no better title to the land than any single individual outside of it; and the argument which Egoist uses in behalf of the community this outside individual, if he but had the strength to back it up, might cite with equal propriety in his own behalf. He might say: "The right of possession of land consists in an agreement on my part to forego the special advantages which the use of such land affords to an undisturbed possessor. It represents a giving-up, by me, of that which I could obtain for myself,—the cost to me being certainly that which I have relinquished, and equals in value the special advantage which is the cause of rent. In view of this, it seems to me that affording this protection is to me an expense equal to the rent." And thereupon he might proceed to collect this rent from the community as compensation for the protection which he afforded it in allowing it to occupy the land. But in his case the supposed condition is lacking; he has not the strength necessary to enforce such an argument as this. The community, or combination of individuals, has this strength. Its only superiority to the single individual, then, in relation to the land, consists in the right of the strongest,—a perfectly valid right, I admit, but one which, if exercised, leads to serious results. If the community proposes to exercise its right of the strongest, why stop with the collection of economic rent? Why not make the individual its slave outright? Why not strip him of everything but the bare necessities of life? Why recognize him at all, in any way, except as a tool to be used in the interest of the community? In a word, why not do precisely what capitalism is doing now, or else what State Socialism proposes to do when it gets control of affairs? But if the community does not proprose to go to this extreme; if it proposes to recognize the individual and treat with him,—then it must forego entirely its right of the strongest, and be ready to contract on a basis of equality of rights, by which the individual's title to the land he uses and to what he gets out of it shall be held valid as against the world. Then, if the individual consents to pool his rent with others, well and good; but, if not— why, then, he must be left alone. And it will not do for the community to turn upon him and demand the economic rent of his land as compensation for the "protection" which it affords him in thus letting him alone. As well might the burglar say to the householder: "Here, I can, if I choose, enter your house one of these fine nights and carry off your valuables; I therefore demand that you immediately hand them over to me as compensation for the sacrifice which I make and the protection which I afford you in not doing so."

Egoist asserted that it would be difficult to show that the occupier of superior land would be entitled to that part of the production from his land that would be in excess of what, with an equal application of labor, could be produced from inferior land. Mr. Tucker replied:

PRECISELY as difficult as it would be to show that the man of superior skill (native, not acquired) who produces in the ratio of five hundred to another's three hundred is equitably entitled to this surplus exchange value. There is no more reason why we should pool the results of our lands than the results of our hands. And to *compel* such pooling is as meddlesome and tyrannical in one case as in the other. That school of Socialistic economists which carries Henry George's idea to its conclusions, confiscating not only rent but interest and profit and equalizing wages,—a school of which G. Bernard Shaw may be taken as a typical representative,—is more logical than the school to which Mr. George and Egoist belong, because it completes the application of the tyrannical principle.

The cultivator of land who does not ask protection does not expect the community to secure him the opportunity referred to. He simply expects the community not to deprive him of this opportunity. He does not say to the community: "Here! an invader is trying to oust me from my land; come and help me to drive him off." He says to the community: "My right to this land is as good as yours. In fact it is better, for I am already occupying and cultivating it. I demand of you simply that you shall not disturb me. If you impose certain burdens upon me by threatening me with dispossession, I, being weaker than you, must of course submit temporarily. But in the mean time I shall teach the principle of liberty to the individuals of which you are composed, and by and by, when they see that you are oppressing me, they will espouse my cause, and your tyrannical yoke will speedily be lifted from my neck."

If the cost principle of value cannot be realized otherwise than by compulsion, then it had better not be realized. For my part, I do not believe that it is possible or highly important to realize it *absolutely and completely.* But it is both possible and highly important to effect its approximate realization. So much can be effected without compulsion,—in fact, can only be effected by at least partial abolition of compulsion,—and so much will be sufficient. By far the larger part of the violations of the cost principle—probably nine-tenths—result from artificial, law-made inequalities; only a small portion arise from natural inequalities. Abolish the artificial monopolies of money and land, and interest, profit, and the rent of buildings will almost entirely disappear; ground rents will no longer flow into a few hands; and practically the only inequality remaining will be the slight disparity of products due to superiority of soil and skill. Even this disparity will soon develop a tendency to decrease. Under the new economic conditions and enlarged opportunities resulting from freedom of credit and land classes will tend to disappear; great capacities will not be developed in a few at the expense of stunting those of the many; talents will approximate towards equality, though their variety will be greater than ever; freedom of locomotion will be vastly increased; the toilers will no longer be anchored in such large numbers in the present commercial centres, and thus made subservient to the city landlords; territories and resources never before utilized will become easy of access and development; and under all these influences the disparity above mentioned will decrease to a minimum. Probably it will never disappear entirely; on the other hand, it can never become intolerable. It must always remain a comparatively trivial consideration, certainly never to be weighed for a moment in the same scale with liberty.

It was only because I conceived it out of the question that Egoist, in maintaining that "the value of protection in the possession of land is equal to its economic rent," could be discussing value without regard to the law of equal liberty as a prior condition, or soberly advocating the exercise of the right of might regardless of equity, that I interpreted his words as implying a superiority *in equity* in the community's title to land over that of the individual,—a superiority other than that of might; a superiority, in short, other than that by which the highwayman relieves the traveller of his goods. I was bound to suppose (and later statements in his present letter seem to strengthen the supposition) that he looked upon the "giving up, by the community," of its right to land as the giving up of a superior equitable right; for otherwise, in demanding value in return for this sacrifice, he would be compelled in logic to demand, on behalf of a burglar, value in return for the sacrifice made in declining to carry off a householder's wealth by stealth. But Egoist repudiates this supposition (though he does not follow the logic of his repudiation), and I must take him at his word. He thus lays himself open to a retort which I could not otherwise have made. In his previous letter he criticised me for making sentiment a factor in the estimation of value. Whether or not this was a transgression, on my part, of the limits of economic discussion, he certainly has transgressed them much more seriously in making force such a factor. Exchange implies liberty; where there is no liberty there is no exchange, but only robbery; and robbery is foreign to political economy. At least one point, however, is gained. Between Egoist and myself all question of any superior *equitable* right of the community is put aside forever. Equity not considered, we agree that the land belongs to the man or body of men strong enough to hold it. And for all practical purposes his definition of "ownership" suits me, though I view ownership less as the "result of the ability of the community to maintain possession" and an application of this result "for the benefit of individuals," than as a result of the *inability* of the community to maintain itself in peace and security otherwise than by the recognition of only such relations between man and wealth as are in harmony with the law of equal liberty. In other words, ownership arises not from superiority of the community to the individual, but from the inferiority of the community to the facts and powers of nature.

Egoist here stated that he would not agree "that the right of the strongest will lead to serious results, except when applied to create an inequitable relation between individuals"; so Mr. Tucker rejoined:

HERE we have an acknowledgment of a principle of equity and a contemplation of its observance by the mighty, which goes to sustain my original supposition, despite Egoist's protest. It implies an abandonment by the mighty of their right of domination and a willingness to contract with the weak. Now, I agree that the contracts thus entered into will not lead to serious results, unless they create inequitable relations between individuals. But the first of all equities is not equality of material well-being, but equality of liberty; and if the contract places the former equality before the latter, it *will* lead to serious results, for it logically necessitates the arbitrary leveling of all material inequalities, whether these arise from differences of soil or differences of skill. To directly enforce equality of material well-being is meddlesome, invasive, and offensive, but to directly enforce equality of liberty is simply protective and defensive. The latter is negative, and aims only to prevent the establishment of artificial inequalities; the former is positive, and aims at direct and active abolition of natural inequalities. If the former is the true policy, then it is as equitable to enforce the pooling of interest, profit, and wages as the pooling of rent. If the latter is the true policy, we have only to see to it that no artificial barriers against individual initiative are constructed. Under such conditions, if the natural inequalities tend to disappear, as they surely will, then so much the better.

In speaking of skill as "inseparably attached to the individual," Egoist surely does not mean to argue the impossibility of seizing and distributing the results of skill, for that would be a ridiculous contention. Then he can only mean that there is something sacred about the individual which the mighty are bound to respect. But this again is inconsistent with his theory of the right of might. If the strongest is to exercise his might, then he need stop at nothing but the impossible; if, on the other hand, he contracts with the weaker on a basis of equal liberty, then both strong and weak must be left secure in their possession of the products of their labor, whether aided by superior skill or superior soil.

If Malthusianism is true, it is as true after the pooling of rent as before. If the encroachment of population over the limit of the earth's capacity is inevitable, then there is no solution of the social problem. Pooling the rent or organizing credit would only postpone the catastrophe. Sooner or later the masses would find nothing to share but the curses of war rather than the "blessings of peace," and at that stage it would matter but little to them whether they shared equally or unequally.

I hold that, in case rent were to be nationalized by force, liberty would be incomplete; and liberty must be complete, whatever happens.

I hold that superiority will always rule; and it is only when real superiority is known and recognized as such, and therefore allowed to have its perfect work unresisted and unimpeded, that the minimum of evil will result. The really serious results are those that follow the attempts of inferiority, mistaking itself for superiority, to fly in the face of the real article. In other words, when individuals or majorities, seeing that they are stronger for the time being than other individuals or minorities, suppose that they are therefore stronger than natural social laws and act in violation of them, disaster is sure to follow. These laws are the really mighty, and they will always prevail. The first of them is the law of equal liberty. It is by the observance of this law, I am persuaded, rather than by "an equal share in the transferable opportunities," that the ultimate "intelligence of the people" will remove "every reasonable cause of complaint."

I find so little attempt to meet the various considerations which I have advanced that I have not much to add by way of comment. The monopoly of mining gold at a particular point exists in the physical constitution of things, and a pooling of the results thereof (which would be a virtual destruction of the monopoly) can only be directly achieved in one of two ways,—mutual agreement or an invasion of liberty. The monopoly of inventors and authors, on the contrary, has no existence at all except by mutual agreement or an invasion of liberty. It seems to me the difference between the two is sufficiently clear. Egoist's statement of the law of equal liberty is satisfactory. Standing upon it, I would repel, by force if necessary, the confiscator of rent on the ground that he "takes a liberty at the expense of others." I have no objection to forcible measures against transgressors, but the question recurs as to who are the transgressors. If the piece of land which I am using happens to be better than my neighbor's, I do not consider myself a transgressor on that account; but if my neighbor digs some of my potatoes and carries them off, I certainly consider him a transgressor, even though he may name his plunder economic rent. But Egoist, viewing this case, considers me the transgressor and my neighbor the honest man. I believe that education in liberty will bring people to my view rather than his. If it doesn't, I shall have to succumb. It is to be noted that Egoist makes no further reference to my argument regarding skill. I urged that the levelling of inequalities in land logically leads to the levelling of inequalities in skill. Egoist replied that skill is inseparably attached to the individual, while land is not. I rejoined that the results of skill are not inseparably attached to the individual, and that the right of might recognizes nothing sacred about the individual. To this Egoist makes no reply. Hence my argument that the nationalization of rent logically involves the most complete State Socialism and minute regulation of the individual stands unassailed.

It has been stated and restated in these columns, until I have grown weary of the reiteration, that voluntary association for the purpose of preventing transgression of equal liberty will be perfectly in keeping with Anarchism, and will probably exist under Anarchism until it "costs more than it comes to"; that the provisions of such associations will be executed by such agents as it may select in accordance with such methods as it may prescribe, provided such methods do not themselves involve a transgression of the liberty of the innocent; that such association will restrain only the criminal (meaning by criminal the transgressor of equal liberty); that non-membership and non-support of it is not a criminal act; but that such a course nevertheless deprives the non-member of any title to the benefits of the association, except such as come to him incidentally and unavoidably. It has also been repeatedly affirmed that, in proposing to abolish the State, the Anarchists expressly exclude from their definition of the State such associations as that just referred to, and that whoever excludes from his definition and championship of the State everything except such associations has no quarrel with the Anarchists beyond a verbal one. I should trust that the "understanding on these points" is now clear, were it not that experience has convinced me that my command of the English language is not adequate to the construction of a foundation for such trust.

The fact that Egoist points out a similarity between the monopoly of a gold-mine and that of an invention by no means destroys *the* difference between them which I pointed out,—this difference being that, whereas in the former case it is impossible to prevent or nullify the monopoly without restricting the liberty of the monopolist, in the latter it is impossible to sustain it without restricting the liberty of the would-be competitors. To the Anarchist, who believes in the minimum of restriction upon liberty, this difference is a vital one,—quite sufficient to warrant him in refusing to prevent the one while refusing to sustain the other.

Egoist says that "an occupier is not a transgressor of equal liberty unless he claims and receives the right of undisturbed possession without giving an equivalent in return." Anarchism holds, on the contrary, in accordance with the principles stated at the outset of this rejoinder, that an occupier is not a transgressor even if, not claiming it or paying for it, he does receive this right.

The assertion that "the distribution of skill is absolutely independent of social agreement" is absolutely erroneous. In proof of this I need only call attention to the apprenticeship regulations of the trade unions and the various educational systems that are or have been in vogue, not only as evidence of what has already been done in the direction of controlling the distribution of skill, but also as an indication of what more may be done if State Socialism ever gets a chance to try upon humanity the interesting experiments which it proposes. On the other hand, the collection of rent by the collectivity does not necessarily affect the distribution of land. Land titles will remain unchanged as long as the tax (or rent) shall be paid. But it does distribute the products resulting from differences of land, and it is likewise possible to distribute the products resulting from differences of skill. Now until this position is overthrown (and I defy any one to successfully dispute it), it is senseless to liken "dissatisfaction with the distribution of skill" to "the crying of a child because it cannot fly." The absurdity of this analogy, in which the possibility of distributing products is ignored, would have been apparent if it had been immediately followed by the admission of this possibility which Egoist places several paragraphs further down. To be sure, he declares even there that it is impossible, but only in the sense in which Proudhon declares interest-bearing property impossible,—that of producing anti-social results which eventually kill it or compel its abandonment. I contend that similarly anti-social results will follow any attempt to distribute by law the products arising from differences of land; and I ask, as I have asked before without obtaining an answer, why the collectivity, if in its right of might it may see fit to distribute the rent of land, may not find it equally expedient to distribute the rent of skill; why it may not reduce all differences of wealth to an absolute level; in short, why it may not create the worst and most complete tyranny the world has ever known?

In regard to the attitude of Anarchistic associations towards rent and its collection, I would say that they might, consistently with the law of equal freedom, except from their jurisdiction whatever cases or forms of transgression they should not think it expedient to attempt to prevent. These exceptions would probably be defined in their constitutions. The members could, if they saw fit, exempt the association from enforcing gambling debts or rent contracts. On the other hand, an association organized on a different basis which should enforce such debts or contracts would not thereby become itself a transgressor. But any association would be a transgressor which should attempt to prevent the fulfilment of rent contracts or to confiscate rent and distribute it. Of the three possibilities specified by Egoist the third is the only one that tends to establish an artificial inequality; and that the worst of all inequalities,—the inequality of liberty, or perhaps it would be more accurate to call it the equality of slavery. The first or second would at the worst fail to entirely abolish *natural* inequalities.

The possibility of valuable land becoming vacant is hardly worth consideration. Still, if any occupant of valuable land should be foolish enough to quit it without first selling it, the estate would be liable to seizure by the first comer, who would immediately have a footing similar to that of other landholders. If this be favoritism, I can only say that the world is not destined to see the time when some things will not go by favor.

Egoist's argument that free competition will tend to distribute rent by a readjustment of wages is exactly to my purpose. Have I not told him from the start that Anarchists will gladly welcome any tendency to equality *through liberty?* But Egoist seems to object to reaching equality by this road. It must be reached by law or not at all. If reached by competition, "competition would be harassed." In other words, competition would harass competition. This wears the aspect of another absurdity. It is very likely that competitors would harass competitors, but competition without harassed competitors is scarcely thinkable. It is even not improbable that "class distinctions" would be developed, as Egoist says. Workers would find the places which their capacities, conditions, and inclinations qualify them to fill, and would thus be classified, or divided into distinct classes. Does Egoist think that in such an event life would not be worth living? Of course the words "harass" and "class distinction" have an ugly sound, and competition is decidedly more attractive when associated instead with "excel" and "organization." But Anarchists never recoil from disagreeable terms. Only their opponents are to be frightened by words and phrases.

PROPERTY UNDER ANARCHISM

A discussion in *The Free Life* (London) between its editor, Mr. Auberon Herbert, and an Anarchistic correspondent, Mr. Albert Tarn, involved an objection to Anarchism that it would throw property titles (especially land titles) into hopeless confusion, which led Mr. Tucker to enter the controversy in *Liberty* in the following manner:

THIS criticism of Anarchism, reduced to its essence, is seen to be twofold. First, the complaint is that it has no fixed standard of acquiring or owning. Second, the complaint is that it necessarily results in a fixed standard of acquiring or owning. Evidently Mr. Herbert is a very hard man to please. Before he criticises Anarchism further, I must insist that he make up his mind whether he himself wants or does not want a fixed standard. And whatever his decision, his criticism falls. For if he wants a fixed standard, that which he may adopt is as liable to become a "rigid crystalline custom" as any that Anarchism may lead to. And if he does not want a fixed standard, then how can he complain of Anarchism for having none?

If it were my main object to emerge from this dispute victorious, I might well leave Mr. Herbert in the queer predicament in which his logic has placed him. But as I am really anxious to win him to the Anarchistic view, I shall try to show him that the fear of scramble and rigidity with which Anarchism inspires him has little or no foundation.

Mr. Herbert, as I understand him, believes in voluntary association, voluntarily supported, for the defence of person and property. Very well; let us suppose that he has won his battle, and that such a state of things exists. Suppose that all municipalities have adopted the voluntary principle, and that compulsory taxation has been abolished. Now, after this, let us suppose further that the Anarchistic view that occupancy and use should condition and limit landholding becomes the prevailing view. Evidently then these municipalities will proceed to formulate and enforce this view. What the formula will be no one can foresee. But continuing with our suppositions, we will say that they decide to protect no one in the possession of more than ten acres. In execution of this decision, they, on October 1, notify all holders of more than ten acres within their limits that, on and after the following January 1, they will cease to protect them in the possession of more than ten acres, and that, as a condition of receiving even that protection, each must make formal declaration on or before December 1 of the specific ten-acre plot within his present holding which he proposes to personally occupy and use after January 1. These declarations having been made, the municipalities publish them and at the same time notify landless persons that out of the lands thus set free each may secure protection in the possession of any amount up to ten acres after January 1 by appearing on December 15, at a certain hour, and making declaration of his choice and intention of occupancy. Now, says Mr. Herbert, the scramble will begin. Well, perhaps it will. But what of it? When a theatre advertises to sell seats for a star performance at a certain hour, there is a scramble to secure tickets. When a prosperous city announces that on a given day it will accept loans from individuals up to a certain aggregate on attractive terms, there is a scramble to secure the bonds. As far as I know, nobody complains of these scrambles as unfair. The scramble begins and the scramble ends, and the matter is settled. Some inequality still remains, but it has been reduced to a minimum, and everybody has had an equal chance with the rest. So it will be with this land scramble. It may be conducted as peacefully as any other scramble, and those who are frightened by the word are simply the victims of a huge bugbear.

And the terror of rigidity is equally groundless. This rule of ten-acre possession, or any similar one that may be adopted, is no more rigid crystalline custom than is Mr. Herbert's own rule of protecting title transferred by purchase and sale. Any rule is rigid less by the rigidity of its terms than by the rigidity of its enforcement. Now it is precisely in the tempering of the rigidity of enforcement that one of the chief excellences of Anarchism consists. Mr. Herbert must remember that under Anarchism all rules and laws will be little more than suggestions for the guidance of juries, and that all disputes, whether about land or anything else, will be submitted to juries which will judge not only the facts, but the law, the justice of the law, its applicability to the given circumstances, and the penalty or damage to be inflicted because of its infraction. What better safeguard against rigidity could there be than this? "Machinery for altering" the law, indeed! Why, under Anarchism the law will be so flexible that it will shape itself to every emergency and need no alteration. And it will then be regarded as *just* in proportion to its flexibility, instead of as now in proportion to its rigidity.

OCCUPANCY AND USE VERSUS THE SINGLE TAX

In December, 1894, Mr. Steven T. Byington, still a Single Taxer, started a discussion with the editor of *Liberty* (Mr. John Beverley Robinson and Miss Katharine J. Musson participating) on certain factors in the land tenure and rent problems. Mr. Byington, an expert mathematician, carried the discussion into quite an intricate maze of figures, which are rather hard for the reader to understand without complete reproduction, here impossible. But, since Mr. Tucker's replies embodied some very pertinent and valuable explanations and arguments, it has been attempted to give as many of these as will be coherent without a full presentation of the other side. The discussion extends over a period of more than a year:

IT is not my purpose to lose myself in the mathematical maze through which Comrades Robinson and Byington are now gropingly threading their way. But I may point out to the latter, anent the dire perplexities in which he has involved 111 coal miners, that political economy knows not only a law of diminishing returns, but a law of increasing returns as well, and that he has ignored this branch of the law in the operation of his second mine.

In the first mine, where 100 men are already at work at the time of Mr. Byington's hypothesis, it may fairly be supposed that the law of diminishing returns begins to apply; but in the second mine, where not even one man works until there are 110 at work in the first, it is equally fair to suppose that the law of increasing returns will be in force until here also there are 100 workers. In that case the second mine, instead of yielding (as Mr. Byington presumes) one workman $900, two $1790, three $2670, &c., would yield one workman $900, two $1810, three $2730, &c. This little fact brings a wonderful change over the spirit of Mr. Byington's dreadful dream. For no sooner will his 111th miner have begun to work the second mine alone than he will be joined by the 110th, and the 109th, and the 108th, and the 107th, &c., &c., each new accession having a tendency to increase the earnings of the 11 men and to reduce the swollen incomes of the original 100, and the movement as a whole achieving, if not a restoration of absolute equality, at least a considerable approach to it. Which again impels me to recall the remark of Bastiat that there are things that we see and things that we don't see.

Again: the hypothesis is unwarrantably violent in predicating the existence of but one first-quality mine. As a matter of fact, there would in most cases be a number of superior mines nearly on a level in point of quality, and as the demand for coal increased, these mines would compete to secure extra labor, the competition forcing them to pay for this labor as much as could be paid without reducing the $1000 income enjoyed by each of the original occupants.

Still again: absolute freedom being the condition of the hypothesis, these mines would compete for this labor, not only with each other, but with all the other branches of industry newly opened or increased in activity by free money, free land, and free conditions generally, which would make it still less possible to obtain labor without awarding it its full product.

And further: it is assuming too much to say that a fair interpretation of the terms occupancy and use could exclude all but 100 men from the mine in question. Here the economic problem becomes complicated with engineering problems which I am incompetent to discuss; but it is not at all sure that the theory of occupancy and use would enable any hundred men to get the grip on subterranean riches that is here presumed.

And—last consideration of all—mining is but one, and the smallest, of the four great classes of labor, and the others are not relieved in the same degree from the equalizing influence of competition; so that, were a considerable inequality proven a necessity of mining, it would not follow that there would be as great inequality, or necessarily any at all, in agriculture, manufactures and commerce.

Thus you see, Mr. Byington, that, do your little sum as nicely as you will, there are still a few other things to be thought of.

It must not be supposed, however, that I share Mr. Robinson's view that economic rent is not a reality. I believe that economic rent exists now, and would continue under freedom, but then with a tendency to decrease and a possibility (though not a probability) of ultimate disappearance. In any event, taking the worst view of the matter, it would be distributed among actual occupants and users,—a *vastly* greater number than now enjoy it,—which would be much better for *all* than to distribute it among those who benefit by political jobbery, or among the people themselves through the agency of a State landlord, which would speedily become, by successive grants and usurpations of power, a State money-lord, a State industry-lord, a State education-lord, a State religion-lord, a State love-lord, and a State art-lord.

Equality if we can get it, but Liberty at any rate!

By compelling Mr. Byington to recognize the law of increasing returns in both mines instead of in one alone, I at the same time compel him to assume, in order to overcome the tendency of this law toward equality, a far greater and more improbable inferiority in the quality of the second mine than he attributed to that mine in his first hypothesis. And, as these sudden drops in quality are not, as a general thing, typical of the actual fact, Mr. Byington's new figures greatly weaken his argument.

It is not altogether a question of how much these laborers are worth to employers engaged in coal-mining. Their worth to employers in other lines must be taken into account. Under freedom, when the availability of capital will furnish new avenues for labor, Mr. Byington's 111th man who goes to work in the second mine for $900 instead of accepting offers of $1000 from men in other lines of business will be a fool who deserves his fate.

But, says Mr. Byington, the demand for coal finally making it worth while to pay the 111th man $1000 to go to work in the second mine, this demand and consequent rise in price will correspondingly increase the reward of the operators of the first mine, and the inequality will be as great as ever. Which means, at the worst, that, while none are paid any less than formerly, some are paid more. Dreadful thing! As Mr. Donisthorpe has pointed out in a way that evidently appeals with force to my Christian friend, Mr. Byington, the accidental benefiting of another is, "in the present state of Christian fraternity, a consummation to be carefully shunned."

Whether the neighboring farmers should sink shafts themselves or part with their land to others wishing to do so, in either case there would be an introduction of a new competitive factor tending toward equality. The article to which Mr. Byington now replies was one calling his attention to factors in the rent problem which he seemed to neglect. The liability of access to the first coal vein through a new shaft was one of these factors, and Mr. Byington's answer does not get rid of it. His nearest approach to it is a suggestion of the Malthusian argument, to which I can only respond that, if Malthusianism be true, it militates as strongly against the single tax as against any other reformatory proposal. I may add—though this matter is not strictly pertinent to the present discussion, but an engrafting upon it of an old discussion —that I would not, under any ordinary circumstances, oust an occupant and user to get either mining land or a right of way thereto. But I can conceive of circumstances, not only in the relations of men to the land, but in the relations of men to each other, where I would, for the moment, trample ruthlessly upon all the principles by which successful society must as a general thing be guided. I would advise Mr. Byington to consider for a while whether he himself is superior to necessity before too confidently assuming that there is any single rule to which he can *always* conform his conduct.

I know of no domain that occupies a higher eminence than that occupied by the domain which says to every user of land: "Hand over to me all that your land yields you over and above what the most barren of wastes yields to your most unfortunate fellowman, or else I will throw you neck and heels into the street." The "eminent domain" that I believe in, if Mr. Byington insists on so denominating it, would assume no rights in any land whatsoever, but would simply decline to protect the dominion of any one over land which he was not using.

To block up a narrow passage not regularly occupied and used for purposes of travel is one thing; to barricade an improved, claimed, and constantly used highway is another thing. Admission of the former requires no reconciliation with denial of the latter.

The value of land under the present system of land tenure has no bearing whatever on my assertion that under freedom the equalizing influence of competition is felt less in mining than in other branches of labor. If A has a mine in which his day's labor will yield him ten per cent. more coal than B's day's labor will yield B in another mine, A will derive ten per cent. more from the sale of his coal than B will derive from the sale of his, because all the coal, assuming it to be of equal quality, will bring the same price per ton, so far as the mine-owner is concerned. But commercial competition in cities is a different matter. In the lower and busy section of New York city there are perhaps a hundred drugstores occupying sites which may vary slightly in suitability for the drug trade, but all of which are excellent. In the upper parts of the city there are other drug-stores, most of which occupy vastly inferior sites. There is always a stiff competition in progress between the down-town druggists, but, in spite of this, the high rents which they have to pay prevent them from putting their prices much below the prices prevailing up town. Now, if the present system of land tenure should be changed to one of occupancy and use, what would happen? Why, the down-town druggists, relieved of the burden of rent, would lower their prices in competition with each other until all or nearly all the rent which they now pay landlords would be flowing into the pockets of their customers. The profits of the down-town druggist doing a large business at low prices could be little or no more than normal wages, and those of the up-town druggist doing a small business at high prices could be little or no less. In this typical commercial example competition under freedom shows a strong tendency to take from the occupants of superior sites their advantage. The occupants of inferior commercial sites can in most cases obtain for their goods prices proportionately higher, but the owner of a mine yielding an inferior quantity of coal can get no more per ton for his product than can his more fortunate rivals. This is the difference that I pointed out to Mr. Byington, and his remark regarding the present value of city land is no answer.

Certainly no land, except the very poorest, will be free under the single tax, for every occupant of land that is good for anything will have to pay tribute to the State. Evidently free land is one thing to Mr. Byington and another thing to me. I consider a potato patch whose cultivator pays no rent free land, even though it be a city corner-lot; and I should consider the same piece of land not free, but monopolized, if it were occupied by a confectioner obliged to pay tribute either to an individual or to the State.

The man who plants himself in a passage-way simply takes up vacant land and becomes an occupant thereof in good faith for ordinary and legitimate purposes, and not with a view to unnecessarily and maliciously embarrassing and crippling others. But, though the intent were not malicious, if the result were not merely inconvenience for others but complete imprisonment, I should regard the emergency as sufficiently critical to warrant a violation of principle. Not for gods, devils, society, men or principles would I allow myself to be imprisoned, completely crippled, and virtually killed, if I could in any way avoid it. But I would suffer a great deal of embarrassment in order to avoid the violation of a principle the general observance of which I consider essential to the closest possible approximation to that social harmony which I deem of high value to myself.

By all means kick for your full product, Mr. Byington, and

kick hard. I wish you to get it if you can, as I too wish to get mine. But I am not willing to pay too much for it. I am not willing to part with my liberty to get my full product, unless that part of my product which I do get is insufficient to keep me from starving. And even then I personally might prefer death; I do not know. Besides, Mr. Byington does not fairly represent his fellow Single-Taxers. He wants his own product, but *their* chief worry is because their product goes in part to a neighbor whom they hate,— the landlord; and they will be abundantly satisfied when it shall be taken from this hated neighbor and given to another whom they love,—the tax-collector.

Mr. Byington said that, whatever relief might come from the opening of new mines, the needs of civilization would soon press upon the limits of these mines. This is simply a form of saying that, whatever new opportunities may be opened for labor, the tendency of population to outstrip the means of subsistence is sure to ultimately neutralize them. That is Malthusianism; and, if it is true, all economic reforms, including the Single Tax, are a delusion and a snare.

I have not urged that society should make any exceptions in favor of the man who commits an invasion under circumstances that go far to excuse him. This would be a matter entirely for the jury. If I were on a jury to try the case of a man who had stolen bread when starving, I would vote in favor of a formal penalty, too light to be burdensome, and yet sufficient to stamp the act as invasive.

The simple fact is this,—that necessity, and only necessity, may excuse the coercion of the innocent. Now, necessity knows no law, and it knows no "aims"; it does not inquire whether the coercion to be exercised will be direct or indirect, incidental or essential; it just coerces, whether or no, and because it cannot do otherwise.

I believe that all vacant land should be free in Mr. Byington's sense of the word,—that is, open to be freely occupied by any comer. I believe that all occupied land should be free in my sense of the word,—that is, enjoyed by the occupant without payment of tribute to a nonoccupant. Whether the achievement of these two freedoms will tend to reduce rental values we shall know better when Mr. Byington has "seen about those drug-stores."

In this sense [evicting occupants contrary to the principle of liberty, under the plea of a higher law of necessity] I declare my willingness to stand for eminent domain. But I insist that Mr. Byington does not, as he claims, get rid of eminent domain, but on the contrary gives it the most rigorous and universal application, when he proposes to exact from each land-occupant a portion of his product under penalty of eviction.

I accept Mr. Byington's amendment. I think myself that it is better to exclude the matter of good faith. It is simpler and truer to say that any man who uses his land for the commission of a plainly invasive act may be dispossessed and treated as a criminal. If the act committed is of a doubtful character, then the same rule applies here that applies to all other doubtful cases: that is, the troublesome party should be given the benefit of the doubt, either until his course becomes clearly invasive, when he should be dispossessed as an invader, or until it becomes a peremptory menace to the community's safety, when he should be dispossessed in the name of necessity, though it be still doubtful whether he is an invader.

I deny that the thing fundamentally desirable is the minimum of invasion. The ultimate end of human endeavor is the minimum of pain. We aim to decrease invasion only because, as a rule, invasion increases the total of pain (meaning, of course, pain suffered by the ego, whether directly or through sympathy with others.) But it is precisely my contention that this rule, despite the immense importance which I place upon it, is not absolute; that, on the contrary, there are exceptional cases where invasion—that is, coercion of the non-invasive—lessens the aggregate pain. Therefore coercion of the non-invasive, when justifiable at all, is to be justified on the ground that it secures, not a minimum of invasion, but a minimum of pain. The position, then, which Mr. Byington seems to take that coercion of the non-invasive is allowable only as an unavoidable incident in the coercion of invaders, and not allowable when it is an unavoidable incident in the prevention of impending cataclysmic disaster not the work of invaders, is seen at once to be inconsistent with my fundamental postulate—to me axiomatic—that the ultimate end is the minimum of pain. If Mr. Byington believes that the minimum of invasion is always desirable, I summon him to deal specifically with the case cited by me in my discussion with Mr. Yarros,—the case, that is, of a burning city which can be saved from total destruction only by blowing up the houses on a strip of territory inhabited by non-invasive persons who refuse their consent to such disposition of their property. If Mr. Byington thinks that these houses should not be blown up, I ask him to tell us why. If, on the other hand, he admits that they should be blown up, I ask him if such action would not be "injury to non-invaders without the resistance of invasion,"—a policy to which he declares himself opposed under any circumstances. Can he maintain his abstract proposition in face of the concrete illustration? Moreover, the illustration, though not framed originally for this discussion, is a most happy one for the purpose, since here it is the innocent act of land-occupancy which constitutes the obstacle to social welfare. I hold, then, to my claim that occupancy and use as the title to land is not vitiated by the fact that it is a rule which, like all others, must sometimes be trodden underfoot.

Either Mr. Byington has not understood me, or I do not understand him. His answer to me seems to be based on an assumption that my previous answer to him was just the opposite of what it really was. He had put to me this question: "If A builds a house, and rents it to B, who thereupon lives or works in it under the lease, will you regard A or B as the 'occupier and user' of the land on which that house stands?" I answered: "I would regard B as the occupant and user of the land on which the house stands, and as the owner of the house itself." To this Mr. Byington rejoins: "Then houses will be rented under your system just as now, and the sum charged for rent will include the rental value of the land as well as payment for the use of the house." A most remarkable conclusion, surely! To my own mind the logical conclusion is precisely the contrary. It is perfectly clear to me that A will not build a house to rent to B, if he knows that the protective association will recognize B as the owner of both land and house as soon as he becomes the occupant. I utterly repudiate the idea that unused land, if usable, would remain idle under an occupancy-and-use *régime*. How could it, when any one would be free to take it and would not be forced to pay rent for it?

As a result of the misunderstanding, Mr. Byington has failed to "see about the drug-stores." All his present remarks upon them are *mal à propos*. Under an occupancy-and-use system all ground-floor druggists—that is, all retail druggists —will be owners of both land and store, and competition will proceed among them with the effect described by me and my argument that "competition under freedom shows a strong tendency to take from the occupants of superior sites their advantage" remains intact. Mr. Byington will have to try again. First, however, let me answer his puerile question: "Why does not the man who now pays no rent because he is on his own land now undersell his rent-paying competitors." For precisely the same reason that the man who pays no interest because he is using his own capital does not undersell his interest-paying competitors. Is Mr. Byington really unaware that the man who uses that which he could lend to another for a price insists on getting as much profit from it (in addition to the reward of his labor and enterprise) as he would get if he should lend it?

Mr. Byington may understand that the man who builds a cage over the sleeper is an invader. The man who blocks up an improved, claimed, and constantly used highway is also an invader. The man who takes possession of an unoccupied, unimproved, unused passage is not an invader, and does not become one simply because, afterward, somebody else wishes to make a highway of it. Such a man is not to be dispossessed except in one of those rare emergencies when necessity, which knows no law, compels it.

Regarding protection of occupancy, I answer Mr. Byington that undoubtedly the protective association would insist on registration of all titles to real estate as a condition of protection. Then, in case of dispute between claimants and a failure of the jury to agree, the protective association would regard as the occupant the party whose registration of title it had already accepted.

The picket note to which Mr. Byington alludes was a criticism upon Miss Katharine J. Musson. The paragraph being short, I reproduce it:

The statement that a State can have no rights except those

delegated to it by individuals is singular doctrine on the lips of a Single Taxer. Miss Musson acknowledges the right of the State to collect rent from every land-occupant, this rent being in her eyes the just due of all individuals, since all have an equal right to the use of every part of the earth. It follows from these two positions that the State, if it collects my share of this rent, commits an act of usurpation, for I have not delegated to it the right to collect my rent. And yet I have not heard that Miss Musson or any other Single Taxer would limit the State, in the exercise of its rent-collecting function, to the collection of only such portion of the total rent as is properly due to the persons who have appointed the State their rent-collector. It follows further that all individuals who, like myself, have not appointed the State their rent-collector may, if they choose, go about, each individually, from one land-occupant to another, collecting their respective shares of the rent due. According to this, I have the right to at once start on a tour among my neighbors (or even among all the land-occupying inhabitants of the earth) and demand of each the delivery into my hands of that greater or smaller fraction of a cent which each owes me for the current quarter. Or, if I find this course too expensive, all those who ignore the State may unite in appointing a private force of rent-collectors to collect their share of the total rent. Does Miss Musson accept these logical inferences from her position?

Mr. Byington admits that the State is a usurper if it collects my share of rent without getting from me a power of attorney. He claims neither for himself or for any other person or for any association of persons the right to collect my share of rent without authorization from me. Accordingly he expresses a willingness to enter into an arrangement with me for the collection of our rents; that is, he invites me to give a power of attorney. I must admit that this is very accommodating on Mr. Byington's part; nevertheless, I churlishly decline. If any part of the money in the hands of land-users belongs to me (which is the hypothesis just now), I prefer to leave it where it is. Now, Mr. Byington, what are you and your Single-Tax friends going to do about it? I do not call upon you to determine *my* share; so far as I am concerned, it may remain undetermined. But, if you are going to collect *your* share, you will have to determine first what *your* share is. At any rate, I bid you take good care not to touch mine. By your own confession you Single Taxers are entitled to collect only such rent as is the rightful share of the Single Taxers, all others refusing to delegate their rights. Do you tell me that such a task is insuperably difficult and intrinsically absurd? Very well, I answer; that fact is not my fault; it is simply the misfortune of the Single-Tax theory.

The collection of rent by each individual from all land-users on earth, which Mr. Byington accepts so complacently, is an absurdity which Miss Musson cannot stand. So she attempts to dispute my conclusion. I am not debating with her now regarding the Single-Tax theory. For the nonce I am accepting it; I am supposing that I have a right in certain funds now in the hands of land-users. So never mind the Single-Tax theory. Then she tells me of the dreadful things that would happen if, under an occupancy-and-use *régime,* I should refuse to delegate my right. But I am not discussing occupancy and use either. Miss Musson is supposed to know nothing of my opinions on the land question. I present myself to her simply as the individual, Tucker, who declines to delegate his rights, just as I might have presented a hypothetical individual, Smith. But, argues Miss Musson, you have no separate right to rent. Very well; we will not dispute about that either. The only thing that concerns me at present is Miss Musson's specific declaration, in the last sentence of her article, that I have a share in the aggregate right to rent, and that *I can delegate this to the State.* Here I have all that I want,—all that is necessary to the main purpose of my original criticism. Delegation of rights is an act of pure volition, and, as such, implies the power to refuse such delegation. Then, if I can delegate to the State my share in the aggregate right to rent, I can also decline to delegate it. Now, I do so decline. But Miss Musson has previously and fundamentally declared that a State can have no rights except those delegated to it by individuals. Therefore, since I refuse to delegate to the State my share in the aggregate right to rent, the State has no right to take my share in the aggregate right to rent. Q. E. D. And there is no escape from the demonstration. Miss Musson may as well "acknowledge the corn" first as last, and make her choice between individualism and the Single Tax. The two are incompatible.

I can readily forgive Mr. Byington for mistaking B for A in my answer to his question. Such a slip the most careful man may make at any time. But his more fundamental misconception of what the occupancy-and-use doctrine really is I find it more difficult, if not to pardon, at least to account for. Certainly in no writing of mine have I given him warrant for supposing me to hold that a man should be allowed a title to as much of the earth as he, in the course of his life, with the aid of all the workmen that he can employ, may succeed in covering with buildings. It is occupancy *and* use that Anarchism regards as the basis of land ownership,—not occupany *or* use, as Mr. Byington seems to have understood. A man cannot be allowed, merely by putting labor, to the limit of his capacity and beyond the limit of his personal use, into material of which there is a limited supply and the use of which is essential to the existence of other men, to withhold that material from other men's use; and any contract based upon or involving such withholding is as lacking in sanctity or legitimacy as a contract to deliver stolen goods. As I have never held that freedom of contract includes a right to dispose of the property of others, I do not, in denying such right, "yield the sanctity of contract," as Mr. Byington puts it. Yes, the object of Anarchism is, sure enough, to let every man "control self and the results of self-exertion"; but this by no means implies that a man may store upon another's land the results of his self-exertion. If a man exerts himself by erecting a building on land which afterward, by the operation of the principle of occupancy and use, rightfully becomes another's, he must, upon the demand of the subsequent occupant, remove from this land the results of his self-exertion, or, failing so to do, sacrifice his property right therein. The man who persists in storing his property on another's premises is an invader, and it *is* his *crime* that alienates his control of this property. He is "fined one house," not "for building a house and then letting another man live in it," but for invading the premises of another. If there were nothing in the "Beauties of Government" to beat that, then indeed would government be a really beautiful thing.

The objection advanced by Mr. Byington that adherence to this principle must cause a degree of embarrassment to persons desirous of using an entire edifice for a period too short to warrant building or buying has some validity, and should be accorded all the weight that properly belongs to it. But its gravity is insufficient to balance that of considerations in the other scale. It must be remembered that comparatively few persons desire to rent an *entire* building for a *short* time. As a rule, those who want quarters for a short time prefer parts of buildings, and there is nothing in the occupancy-and-use plan to prevent them from realizing their desire. As a rule, again, those who want an entire building want it for a long time, and therefore can afford to build or buy. The exceptional person who does not come under these heads will undoubtedly have to pay something for the realization of his exceptional desires. He will have to make it worth the while of the occupying owner of the desired building to part with it; that is to say, he will have to buy the building at something above its normal value. Perhaps, to avoid the embarrassment of looking for a purchaser at the expiration of the time for which he desires the building, he will be able to effect a contract with the seller whereby the latter shall agree to buy back the building at a given date at its normal value. If the seller should fail to keep this agreement, the building would still be the property of the buyer, and he could sell it to another party. The difference between the buying and the selling price might not exceed the rent exacted for such buildings under the present *régime*. But, assuming that these exceptional persons would be, for occasional brief periods, under a greater burden in this respect than at present, this could not offset the far more important fact that the great body of people would be occupying their own buildings, paying no rent for their use and no interest on the money with which they were built. The entire race's steady and imperative need of free access to the land cannot be subordinated to the occasional convenience of a small fraction of the race.

The adjustment of the conditions upon which an occupant and user can secure his premises against being considered as abandoned while he is on a vacation or a visit, or of the conditions upon which an occupying owner who desires to sell may hold his property while seeking a purchaser, or of the conditions upon which a man who builds houses, not to rent but to sell, may likewise be accommodated in his search for purchasers, is a mere matter of human device or administrative detail, not to be discussed in these columns unless the attempt be to show that such device is impossible.

Probably my language regarding ground-floor occupants was not sufficiently clear. In my assertion that they would own *both land and store* the intended emphasis was on the words here italicized, and I neglected to consider the fact that not all occupying owners would, on erecting a building, prefer to occupy the ground floor themselves, my view being colored by the knowledge that retail druggists, apropos of whom my point was made, so far as I have observed, do business on the ground floor. It was not in my mind at all to deny that a registered occupying owner would lose his claim to protection of his title should he choose to personally occupy only the attic of his building. It would be required only that he should occupy and use some portion or portions practically equal to the ground floor in area. It is probable that in an occupancy-and-use system there would be many cases of rent-paying by tenants of rooms or floors. But the amount of this rent would be greatly influenced by the competition that would prevail in consequence of the freeing of unused land, and the ability to build with non-interest-bearing capital that free money would insure, as well as by the non-intervention of the protective association in the relations of owner and tenant. I question whether, under such circumstances, the rent that could be obtained would often much exceed the loss through wear and tear and care of the premises rented.

In his present remarks about price-cutting and its relation to rent Mr. Byington leaves entirely out of the account the element of competition on which my argument rests. Does he suppose that there is any sharply competitive trade in existence in which the tradesman does not constantly ask himself the question how he can manage to lower his prices in order to secure some of the patronage that is going to his competitors? And does he suppose that, in considering this problem, this tradesman fails to ask himself if he cannot reduce his expenses and thereby manage to lower his prices? And is not rent one of these expenses? And, if it were lifted from his shoulders, would he not lower his prices at once? And, if he did, would not his competitor, who has all the time been doing business in a building of his own and paying rent to nobody, be forced to lower his prices also in order to retain his trade,—a thing which now he does not have to do because his rent-paying competitor cannot lower his prices? It is as clear as daylight.

The man who builds a cage over a sleeper prevents the sleeper from exercising his unquestionable right to *step off* of premises that belong to another, and therefore is an invader. The man who becomes by occupancy and use the owner of a previously unoccupied, unimproved, and unused passage, and in the exercise of his ownership blocks the passage, simply prevents other men from doing what they have no right to do, —that is, *step on* to premises that belong to another,—and therefore is not an invader.

Mr. Byington's answer to my contention that there may be circumstances under which it is advisable to do violence to equal freedom amounts in its conclusion to a statement that no evil can be as disastrous as an act of invasion; that justice should be done though the heavens fall, for a precedent of injustice would lead to a worse disaster than the falling of the heavens; and that, if he were the guardian of a city most of whose inhabitants found themselves under the necessity of a choice between death by fire on the one hand and death by drowning on the other, he would not relieve them from this choice if he could do so only by violating the property rights of a portion of his fellow-citizens. Discussion is hopeless here.

In May, 1895, Mr. Louis F. Post delivered a lecture at Cincinnati on the Single Tax, in which he made the statement that occupancy and use was really the only true title to land. After the lecture, in reply to a question from one of his auditors, he explained that his advocacy of the Single Tax was as the best method of reaching the occupancy-and-use title. When Mr. Tucker's attention was called to Mr. Post's statement, he hailed it as very significant, since the other prominent champions of the Single Tax denied that the land belongs to the occupant and user and affirmed that all land belongs equally to all the people; and he stated that, if Mr. Post had not been misunderstood, the latter had taken a position which involved the rejection of the Single-Tax theory and pledged him to the Single Tax only as a measure of expediency and as a stepping-stone. Mr. Post replied that he did not mean to imply that he advocated the Single Tax as a stepping-stone in the sense of a temporary expedient, but as the only way of obtaining and maintaining the title of occupancy and use. That explanation called forth the following from the editor of *Liberty*:

Mr. Post admits the utterances attributed to him, and then proceeds to emasculate them. It appears that the phrase occupancy and use is used by Mr. Post simply as an equivalent of the right of possession. In that case it is nonsense to talk about the Single Tax or any other measure as the best method of reaching the occupancy-and-use title, for in Mr. Post's sense that title already exists. Today the occupant of land is its *possessor*, in right and in fact. The aim of the occupancy-and-use agitation is not to secure for the occupant a possession which is already his, but an ownership and control which in most cases is not his, but his landlord's,—an ownership and control which shall end when occupancy and use end, but which shall be absolute while occupancy and use continue.

In another part of his letter Mr. Post virtually denies the equivalence of occupancy with possession by declaring that landlords, even those who rent land and buildings in their entirety, are occupants and users. If this be true, then the Astor estate is occupying and using a very large portion of the city of New York. But to assert that the Astors are either occupants or possessors is an utter misuse of language. Besides, if the Astors are occupants and users, and if the Single Tax will virtually compel the Astors to relinquish their lands, then the Single Tax, instead of being a means of getting to an occupancy-and-use tenure, will be a means of destroying such tenure. Mr. Post's position bristles at every point with inconsistency and absurdity.

It is so long since I read Mr. George's book that I do not remember whether Mr. Post is right in denying that Mr. George teaches the doctrine of equal ownership of land by all the people. One thing, however, is certain,—that the equal right of *all* people to *every* piece of land is asserted by many of the foremost Single Taxers, some of whom are on the national executive committee of the party. And it is on the strength of this that the Single Tax is defended. How often we hear Single Taxers deploring the name by which their idea is known! "It is very unfortunate," they will tell you, "that our plan is called a tax. It is not a tax at all. We believe in the utter abolition of taxation. Taxation is robbery,—a taking from the producer of his product. We do not propose to rob; in collecting rent we take only what is ours, for that which comes, not from labor, but from land, belongs, not to the laborer, but to us, the people." If occupancy and use is not a title to land, then this position is sound; on the other hand, if it is a title to land, then the Single Tax is robbery. Mr. Post cannot escape from this dilemma.

If there must be Single Taxers, I prefer those of the Philadelphia sort, who attack occupancy and use with hammer and tongs, maintaining that it is unscientific and diametrically opposite to their fundamental principles. Relieve me, pray, of opponents like Mr. Post, who, using my own phraseology in a distorted sense, strive to make it appear to the people that their ideas are mine. Let Anarchists be on their guard. Don't bite at phrases.

In considering the letters of Mr. Alexander Horr, I notice at the outset that they betray a singular contradiction. In the first we are told that the occupancy-and-use theory of land tenure "has not risen to the dignity of respectable empiricism." In the second we are told that of the four systems of land tenure now advocated there are two which "deserve the most careful consideration," and that one of the two is the occupancy-and-use theory. The question arises: why does that which has not risen to the dignity of respectable empiricism deserve to be considered with care?

Mr. Horr complains of the indefiniteness with which the advocates of the occupancy-and-use theory explain it. My opinion is that the larger share of the indefiniteness regarding it that exists in his own mind is due to a failure on his part to weigh and understand what has been said in defense of the theory. In a recent conversation with me, Mr. Horr naïvely assumed the ownership by an Astor of the whole of Manhattan Island, and the renting of the same in parcels to tenants, as a possibility quite consistent with the occupancy-and-use theory and one which the theory's advocates would so regard. Such an assumption on his part showed beyond question that he has failed to consider the positions that have been taken in *Liberty* as to the nature of occupancy and use. These positions have been stated in English plain enough to be definitely grasped. If Mr. Horr had taken pains to understand them, he could not interpret the occupancy-and-use theory in a manner squarely contradictory of them. There will be no motive for *Liberty* to attempt a completer exposition of its doctrine for Mr. Horr's benefit, until he understands the perfectly definite things that *Liberty* has already said.

Agreeing to my claim that equal freedom is not a law, but simply a rule of social life which we find it expedient to follow, Mr. Horr asks me why, if it is expedient to enforce equal freedom in other things, it is not also expedient to enforce equal rights to the use of the earth. As appropriately might I ask him why it is not expedient to enforce equal rights to the use of brain power. Equal freedom as defined and advocated in *Liberty* covers only the control of self and the results of self-exertion. "Equal rights in other things" is a phrase of Mr. Horr's coinage. I uphold equal freedom, as I define it, because it secures individuality, the definition and encouragement of which are essential to social development and prosperity and to individual happiness. I oppose Mr. Horr's policy loosely described as "equal rights in other things" because it tends to obliterate individuality. The enforcement of equal rights to the use of the earth, for instance, by a single tax on land values means a confiscation of a portion of the individual's product, a denial of the liberty to control the results of self-exertion, and hence a trampling upon individuality. If an equal distribution or common ownership of wealth, with the accompanying destruction of individuality, is a good thing, then let us become Communists at once, and confiscate every excess, whether its source be land value, brain value, or some other value. If, on the other hand, the protection of the individual is the thing paramount and the main essential of happiness, then let us defend the equal liberty of individuals to control self and the results of self-exertion, and let other equalities take care of themselves.

An instance of the peculiar manner in which Mr. Horr interprets his opponent's utterances may be seen in his comments on Mr. Yarros's statement that, while voluntary taxation of economic rent might not be a good thing, "the use of force to bring it about would be extremely unwise." Mr. Horr thinks that this statement is "not quite clear." It is true that it is not quite exact. Mr. Yarros had better have said "the use of force to effect it," or, more simply still, "the enforcement of it," than "the use of force to bring it about." But even from the sentence as it stands it seems to me that no intelligent reader should have failed to extract the evident meaning that, though men might well agree to pay rent into a common treasury, no man should be forced to do so. Yet Mr. Horr takes it to mean that force should not be used to collect rent in special and abnormal cases. I do not see the slightest warrant for this extraordinary and senseless construction of Mr. Yarros's words.

Mr. Horr defends State collection of rent on the ground that, if equal rights to land be admitted, "all men have a right to collect rent from those who use better than free land, because each individual would collect such rent himself, if he had the power." Logic does not warrant the inference. I showed clearly, in my discussion with Miss Musson, that, even granting Single-Tax ethics, still State collection of every individual's share of rent, without delegation by each individual of his right to collect, cannot be advocated consistently by any individualist. The fact that an individual would collect the rent rightfully due him, if he had the power, does not warrant another man, or all other men, in proceeding unauthorized to collect this rent. There are some creditors who believe that the State should not collect debts. Would Mr. Horr claim that the State is entitled to collect the debts due these creditors, regardless of their wishes in the matter? Now rent is nothing but a debt, under Single-Tax ethics. Consequently any parties who contract for the collection of their rents in common must see to it that they collect only their own shares of the total rent due. If they collect other people's shares, even the Single Taxer, if he be an individualist, is bound to consider them thieves.

All that Mr. Horr has to say about the difficulty of sustaining an occupancy-and-use system by jury decisions is based on silly and gratuitous assumptions. In the first place, it is pure assumption to say that juries will be recruited solely from tax-payers. No believer in the original form of jury trial as explained by Spooner ever advanced such a proposition. In the second place, it is pure assumption to say that, when taxation is voluntary, only land-owners will pay taxes, because they alone benefit by the expenditure of the taxes. It is not true that they alone benefit. Every individual benefits whose life, liberty, and property is protected. In the third place, it is pure assumption to say that jurors do not, in the main, render verdicts in accordance with their own conceptions of equity and social living. A jury of thieves is quite as likely as a jury of honest men to convict a prisoner justly accused of theft. Now, no advocate of occupancy-and-use tenure of land believes that it can be put in force, until as a theory it has been as generally, or almost as generally, seen and accepted as is the prevailing theory of ordinary private property. But, when the theory has been thus accepted, jurors may be relied on, in the main, to render verdicts in accordance therewith, no matter what their status or situation in life. Were it not so, no society would be possible.

Mr. Horr finally defends the Single Tax, against the objection that under it the land occupant is at the mercy of the community, by claiming that "changes due to social growth which are just as inevitable as any other phenomena of nature must be submitted to." I suppose, then, that, because I must submit to the tornado that destroys my crop, I must also submit to the depredations of people who choose to settle in my vicinity and then rob me of a part of my crop by what they call a tax on my land value. Well, of course I must, if my fellow-citizens all turn thieves,—that is, Single Taxers. Consequently I am trying to persuade them to be honest.

GEORGE AND THE SINGLE TAX

Following are some fragmentary paragraphs relating to different phases of the Single Tax and to Henry

George's perplexities concerning his economic theories. The editor of *Liberty* took great delight in pointing out his inconsistencies:

SOME of Henry George's correspondents have been pestering him a good deal with embarrassing questions as to what will become, under his system, of the home of a man who has built a house upon a bit of land which afterwards so rises in value that he cannot afford to pay the taxes on it. Unable to deny that such a man would be as summarily evicted by the government landlord as is the Irish farmer in arrears by the individual landlord, and yet afraid to squarely admit it, Mr. George has twisted and turned and doubled and dodged, attempting to shield himself by all sorts of irrelevant considerations, until at last he is reduced to asking in rejoinder if this argument has not "a great deal of the flavor of the Georgia deacon's denunciation of abolitionists because they wanted to deprive the widow Smith of her solitary 'nigger,' her only means of support." That is, Mr. George virtually asserts that the claim to own a human being is no more indefensible than the claim of the laborer to own the house he has built and to the unincumbered and indefinite use of whatever site he may have selected for it without dispossessing another. The editor of the *Standard* must have been reduced to sore straits when he resorted to this argument. With all his shuffling he has not yet escaped, and never can escape, the fact that, if government were to confiscate land values, any man would be liable to be turned out of doors, perhaps with compensation, perhaps without it, and thus deprived, maybe, of his dearest joy and subjected to irreparable loss, just because other men had settled in his vicinity or decided to run a railroad within two minutes' walk of his door. This in itself is enough to damn Mr. George's project. That boasted craft, Land Nationalization, is floundering among the rocks, and the rock of individual liberty and the inalienable homestead has just made an enormous hole in its unseaworthy bottom which will admit all the water necessary to sink it.

Henry George's correspondents continue to press him regarding the fate of the man whose home should so rise in value through increase of population that he would be taxed out of it. At first, it will be remembered, Mr. George coolly sneered at the objectors to this species of eviction as near relatives of those who objected to the abolition of slavery on the ground that it would "deprive the widow Smith of her only 'nigger.'" *Liberty* made some comments on this, which Mr. George never noticed. Since their appearance, however, his analogy between property in "niggers" and a man's property in his house has lapsed, as President Cleveland would say, into a condition of "innocuous desuetude," and a new method of settling this difficulty has been evolved. A correspondent having supposed the case of a man whose neighborhood should become a business centre, and whose place of residence, therefore, as far as the land was concerned, should rise in value so that he could not afford or might not desire to pay the tax upon it, but, as far as his house was concerned, should almost entirely lose its value because of its unfitness for business purposes, Mr. George makes answer that the community very likely would give such a man a new house elsewhere to compensate him for being obliged to sell his house at a sacrifice. That this method has some advantages over the "nigger" argument I am not prepared to deny, but I am tempted to ask Mr. George whether this is one of the ways by which he proposes to "simplify government."

Henry George, in the *Standard*, calls Dr. Cogswell of San Francisco, who has endowed a polytechnic college in that city, and for its maintenance has conveyed certain lands to trustees, a "philanthropist by proxy," on the ground that the people who pay rent for these lands are really taxed by Dr. Cogswell for the support of the college. But what are Henry George himself, by his theory, and his ideal State, by its practice, after realization, but "philanthropists by proxy"? What else, in fact, is the State as it now exists? (Oftener a cannibal than a philanthropist, to be sure, but in either case by proxy.) Does not Mr. George propose that the State shall tax individuals to secure "public improvements" which they may not consider such, or which they may consider less desirable to them than private improvements? Does he not propose that individuals shall "labor gratis" for the State, "whether they like it or not"? Does he not maintain that what the State "does with

their labor is simply none of their business"? Mr. George's
criticism of Dr. Cogswell is equally a criticism of every form
of compulsory taxation, especially the taxation of land values.
He has aptly and accurately described himself.

There must be a limitation to great fortunes, says Henry
George, "but that limitation must be natural, not artificial.
Such a limitation is offered by the land value tax." What in
the name of sense is there about a tax that makes it natural
as distinguished from artificial? If anything in the world is
purely artificial, taxes are. And if they are collected by force,
they are not only artificial, but arbitrary and tyrannical.

Henry George answers a correspondent who asks if under
the system of taxing land values an enemy could not compel
him to pay a higher tax on his land simply by making him
an offer for the land in excess of the existing basis of taxation,
by saying that no offers will change the basis of taxation unless they are made in good faith and for other than sentimental
motives. It seems, then, that the tax assessors are to be in-
quisitors as well, armed with power to subject men to examination of their motives for desiring to effect any given
transaction in land. What glorious days those will be for
"boodlers"! What golden opportunities for fraud, favoritism,
bribery, and corruption! And yet Mr. George will have it
that he intends to reduce the power of government.

The idiocy of the arguments employed by the daily press in
discussing the labor question cannot well be exaggerated, but
nevertheless it sometimes makes a point on Henry George
which that gentleman cannot meet. For instance, the New
York *World* lately pointed out that unearned increment attaches not only to land, but to almost every product of labor.
"Newspapers," it said, "are made valuable properties by the
increase of population." Mr. George seems to think this ridiculous, and inquires confidently whether the *World's* success is due to increase of population or to Pulitzer's business
management. As if one cause excluded the other! Does Mr.
George believe, then, that Pulitzer's business management
could have secured a million readers of the *World* if there had
been no people in New York? Of course not. Then, to follow his own logic, Mr. George ought to discriminate in this
case, as in the case of land, between the owner's improvements

and the community's improvements, and tax the latter out of the owner's hands.

Henry George was recently reminded in these columns that his own logic would compel him to lay a tax not only on land values, but on all values growing out of increase of population, and newspaper properties were cited in illustration. A correspondent of the *Standard* has made the same criticism, instancing, instead of a newspaper, "Crusoe's boat, which rose in value when a ship appeared on the horizon." To this correspondent Mr. George makes answer that, while Crusoe's boat might have acquired a value when other people came, "because value is a factor of trading, and, when there is no one to trade with, there can be no value," yet "it by no means follows that growth of population increases the value of labor products; for a population of fifty will give as much value to a desirable product as a population of a million." I am ready to admit this of any article which can be readily produced by any and all who choose to produce it. But, as Mr. George says, it is not true of land; and it is as emphatically not true of every article in great demand which can be produced, in approximately equal quality and with approximately equal expense, by only one or a few persons. There are many such articles, and one of them is a popular newspaper. Such articles are of small value where there are few people and of immense value where there are many. This extra value is unearned increment, and ought to be taxed out of the individual's hands into those of the community if any unearned increment ought to be. Come, Mr. George, be honest! Let us see whither your doctrine will lead us.

Cart and horse are all one to Henry George. He puts either first to suit his fancy or the turn his questioner may take, and no matter which he places in the lead, he "gets there all the same"—on paper. When he is asked how taxation of land values will abolish poverty, he answers that the rush of wage-laborers to the land will reduce the supply of labor and send wages up. Then, when somebody else asks him how wage-laborers will be able to rush to the land without money to take them there and capital to work the land afterwards, he answers that wages will then be so high that the laborers will soon be able to save up money enough to start with. Sometimes, indeed, as if dimly perceiving the presence of some inconsistency lurking between these two propositions, he volunteers an additional suggestion that, after the lapse of a generation, he will be a phenomenally unfortunate young man who shall have no relatives or friends to help him start upon the land. But we are left as much in the dark as ever about the method by which these relatives or friends, during the generation which must elapse before the young men get to the land, are to save up anything to give these young men a start, in the absence of that increase of wages which can only come as a consequence of the young men having gone to the land. Mr. George, however, has still another resource in reserve, and, when forced to it, he trots it out,—namely, that, there being all grades between the rich and the very poor, those having enough to start themselves upon the land would do so, and the abjectly poor, no longer having them for competitors, would get higher wages. Of course one might ask why these diminutive capitalists, who even now can go to the land if they choose, since there is plenty to be had for but little more than the asking, refrain nevertheless from at once relieving an over-stocked labor market; but it would do no good. You see, you can't stump Henry George. He always comes up blandly smiling. He knows he has a ready tongue and a facile pen, and on these he relies to carry him safely through the mazes of unreason.

Henry George thinks the New York *Sun's* claim, that it is "for liberty first, last and forever," pretty cool from a paper that supports a protective tariff. So it is. But the frigidity of this claim is even greater when it comes from a man who proposes on occasion to tax a man out of his home, and to "simplify" government by making it the owner of all railroads, telegraphs, gas-works, and water-works, so enlarging its revenues that all sorts of undreamed-of public improvements will become possible, and unnumbered public officials to administer them necessary.

Perhaps no feature of Henry George's scheme is so often paraded before the public as a bait as the claim that with a tax levied on land values all other taxes will be abolished. But now it is stated in the *Standard* that, if any great fortunes remain after the adoption of the land tax, it will be "a mere detail to terminate them by a probate tax." This is offered for the benefit of those who believe that interest no less than rent causes concentration of wealth. To those who fear the effects upon home industry in case of an abolition of the tariff Mr. George hints that he will be perfectly agreeable to the offering of bounties to home industries. To be sure, he would pay the bounties out of the land tax; but the use of the proceeds of the land tax for a new purpose, after existing governmental expenses had been met, would be equivalent to a new tax. So we already have three taxes in sight where there was to be but one,—the land tax, the probate tax, and the bounty tax. Presently, as new necessities arise, a fourth will loom up, and a fifth, and a sixth. Thus the grand work of "simplifying government" goes on.

The Single Taxer starts with the proposition that "each individual has a just claim to the use of every part of the earth," and, thus starting, he arrives at this conclusion: "When land has no value,—that is, when only one man wants to use it,— we would exact no tax, but, when it acquires a value, our principle that each has an equal right to the earth demands that its rental value should be paid into the public treasury." These two propositions are made in so many words by Mr. A. H. Stephenson, than whom the Single Tax has no abler advocate, not excepting Henry George himself. And yet truth requires the assertion that a more absurd *non sequitur* than this it is not possible for the human mind to conceive. It has the form of reasoning, but, instead of reasoning, it is flat and absolute contradiction. It is exactly paralleled in its essential by such an argument as the following: "This watch belongs to you; therefore it should be put into my pocket." How does this differ, so far as logic and equity are concerned, from the Single-Tax argument: "To the use of this corner-lot you have a just claim; therefore the rental value of this lot should be put into the public treasury"? If I have a just claim to the use of every piece of land on the globe, then of course I have a just claim to the use of any particular piece of land. If I have this latter claim, I, and I alone, have the right to sell this claim. Whoever sells my claim without my consent is a robber. Since every Single Taxer favors such sale of my claim, whether I consent or not, every Single Taxer is an advocate of robbery.

Again: since I have the sole right to sell my claim, I have the sole right to decide at what price it shall be offered in the market. Whoever sells it, even with my consent, is a robber, unless he exacts as great a price as that fixed by me. Since the Single Taxer proposes to sell it without even asking what I am willing to take for it, the Single Taxer is an advocate of robbery.

If my just claim to a particular piece of land is sold, the proceeds of the sale must go into my pocket. If, after putting them in my pocket, I then see fit to take them out again and turn them over to the public treasury in exchange for police or other services that I may desire, well and good. But this must be entirely optional with me. I may keep these proceeds, if I choose; I may spend them, if I choose; and, in the latter case, I may choose how I will spend them. Any one who attempts to substitute his choice for mine in this matter is a robber. Any one who lays violent hands on the proceeds of this sale and deposits them in the public treasury without my consent is a robber. Nearly every Single Taxer proposes to do precisely that, and therefore nearly every Single Taxer is an advocate of robbery.

But even if I were to allow that it would not be robbery to deposit in the *United States* treasury without my consent the proceeds of the sale of my just claim to a particular piece of land (on the ground that I get an equivalent in the use of streets, etc.), it would still be robbery to deposit such proceeds in the treasury of Great Britain or France or Russia or China or Peru. If I have a just claim to the use of *every* piece of land on the globe, then I have a just claim to the use of any particular piece of land in Peru. If this claim is sold, whoever lays hands on the proceeds and deposits them in the Peruvian treasury is a robber. But nearly every Single Taxer says that such a course as this ought to be followed, and hence nearly every Single Taxer is an advocate of robbery.

Bear in mind that I claim no right to any part of the earth. But a right to every part of it is asserted for me by the Single Taxers. The objection that I am now urging is to their use of their own assertion that a certain thing is mine as a foundation for stealing it from me. Their doctrine may be summed up in three words: Property justifies robbery. Proudhon's paradox is eclipsed.

Mr. Bolton Hall has expressed the opinion that I am increasingly worried as to the Single Tax. Well, Mr. Hall, you are right. I *am* worried as to the Single Tax,—not "increasingly," but worried to the extent that I have been ever since "Progress and Poverty" made its appearance. Whenever an intelligent man announces a purpose to tyrannize by force over peaceable folk, it worries me. And it especially worries me when a dishonest man like Henry George uses the pull of hypocritical piety, and an honest man like G. F. Stephens uses the pull of high moral appeal, to induce others to join them in their criminal effort to forcibly take from men the products of their labor. Every form of authority worries me, every *attempt* at authority worries me. State Socialism worries me, Prohibition worries me, Comstockism worries me, the custom houses worry me, the banking monopoly worries me, landlordism worries me, and the Single Tax worries me. Do you suppose for a moment, Mr. Hall, that, if these things did not worry me, I should be publishing *Liberty?* Why, my good sir, I am bending all my energies to the thwarting of you and all others who propose, from whatever sincere and generous motives, to enforce their will upon non-invasive people. You worry me; indeed you do. I wish most heartily that you would let me and other peaceable people alone, abandon your menacing attitude toward our property, and quit worrying us, so that we might go about our business.

So much for the charge of worry, which Mr. Hall used as an introduction to a complaint against me for printing, and against Mr. Yarros for writing, an article containing the following passages: "Wherever it is profitable to improve land, it is generally improved without the compulsion of the Single Tax"; "How would the Single Tax help labor in England, Scotland, Ireland, Germany, Italy, and France? There is no land speculation in those countries worth mentioning." With Mr. Hall's objections to these passages I do not propose to deal elaborately; perhaps Mr. Yarros will do so later. But, in vindication of myself, I may say that to point out vacant lots does not overthrow Mr. Yarros's statement that *generally* that land is improved which it is profitable to improve, and that to point to instances of land speculation in European countries does not overthrow Mr. Yarros's other statement that land speculation in Europe is so much less frequent than in newer countries that it is not worth mentioning. The comparative and qualified statements of Mr. Yarros are construed by Mr. Hall into positive and sweeping ones, and then criticized as such. Mr. Yarros's claims amount simply to this,—that land speculation is an overrated evil even in this country, and that in older countries, where the land question is much more serious than here, speculation in land is so small an element in the problem that it may be neglected. Mr. Hall's surprise that I should print such statements is paralleled by my surprise at his hasty and careless reading of them.

It appears further from Mr. Hall's letter that the Single Taxers propose first to capture Delaware, and then to capture the Anarchists. Like the theatrical manager who prefers to test his new play in a country town before making a venture in the city, the Single Taxers will begin by "trying it on a dog." If they succeed with the dog, then they will accept our challenge. Our chances for a fight would be very bad, were it not that the dog, instead of giving bark for bark, is snapping at the Single Taxers' heels. If Delaware continues to send Single Taxers to the lock-up, there is a bare chance that Delaware will be captured through its own stupidity, and then the Anarchists' innings will begin. In view of Mr. Hall's honest admission that the Single Taxers are less intelligent than the Anarchists, the promised attempt of the less to swallow the greater is indicative of more valor than discretion. It is one thing for the less to worry the greater; it is quite another to swallow it.

METHODS

REFUSAL TO PAY RENT

In the matter of freeing the land, no less than in the other aspects of liberty, has there been a constant clamor for an explanation of the means to be adopted to secure the ends aimed at. It is notorious that, at one time, the Irish Land League had the landlords whipped if the League had had but sense and courage enough to follow up its advantage. It was not difficult, therefore, for the editor of *Liberty* to find conspicuous instances of an effective method of securing results, as he here pointed out:

IRELAND's chief danger: the liability of her people—besotted with superstition; trampled on by tyranny; ground into the dust beneath the weight of two despotisms, one religious, the other political; victims, on the one hand, of as cruel a Church and, on the other, of as heartless a State as have ever blackened with ignorance or reddened with blood the records of civilized nations—to forget the wise advice of their cooler leaders, give full vent to the passions which their oppressors are aiming to foment, and rush headlong and blindly into riotous and ruinous revolution.

Ireland's true order: the wonderful Land League, the nearest approach, on a large scale, to perfect Anarchistic organization that the world has yet seen. An immense number of local groups, scattered over large sections of two continents separated by three thousand miles of ocean; each group autonomous, each free; each composed of varying numbers of individuals of all ages, sexes, races, equally autonomous and free; each inspired by a common, central purpose; each supported entirely by voluntary contributions; each obeying its own judgment; each guided in the formation of its judgment and the choice of its conduct by the advice of a central council of picked men, having no power to enforce its orders except that inherent in the convincing logic of the reasons on which the orders are based; all coördinated and federated, with a minimum of machinery and without sacrifice of spontaneity, into a vast working unit, whose unparalleled power makes tyrants tremble and armies of no avail.

Ireland's shortest road to success: no payment of rent now *or hereafter;* no payment of compulsory taxes now or hereafter; utter disregard of the British parliament and its so-called laws; entire abstention from the polls henceforth; rigorous but non-invasive "boycotting" of deserters, cowards, traitors, and oppressors; vigorous, intelligent, fearless prosecution of the land agitation by voice and pen; passive but stubborn resistance to every offensive act of police or military; and, above all, universal readiness to go to prison, and promptness in filling the places made vacant by those who may be sent to prison. Open revolution, terrorism, and the policy above outlined, which is Liberty, are the three courses from which Ireland now must choose one. Open revolution on the battle-field means sure defeat and another century of misery and oppression; terrorism, though preferable to revolution, means years of demoralizing intrigue, bloody plot, base passion, and terrible revenges,—in short, all the horrors of a long-continued national vendetta, with a doubtful issue at the end; Liberty means certain, unhalting, and comparatively bloodless victory, the dawn of the sun of justice, and perpetual peace and prosperity for a hitherto blighted land.

To the editor of the San Francisco *People*, Anarchism is evidently a new and puzzling doctrine. It having been propounded by an Anarchist from a public platform in that city that Anarchism must come about by peaceful methods and that physical force is never justifiable except in self-defense, the *People* declares that, except physical force, it can see but two methods of settling the labor question: one the voluntary surrender of privileges by the privileged class, which it thinks ridiculous, and the other the ballot, which it rightly describes as another form of force. Therefore the *People*, supposing itself forced to choose between persuasion, the ballot, and direct physical force, selects the last. If I were forced to the alternative of leaving a question unsettled or attempting one of three ineffectual means of settling it, I think I should leave it unsettled. It would seem the wiser course to accept the situation. But the situation is not so hopeless. There is a fourth method of settling the difficulty, of which the *People* seems never to have heard,—the method of passive resistance, the most potent weapon ever wielded by man against oppression. Power feeds on its spoils, and dies when its victims refuse to be despoiled. They can't persuade it to death; they can't vote it to death; they can't shoot it to death; but they can always starve it to death. When a determined body of people, sufficiently strong in numbers and force of character to command respect and make it unsafe to imprison them, shall agree to quietly close their doors in the faces of the tax-collector and the rent-collector, and shall, by issuing their own money in defiance of legal prohibition, at the same time cease paying tribute to the money-lord, government, with all the privileges which it grants and the monopolies which it sustains, will go by the board. Does the *People* think this impracticable? I call its attention, then, to the vast work that was done six years ago in Ireland by the old Irish Land League, in defiance of perhaps the most powerful government on earth, simply by shutting the door in the face of the rent-collector alone. Within a few short months from the inauguration of the "No-Rent" policy landlordry found itself upon the verge of dissolution. It was at its wits end. Confronted by this intangible power, it knew not what to do. It wanted nothing so much as to madden the stubborn peasantry into becoming an actively belligerent mob which could be mowed down with Gatling guns. But, barring a paltry outbreak here and there, it was impossible to goad the farmers out of their quiescence, and the grip of the landlords grew weaker every day.

"Ah! but the movement failed," I can hear the *People* reply. Yes, it did fail; and why? Because the peasants were acting, not intelligently in obedience to their wisdom, but blindly in obedience to leaders who betrayed them at the critical moment. Thrown into jail by the government, these leaders, to secure their release, withdrew the "No-Rent Manifesto," which they had issued in the first place not with any intention of freeing the peasants from the burden of an "immoral tax," but simply to make them the tools of their political advancement. Had the people realized the power they were exercising and understood the economic situation, they would not have resumed the payment of rent at Parnell's bidding, and today they might have been free. The Anarchists do not propose to repeat their mistake. That is why they are devoting themselves entirely to the inculcation of principles, especially of economic principles. In steadfastly pursuing this course regardless of clamor, they alone are laying a sure foundation for the success of the revolution, though to the *People* of San Francisco, and to all people who are in such a devil of a hurry that they can't stop to think, they seem to be doing nothing at all.

III—TRADE AND INDUSTRY

THE ATTITUDE OF ANARCHISM TOWARD INDUSTRIAL COMBINATIONS

FROM September 13 to 16, 1899, the Civic Federation held a Conference on Trusts, in Chicago, before which it invited about one hundred individuals from every walk of life and of various political and economic beliefs to discuss the question of trusts from every angle. Mr. Tucker was one of those invited to address the assembly, and his paper, which is here reproduced in full, excited more interest and comment, according to the newspaper accounts at the time, than the remarks of any other speaker at the conference:

HAVING to deal very briefly with the problem with which the so-called trusts confront us, I go at once to the heart of the subject, taking my stand on these propositions: That the right to coöperate is as unquestionable as the right to compete; that the right to compete involves the right to refrain from competition; that coöperation is often a method of competition, and that competition is always, in the larger view, a method of coöperation; that each is a legitimate, orderly, non-invasive exercise of the individual will under the social law of equal liberty; and that any man or institution attempting to prohibit or restrict either, by legislative enactment or by any form of invasive force, is, in so far as such man or institution may fairly be judged by such attempt, an enemy of liberty, an enemy of progress, an enemy of society, and an enemy of the human race.

Viewed in the light of these irrefutable propositions, the trust, then, like every other industrial combination endeavoring to do collectively nothing but what each member of the combination rightfully may endeavor to do individually, is *per se*, an unimpeachable institution. To assail or control or deny this form of coöperation on the ground that it is itself a denial of competition is an absurdity. It is an absurdity, because it proves too much. The trust is a denial of competition in no other sense than that in which competition itself is a denial of competition. The trust denies competition only by producing and selling more cheaply than those outside of the trust can produce and sell; but in that sense every successful individual competitor also denies competition. And if the trust is to be suppressed for such denial of competition, then the very competition in the name of which the trust is to be suppressed must itself be suppressed also. I repeat: the argument proves too much. The fact is that there is one denial of competition which is the right of all, and that there is another denial of competition which is the right of none. All of us, whether out of a trust or in it, have a right to deny competition by competing, but none of us, whether in a trust or out of it, have a right to deny competition by arbitrary decree, by interference with voluntary effort, by forcible suppression of initiative.

Again: To claim that the trust should be abolished or controlled because the great resources and consequent power of endurance which it acquires by combination give it an undue advantage, and thereby enable it to crush competition, is equally an argument that proves too much. If John D. Rockefeller were to start a grocery store in his individual capacity, we should not think of suppressing or restricting or hampering his enterprise simply because, with his five hundred millions, he could afford to sell groceries at less than cost until the day when the accumulated ruins of all other grocery stores should afford him a sure foundation for a profitable business. But, if Rockefeller's possession of five hundred millions is not a good ground for the suppression of his grocery store, no better ground is the control of still greater wealth for the suppression of his oil trust. It is true that these vast accumulations under one control are abnormal and dangerous, but the reasons for them lie outside of and behind and beneath all trusts and industrial combinations,—reasons which I shall come to presently,—reasons which are all, in some form or other, an arbitrary denial of liberty; and, but for these reasons, but for these denials of liberty, John D. Rockefeller never could have acquired five hundred millions, nor would any combination of men be able to control an aggregation of wealth that could not be easily and successfully met by some other combination of men.

Again: There is no warrant in reason for deriving a right to control trusts from the State grant of corporate privileges under which they are organized. In the first place, it being pure usurpation to presume to endow any body of men with rights and exemptions that are not theirs already under the social law of equal liberty, corporate privileges are in themselves a wrong; and one wrong is not to be undone by attempting to offset it with another. But, even admitting the justice of corporation charters, the avowed purpose in granting them is to encourage coöperation, and thus stimulate industrial and commercial development for the benefit of the community. Now, to make this encouragement an excuse for its own nullification by a proportionate restriction of coöperation would be to add one more to those interminable imitations of the task of Sisyphus for which that stupid institution which we call the State has ever been notorious.

Of somewhat the same nature, but rather more plausible at first blush, is the proposition to cripple the trusts by stripping them of those law-created privileges and monopolies which are conferred, not upon trusts as corporate bodies, but upon sundry individuals and interests, ostensibly for protection of the producer and inventor, but really for purposes of plunder, and which most trusts acquire in the process of merging the original capitals of their constituent members. I refer, of course, to tariffs, patents, and copyrights. Now, tariffs, patents, and copyrights either have their foundations in justice, or they have not their foundations in justice. If they have their foundations in justice, why should men guilty of nothing but a legitimate act of coöperation and partnership be punished therefor by having their just rights taken from them? If they have not their foundations in justice, why should men who refrain from coöperation be left in possession of unjust privileges that are denied to men who coöperate? If tariffs are unjust, they should not be levied at all. If patents and copyrights are unjust, they should not be granted to anyone whomsoever. But, if tariffs and patents and copyrights are just, they should be levied or granted in the interest of all who are entitled to their benefits from the viewpoint of the motives in which these privileges have their origin, and to make such levy or grant dependent upon any foreign motive, such, for instance, as willingness to refrain from coöperation, would be sheer impertinence.

Nevertheless, at this point in the hunt for the solution of the trust problem, the discerning student may begin to realize that he is hot on the trail. The thought arises that the trusts, instead of growing out of competition, as is so generally supposed, have been made possible only by the absence of competition, only by the difficulty of competition, only by the obstacles placed in the way of competition,—only, in short, by those arbitrary limitations of competition which we find in those law created privileges and monopolies of which I have just spoken, and in one or two others, less direct, but still more far-reaching and deadly in their destructive influence upon enterprise. And it is with this thought that Anarchism, the doctrine that in all matters there should be the greatest amount of individual liberty compatible with equality of liberty, approaches the case in hand, and offers its diagnosis and its remedy.

The first and great fact to be noted in the case, I have already hinted at. It is the fact that the trusts owe their power to vast accumulation and concentration of wealth, unmatched, and, under present conditions, unmatchable, by any equal accumulation of wealth, and that this accumulation of wealth has been effected by the combination of several accumulations only less vast and in themselves already gigantic, each of which owed its existence to one or more of the only means by which large fortunes can be rolled up,—interest, rent, and monopolistic profit. But for interest, rent, and monopolistic profit, therefore, trusts would be impossible. Now, what causes interest, rent, and monopolistic profit? For all there is but one cause,—the denial of liberty, the suppression or restriction of competition, the legal creation of monopolies.

This single cause, however, takes various shapes.

Monopolistic profit is due to that denial of liberty which takes the shape of patent, copyright, and tariff legislation, patent and copyright laws directly forbidding competition, and tariff laws placing competition at a fatal disadvantage.

Rent is due to that denial of liberty which takes the shape of land monopoly, vesting titles to land in individuals and associations which do not use it, and thereby compelling the non-owning users to pay tribute to the non-using owners as a condition of admission to the competitive market.

Interest is due to that denial of liberty which takes the shape of money monopoly, depriving all individuals and associations, save such as hold a certain kind of property, of the right to issue promissory notes as currency, and thereby compelling all holders of property other than the kind thus privileged, as well as all non-proprietors, to pay tribute to the holders of the privileged property for the use of a circulating medium and instrument of credit which, in the complex stage that industry and commerce have now reached, has become the chief essential of a competitive market.

Now, Anarchism, which, as I have said, is the doctrine that in all matters there should be the greatest amount of individual liberty compatible with equality of liberty, finds that none of these denials of liberty are necessary to the maintenance of equality of liberty, but that each and every one of them, on the contrary, is destructive of equality of liberty. Therefore it declares them unnecessary, arbitrary, oppressive, and unjust, and demands their immediate cessation.

Of these four monopolies—the banking monopoly, the land monopoly, the tariff monopoly, and the patent and copyright monopoly—the injustice of all but the last-named is manifest even to a child. The right of the individual to buy and sell without being held up by a highwayman whenever he crosses an imaginary line called a frontier; the right of the individual to take possession of unoccupied land as freely as he takes possession of unoccupied water or unoccupied air; the right of the individual to give his I O U, in any shape whatsoever, under any guarantee whatsoever, or under no guarantee at all, to anyone willing to accept it in exchange for something else,—all these rights are too clear for argument, and any one presuming to dispute them simply declares thereby his despotic and imperialistic instincts.

For the fourth of these monopolies, however,—the patent and copyright monopoly,—a more plausible case can be presented, for the question of property in ideas is a very subtle one. The defenders of such property set up an analogy between the production of material things and the production of abstractions, and on the strength of it declare that the manufacturer of mental products, no less than the manufacturer of material products, is a laborer worthy of his hire. So far, so good. But, to make out their case, they are obliged to go further, and to claim, in violation of their own analogy, that the laborer who creates mental products, unlike the laborer who creates material products, is entitled to exemption from competition. Because the Lord, in his wisdom, or the Devil, in his malice, has so arranged matters that the inventor and the author produce naturally at a disadvantage, man, in his might, proposes to supply the divine or diabolic deficiency by an artificial arrangement that shall not only destroy this disadvantage, but actually give the inventor and author an advantage that no other laborer enjoys,—an advantage, moreover, which, in practice, goes, not to the inventor and the author, but to the promoter and the publisher and the trust.

Convincing as the argument for property in ideas may seem at first hearing, if you think about it long enough, you will begin to be suspicious. The first thing, perhaps, to arouse your suspicion will be the fact that none of the champions of such property propose the punishment of those who violate it, contenting themselves with subjecting the offenders to the risk of damage suits, and that nearly all of them are willing that even the risk of suit shall disappear when the proprietor has enjoyed his right for a certain number of years. Now, if, as the French writer, Alphonse Karr, remarked, property in ideas is a property like any other property, then its violation, like the violation of any other property, deserves criminal punishment, and its life, like that of any other property, should be secure in right against the lapse of time. And, this not being claimed by the upholders of property in ideas, the suspicion arises that such a lack of the courage of their convictions may be due to an instinctive feeling that they are wrong.

The necessity of being brief prevents me from examining this phase of my subject in detail. Therefore I must content myself with developing a single consideration, which, I hope, will prove suggestive.

I take it that, if it were possible, and if it had always been possible, for an unlimited number of individuals to use to an unlimited extent and in an unlimited number of places the same concrete things at the same time, there never would have been any such thing as the institution of property. Under those circumstances the idea of property would never have entered the human mind, or, at any rate, if it had, would have been summarily dismissed as too gross an absurdity to be seriously entertained for a moment. Had it been possible for the concrete creation or adaptation resulting from the efforts of a single individual to be used contemporaneously by all individuals, including the creator or adapter, the realization, or impending realization, of this possibility, far from being seized upon as an excuse for a law to prevent the use of this concrete thing without the consent of its creator or adapter, and far from being guarded against as an injury to one, would have been welcomed as a blessing to all,—in short, would have been viewed as a most fortunate element in the nature of things. The *raison d'être* of property is found in the very fact that there is no such possibility,—in the fact that it is impossible in the nature of things for concrete objects to be used in different places at the same time. This fact existing, no person can remove from another's possession and take to his own use another's concrete creation without thereby depriving that other of all opportunity to use that which he created, and for this reason it became socially necessary, since successful society rests on individual initiative, to protect the individual creator in the use of his concrete creations by forbidding others to use them without his consent. In other words, it became necessary to institute property in concrete things.

But all this happened so long ago that we of today have entirely forgotten why it happened. In fact, it is very doubtful whether, at the time of the institution of property, those who effected it thoroughly realized and understood the motive of their course. Men sometimes do by instinct and without analysis that which conforms to right reason. The institutors of property may have been governed by circumstances inhering in the nature of things, without realizing that, had the nature of things been the opposite, they would not have instituted property. But, be that as it may, even supposing that they thoroughly understod their course, we, at any rate, have pretty nearly forgotten their understanding. And so it has come about that we have made of property a fetich; that we consider it a sacred thing; that we have set up the god of property on an altar as an object of idol-worship; and that most of us are not only doing what we can to strengthen and perpetuate his reign within the proper and original limits of his sovereignty, but also are mistakenly endeavoring to extend his dominion over things and under circumstances which, in their pivotal characteristic, are precisely the opposite of those out of which his power developed.

All of which is to say in briefer compass, that from the justice and social necessity of property in concrete things we have erroneously assumed the justice and social necessity of property in abstract things,—that is, of property in ideas,—with the result of nullifying to a large and lamentable extent that fortunate element in the nature of things, in this case not hypothetical, but real,—namely, the immeasurably fruitful possibility of the use of abstract things by any number of individuals in any number of places at precisely the same time, without in the slightest degree impairing the use thereof by any single individual. Thus we have hastily and stupidly jumped to the conclusion that property in concrete things logically implies property in abstract things, whereas, if we had had the care and the keenness to accurately analyze, we should have found that the very reason which dictates the advisability of property in concrete things denies the advisability of property in abstract things. We see here a curious instance of that frequent mental phenomenon,—the precise inversion of the truth by a superficial view.

Furthermore, were the conditions the same in both cases, and concrete things capable of use by different persons in different places at the same time, even then, I say, the institution of property in concrete things, though under those conditions manifestly absurd, would be infinitely less destructive of individual opportunities, and therefore infinitely less dangerous and detrimental to human welfare, than is the institution of property in abstract things. For it is easy to see that, even should we accept the rather startling hypothesis that a single ear of corn is continually and permanently consumable, or rather inconsumable, by an indefinite number of persons

scattered over the surface of the earth, still the legal institution of property in concrete things that would secure to the
sower of a grain of corn the exclusive use of the resultant
ear would not, in so doing, deprive other persons of the right
to sow other grains of corn and become exclusive users of their
respective harvests; whereas the legal institution of property
in abstract things not only secures to the inventor, say, of the
steam engine the exclusive use of the engines which he actually makes, but at the same time deprives all other persons of
the right to make for themselves other engines involving any
of the same ideas. Perpetual property in ideas, then, which
is the logical outcome of any theory of property in abstract
things, would, had it been in force in the lifetime of James
Watt, have made his direct heirs the owners of at least nine-
tenths of the now existing wealth of the world; and, had it
been in force in the lifetime of the inventor of the Roman
alphabet, nearly all the highly civilized peoples of the earth
would be today the virtual slaves of that inventor's heirs,
which is but another way of saying that, instead of becoming
highly civilized, they would have remained in the state of
semi-barbarism. It seems to me that these two statements,
which in my view are incontrovertible, are in themselves sufficient to condemn property in ideas forever.

If then, the four monopolies to which I have referred are
unnecessary denials of liberty, and therefore unjust denials of
liberty, and if they are the sustaining causes of interest, rent,
and monopolistic profit, and if, in turn, this usurious trinity
is the cause of all vast accumulations of wealth,—for further
proof of which propositions I must, because of the limitations
of my time, refer you to the economic writings of the Anarchistic school,—it clearly follows that the adequate solution
of the problem with which the trusts confront us is to be
found only in abolition of these monopolies and the consequent guarantee of perfectly free competition.

The most serious of these four monopolies is unquestionably
the money monoply, and I believe that perfect freedom in
finance alone would wipe out nearly all the trusts, or at least
render them harmless, and perhaps helpful. Mr. Bryan told
a very important truth when he declared that the destruction
of the money trust would at the same time kill all the other
trusts. Unhappily, Mr. Bryan does not propose to destroy the

money trust. He wishes simply to transform it from a gold trust into a gold and silver trust. The money trust cannot be destroyed by the remonetization of silver. That would be only a mitigation of the monopoly, not the abolishment of it. It can be abolished only by monetizing all wealth that has a market value,—that is, by giving to all wealth the right of representation by currency, and to all currency the right to circulate wherever it can on its own merits. And this is not only a solution of the trust question, but the first step that should be taken, and the greatest single step that can be taken, in economic and social reform.

I have tried, in the few minutes allotted to me, to state concisely the attitude of Anarchism toward industrial combinations. It discountenances all direct attacks on them, all interference with them, all anti-trust legislation whatsoever. In fact, it regards industrial combinations as very useful whenever they spring into existence in response to demand created in a healthy social body. If at present they are baneful, it is because they are symptoms of a social disease originally caused and persistently aggravated by a regimen of tyranny and quackery. Anarchism wants to call off the quacks, and give liberty, nature's great cure-all, a chance to do its perfect work.

Free access to the world of matter, abolishing land monopoly; free access to the world of mind, abolishing idea monopoly; free access to an untaxed and unprivileged market, abolishing tariff monopoly and money monopoly,—secure these, and all the rest shall be added unto you. For liberty is the remedy of every social evil, and to Anarchy the world must look at last for any enduring guarantee of social order.

STRIKES AND FORCE

In the famous Homestead Strike, the rights and interests of both capital and labor were so intermingled and jumbled in the discussions in the daily press that it was difficult for the man on the street to form an impartial opinion; it was not easy even for the student of sociology to reach a rational conclusion. So the editor of *Liberty* stepped into the fray to reprove one of the most vicious of the muddlers:

REGARDING methods, one of the truths that has been most steadily inculcated by this journal has been that social questions cannot be settled by force. Recent events have only confirmed this view. But when force comes, it sometimes leads incidentally to the teaching of other lessons than that of its own uselessness and becomes thereby to that extent useful. The appeal to force at Homestead affords a signal example of such incidental beneficence; for it has forced the capitalistic papers of the country, and notably the New York *Sun*, to take up a bold defense of liberty in order to protect property. Now, all that Anarchism asks is liberty; and when the enemies of liberty can find no way of saving their own interests except by an appeal to liberty, *Liberty* means to make a note of it and hold them to it.

Applied to the conduct of the Homestead strikers, this principle of equal liberty, of which the *Sun's* words are an expression, instead of condemning it as the *Sun* pretends, palliates and even excuses it; for, before these strikers violated the equal liberty of others, their own right to equality of liberty had been wantonly and continuously violated. But, applied to the conduct of capitalists generally, it condemns it utterly, for the original violation of liberty in this matter is traceable directly to them.

This is no wild assertion, but a sober statement of fact, as I will explain. It is not enough, however true, to say that, "if a man has labor to sell, he must find some one with money to buy it"; it is necessary to add the much more important truth that, if a man has labor to sell, he has a right to a free market in which to sell it,—a market in which no one shall be prevented by restrictive laws from honestly obtaining the money to buy it. If the man with labor to sell has not this free market, then his liberty is violated and his property virtually taken from him. Now, such a market has constantly been denied, not only to the laborers at Homestead, but to the laborers of the entire civilized world. And the men who have denied it are the Andrew Carnegies. Capitalists of whom this

Pittsburg forge-master is a typical representative have placed and kept upon the statute-books all sorts of prohibitions and taxes (of which the customs tariff is among the least harmful) designed to limit and effective in limiting the number of bidders for the labor of those who have labor to sell. If there were no tariffs on imported goods; if titles to unoccupied land were not recognized by the State; above all, if the right to issue money were not vested in a monopoly,—bidders for the labor of Carnegie's employees would become so numerous that the offer would soon equal the laborer's product. Now, to solemnly tell these men who are thus prevented by law from getting the wages which their labor would command in a free market that they have a right to reject any price that may be offered for their labor is undoubtedly to speak a formal truth, but it is also to utter a rotten commonplace and a cruel impertinence. Rather tell the capitalists that the laborer is entitled to a free market, and that they, in denying it to him, are guilty of criminal invasion. This would be not only a formal truth, but an opportune application of a vital principle.

Perhaps it will be claimed in answer to this that the laborers, being voters, are responsible for any monopolies that exist, and are thereby debarred from pleading them as an excuse for violating the liberty of their employers. This is only true to the extent to which we may consider these laborers as the "fools" persuaded by the capitalists who are the "scoundrels" that "violence (in the form of enforced monopoly) is a friend of the workmen"; which does not make it less unbecoming in the scoundrels to rebuke and punish the fools for any disastrous consequences that may arise out of this appalling combination of scoundrelism and folly.

Conspicuous among the scoundrels who have upheld these monopolies is the editor of the New York *Sun*. If he tells truth to-day, he tells it as the devil quotes scripture,—to suit his purpose. He will never consent to an application of equal liberty in the interest of labor, for he belongs to the brotherhood of thieves who prey upon labor. If he only would, we Anarchists would meet him with cheerful acquiescence in its fullest application to the interest of capital. Let Carnegie, Dana & Co. first see to it that every law in violation of equal liberty is removed from the statute-books. If, after that, any laborers shall interfere with the rights of their employers, or shall use force upon inoffensive "scabs," or shall attack their employers' watchmen, whether these be Pinkerton detectives, sheriff's deputies, or the State militia, I pledge myself that, as an Anarchist and in consequence of my Anarchistic faith, I will be among the first to volunteer as a member of a force to repress these disturbers of order and, if necessary, sweep them from the earth. But while these invasive laws remain, I must view every forcible conflict that arises as the consequence of an original violation of liberty on the part of the employing classes, and, if any sweeping is done, may the laborers hold the broom! Still, while my sympathies thus go with the under dog, I shall never cease to proclaim my conviction that the annihilation of neither party can secure justice, and that the only effective sweeping will be that which clears from the statute-book every restriction of the freedom of the market.

Of the multitude of novel and absurd and monstrous suggestions called forth from the newspapers by the telegraphers' strike, none have equalled in novelty and absurdity and monstrosity the sober proposal of the editor of the New York *Nation*, that unsentimental being who prides himself on his hard head, that hereafter any and all employees of telegraph companies, railroad companies, and the post-office department who may see fit to strike work without first getting the consent of their employers be treated as are soldiers who desert or decline to obey the commands of their superior officers; in other words (we suppose, though the *Nation* does not use these other words), that they may be summarily court-martialled and shot.

During the rebellion, when all of us, except the much-abused "copperheads," temporarily lost control of our reasoning faculties (we dare say that even the editor of the *Nation* at that time forgot himself and became sentimental for once), we got very angry with Carlyle for patly putting the American Iliad in a nutshell and epigrammatically establishing the substantial similarity between the condition of slave labor at the South and that of so-called "free" labor at the North. England's blunt old sham-hater was answered with much boisterous declamation about "freedom of contract," and his attention was proudly called to the fact that the laborer of the

North could follow his own sweet will, leaving his employer when he saw fit, attaching himself to any other willing to hire him, or, if he preferred, setting up in business for himself and employing others. He was at liberty, it was loudly proclaimed by our abolitionists and free-traders, to work when he pleased, where he pleased, how he pleased, and on what terms he pleased, and no man could say him nay. What are we to think, then, when the chief newspaper exponent of the "freedom of contract" philosophy deliberately sacrifices the only answer that it could make to Carlyle's indictment by proposing the introduction of a military discipline into industry, which, in assimilating the laborer to the soldier, would make him—what the soldier is—a slave? Think? Simply this,—that the hypocritical thieves and tyrants who for years have been endeavoring to make their victims believe themselves freemen see that the game is nearly up, and that the time is fast approaching when they must take by the horns the bull of outraged industry, which, maddened by the discovery of its hitherto invisible chains, is making frantic efforts to burst them it knows not how. It is a point gained. An enemy in the open field is less formidable than one in ambush. When the capitalists shall be forced to show their true colors, the laborers will then know against whom they are fighting.

Fighting, did we say? Yes. For the laborer in these days *is* a soldier, though not in the sense which the *Nation* meant. His employer is not, as the *Nation* would have it, his superior officer, but simply a member of an opposing army. The whole industrial and commercial world is in a state of internecine war, in which the prolétaires are massed on one side and the proprietors on the other. This is the fact that justifies strikers in subjecting society to what the *Nation* calls a "partial paralysis." It is a war measure. The laborer sees that he does not get his due. He knows that the capitalists have been intrusted by society, through its external representative, the State, with privileges which enable them to control production and distribution; and that, in abuse of these privileges, they have seen to it that the demand for labor should fall far below the supply, and have then taken advantage of the necessities of the laborer and reduced his wages. The laborer and his fellows, therefore, resort to the policy of uniting in such numbers in a refusal to work at the reduced rate that the demand for labor becomes very much greater than the supply, and then they take advantage of the necessities of the capitalists and society to secure a restoration of the old rate of wages, and perhaps an increase upon it. Be the game fair or foul, two can play at it; and those who begin it should not complain when they get the worst of it. If society objects to being "paralyzed," it can very easily avoid it. All it needs to do is to adopt the advice which *Liberty* has long been offering it, and withdraw from the monopolists the privileges which it has granted them. Then, as Colonel William B. Greene has shown in his "Mutual Banking," as Lysander Spooner has shown in his works on finance, and as Proudhon has shown in his "Organization of Credit," capital will no longer be tied up by syndicates, but will become readily available for investment on easy terms; productive enterprise, taking new impetus, will soon assume enormous proportions; the work to be done will always surpass the number of laborers to do it; and, instead of the employers being able to say to the laborers, as the unsentimental *Nation* would like to have them, "Take what we offer you, or the troops shall be called out to shoot you down," the laborers will be able to say to their employers, "If you desire our services, you must give us in return an equivalent of their product,"—terms which the employers will be only too glad to accept. Such is the only solution of the problem of strikes, such the only way to turn the edge of Carlyle's biting satire.

LABOR AND ITS PAY

Communists and State Socialists on the one hand and Anarchists and Individualists on the other will never be able to agree on the question of wages, because the reward of labor represents one of the fundamental differences between them. Here is a specimen of the eternal controversy, from the pen of Mr. Tucker:

In No. 121 of *Liberty*, criticising an attempt of Kropotkine to identify Communism and Individualism, I charged him with ignoring "the real question of whether Communism will permit the individual to labor independently, own tools, sell his labor or his products, and buy the labor or products of others." In Herr Most's eyes this is so outrageous that, in reprinting it, he puts the words "the labor of others" in large black type. Most being a Communist, he must, to be consistent, object to the purchase and sale of anything whatever; but why he should particularly object to the purchase and sale of labor is more than I can understand. Really, in the last analysis, labor is the only thing that has any title to be bought or sold. Is there any just basis of price except cost? And is there anything that costs except labor or suffering (another name for labor)? Labor should be paid! Horrible, isn't it? Why, I thought that the fact that it is not paid was the whole grievance. "Unpaid labor" has been the chief complaint of all Socialists, and that labor should get its reward has been their chief contention. Suppose I had said to Kropotkine that the real question is whether Communism will permit individuals to exchange their labor or products on their own terms. Would Herr Most have been so shocked? Would he have printed that in black type? Yet in another form I said precisely that.

If the men who oppose wages—that is, the purchase and sale of labor—were capable of analyzing their thought and feelings, they would see that what really excites their anger is not the fact that labor is bought and sold, but the fact that one class of men are dependent for their living upon the sale of their labor, while another class of men are relieved of the necessity of labor by being legally privileged to sell something that is not labor, and that, but for the privilege, would be enjoyed by all gratuitously. And to such a state of things I am as much opposed as any one. But the minute you remove privilege, the class that now enjoy it will be forced to sell their labor, and then, when there will be nothing but labor with which to buy labor, the distinction between wage-payers and wage-receivers will be wiped out, and every man will be a laborer exchanging with fellow-laborers. Not to abolish wages, but to make *every* man dependent upon wages and secure to every man his *whole* wages is the aim of Anarchistic Socialism. What Anarchistic Socialism aims to abolish is usury. It does not want to deprive labor of its reward; it wants to deprive capital of its reward. It does not hold that labor should not be sold; it holds that capital should not be hired at usury.

But, says Herr Most, this idea of a free labor market from which privilege is eliminated is nothing but "consistent Manchesterism." Well, what better can a man who professes Anarchism want than that? For the principle of Manchesterism is liberty, and consistent Manchesterism is consistent adherence to liberty. The only inconsistency of the Manchester men lies in their infidelity to liberty in some of its phases. And this infidelity to liberty in some of its phases is precisely the fatal inconsistency of the *Freiheit* school,—the only difference between its adherents and the Manchester men being that in many of the phases in which the latter are infidel the former are faithful, while in many of those in which the latter are faithful the former are infidel. Yes, genuine Anarchism is consistent Manchesterism, and Communistic or pseudo-Anarchism is inconsistent Manchesterism. "I thank thee, Jew, for teaching me that word."

Kropotkine, arguing in favor of Communism, says that he has "always observed that workers with difficulty understand the possibility of a wage-system of labor-checks and like artificial inventions of Socialists," but has been "struck on the contrary by the easiness with which they always accept Communist principles." Was Kropotkine ever struck by the easiness with which simple-minded people accept the creation theory and the difficulty with which they understand the possibility of evolution? If so, did he ever use this fact as an argument in favor of the creation hypothesis? Just as it is easier to rest satisfied with the statement, "Male and female created he them," than to trace in the geological strata the intricacies in the evolution of species, so it is easier to say that every man shall have whatever he wants than to find the economic law by which every man may get the equivalent of his product. The ways of Faith are direct and easy to follow, but their goal is a quagmire; whereas the ways of Science, however devious and difficult to tread, lead to solid ground at last. Communism belongs to the Age of Faith, Anarchistic Socialism to the Age of Science.

THE POSTOFFICE AND PRIVATE MAIL SERVICE

THE Winsted *Press* makes a long leader to ridicule the Anarchists for favoring private enterprise in the letter-carrying business. It grounds its ridicule on two claims,—first, that private enterprise would charge high rates of postage, and, second, that it would not furnish transportation to out-of-the-way points. An indisputable fact has frequently been cited in *Liberty* which instantly and utterly overthrows both of these claims. Its frequent citation, however, has had no effect upon the believers in a government postal monopoly. I do not expect another repetition to produce any effect upon the Winsted *Press;* still I shall try it.

Some half-dozen years ago, when letter postage was still three cents, Wells, Fargo & Co. were doing a large business in carrying letters throughout the Pacific States and Territories. Their rate was five cents, more than three of which they expended, as the legal monopoly required, in purchasing of the United States a stamped envelope in which to carry the letter intrusted to their care. That is to say, on every letter which they carried they had to pay a tax of more than three cents. Exclusive of this tax, Wells, Fargo & Co. got less than two cents for each letter which they carried, while the government got three cents for each letter which it carried itself, and more than three cents for each letter which Wells, Fargo & Co. carried. On the other hand, it cost every individual five cents to send by Wells, Fargo & Co., and only three to send by the government. Moreover, the area covered was one in which immensity of distance, sparseness of population, and irregularities of surface made out-of-the-way points unusually difficult of access. Still, in spite of all these advantages on the side of the government, its patronage steadily dwindled, while that of Wells, Fargo & Co. as steadily grew. Pecuniarily this, of course, was a benefit to the government. But for this very reason such a condition of affairs was all the more mortifying. Hence the postmaster-general sent a special commissioner to investigate the matter. He fulfilled his duty and reported to his superior that Wells, Fargo & Co. were complying with the law in every particular, and were taking away the business of the government by furnishing a prompter and securer mail service, not alone to principal points, but to more points and remoter points than were included in the government list of post-offices.

Whether this state of things still continues I do not know. I presume, however, that it does, though the adoption of two-cent postage may have changed it. In either case the fact is one that triumphs over all possible sarcasms. In view of it, what becomes of Editor Pinney's fear of ruinous rates of postage and his philanthropic anxiety on account of the dwellers in Wayback and Hunkertown?

Appreciating the necessity of at least seeming to meet the indisputable fact which I opposed to its championship of government postal monopoly, the Winsted *Press* presents the following ghost of an answer, which may be as convincing to the victims of political superstition as most materializations are to the victims of religious superstition, but which, like those materializations, is so imperceptible to the touch of the hard-headed investigator that, when he puts his hand upon it, he does not find it there.

"The single instance of Wells, Fargo & Co., cited by B. R. Tucker to prove the advantage of private enterprise as a mail carrier, needs fuller explanation of correlated circumstances to show its true significance. As stated by Mr. Tucker, this company half a dozen years ago did a large business carrying letters throughout the Pacific States and Territories to distant and sparsely populated places for five cents per letter, paying more than three to the government in compliance with postal law and getting less than two for the trouble, and, though it cost the senders more, the service was enough better than government's to secure the greater part of the business."

This restatement of my statement is fair enough, except that it but dimly conveys the idea that Wells, Fargo & Co. were carrying, not only to distant and sparsely populated places, but to places thickly settled and easy of access, and were beating the government there also,—a fact of no little importance.

"Several facts may explain this: 1. Undeveloped government service in a new country, distant from the seat of government."

Here the ghost appears, all form and no substance. "John Jones is a better messenger than John Smith," declares the Winsted *Press*, "because Jones can run over stony ground, while Smith cannot." "Indeed!" I answer; "why, then, did Smith outrun Jones the other day in going from San Francisco to Wayback?" "Oh! that may be explained," the *Press* rejoins, "by the fact that the ground was stony." The *Press* had complained against the Anarchistic theory of free competition in postal service that private enterprise would not reach remote points, while government does reach them. I proved by facts that private enterprise was more successful than government in reaching remote points. What sense, then, is there in answering that these points are distant from the government's headquarters and that it had not developed its service? The whole point lies in the fact that private enterprise was the first to develop its service and the most successful in maintaining it at a high degree of efficiency.

"2. Government competition which kept Wells, Fargo from charging monopoly prices."

If the object of a government postal service is to keep private enterprise from charging high prices, no more striking illustration of the stupid way in which government works to achieve its objects could be cited than its imposition of a tax of two (then three) cents a letter upon private postal companies. It is obvious that this tax was all that kept Wells, Fargo & Co. from reducing their letter-rate to three or even two cents, in which case the government probably would have lost the remnant of business which it still commanded. This is guarding against monopoly prices with a vengeance! The competitor, whether government or individual, who must tax his rival in order to live is no competitor at all, but a monopolist himself. It is not government competition that Anarchists are fighting, but government monopoly. It should be added, however, that, pending the transformation of governments into voluntary associations, even government competition is unfair, because an association supported by compulsory taxation could always, if it chose, carry the mails at less than cost and tax the deficit out of the people.

"3. Other paying business which brought the company into contact with remote districts and warranted greater safeguards to conveyance than government then offered to its mail carriers."

Exactly. What does it prove? Why, that postal service and express service can be most advantageously run in conjunction, and that private enterprise was the first to find it out. This is one of the arguments which the Anarchists use.

"4. A difference of two cents was not appreciated in a country where pennies were unknown."

Here the phantom attains the last degree of attenuation. If Mr. Pinney will call at the Winsted post-office, his postmaster will tell—what common sense ought to have taught him—that of all the stamps used not over five per cent. are purchased singly, the rest being taken two, three, five, ten, a hundred, or a thousand at a time. Californians are said to be very reckless in the matter of petty expenditures, but I doubt if any large portion of them would carry their prodigality so far as to pay five dollars a hundred for stamps when they could get them at three dollars a hundred on the next corner.

"These conditions do not exist elsewhere in this country at present. Therefore the illustration proves nothing."

Proves nothing! Does it not prove that private enterprise outstripped the government under the conditions that then and there existed, which were difficult enough for both, but extraordinarily embarrassing for the former?

"We know that private enterprise does not afford express facilities to sparsely settled districts throughout the country."

I know nothing of the kind. The express companies cover practically the whole country. They charge high rates to points difficult of access; but this is only just. The government postal rates, on the contrary, are unjust. It certainly is not fair that my neighbor, who sends a hundred letters to New York every year, should have to pay two cents each on them, though the cost of carriage is but one cent, simply because the government spends a dollar in carrying for me one letter a year to Wayback, for which I also pay two cents. It may be said, however, that where each individual charge is so small, a schedule of rates would cause more trouble and expense than saving; in other words, that to keep books would be poor economy. Very likely; and in that case no one would find it out sooner than the private mail companies. This, however, is not the case in the express business, where parcels of all sizes and weights are carried.

"No more would it mail facilities. A remarkable exception only proves the rule. But, if private enterprise can and will do so much, why doesn't it do it now? The law stands no more in the way of Adams Express than it did in the way of the Wells & Fargo express."

This reminds me of the question with which Mr. Pinney closed his discussion with me regarding free money. He desired to know why the Anarchists did not start a free money system, saying that they ought to be shrewd enough to devise some way of evading the law. As if any competing business could be expected to succeed if it had to spend a fortune in contesting lawsuits or in paying a heavy tax to which its rival was not subject. So handicapped, it could not possibly succeed unless its work was of such a nature as to admit the widest range of variation in point of excellence. This was the case in the competition between Wells, Fargo & Co. and the government. The territory covered was so ill-adapted to postal facilities that it afforded a wide margin for the display of superiority, and Wells, Fargo & Co. took advantage of this to such an extent that they beat the government in spite of their handicap. But in the territory covered by Adams Express it is essentially different. There the postal service is so simple a matter that the possible margin of superiority would not warrant an extra charge of even one cent a letter. But I am told that Adams Express would be only too glad of the chance to carry letters at one cent each, if there were no tax to be paid on the business. If the governmentalists think that the United States can beat Adams Express, why do they not dare to place the two on equal terms? That is a fair question. But when a man's hands are tied, to ask him why he doesn't fight is a coward's question.

Yes, as *The Anti-Monopolist* says, Uncle Sam carries one hundred pounds of newspapers two thousand miles, not for two dollars, but for one dollar, pays the railroad more than its services are worth, and loses about five dollars a trip.

Yes, an express company would charge twenty dollars for the same service, because it knows it would be folly to attempt to compete with the one-dollar rate, and therefore charges for its necessarily limited business such rates as those who desire a guarantee of promptness and security are willing to pay.

Uncle Sam nevertheless continues to carry at the one-dollar rate, knowing that this is a good way to induce the newspapers to wink at his villainies, and that he can and does make up in two ways his loss of five dollars a trip,—1, by carrying one hundred pounds of letters two thousand miles for thirty-two dollars and forbidding anybody else to carry them for less, although the express companies would be glad of the chance to do the same service for sixteen dollars; and, 2, by taking toll from all purchasers of whiskey and tobacco at home, and of various other articles from foreign countries.

And yet some people don't know why the thousands of officeholders who are pulling away at the public teats are getting fat while the people are getting poorer. In fact, some people don't know anything at all except, as Josh Billings said, "a grate menny things that ain't so." It is very unfortunate that such people are intrusted with the editing of newspapers.

In 1907 a Chicago millionaire came forward with an offer to take over the postal service of the country, reduce rates on first and second-class matter one-half, and pay over to the government all surplus earnings above seven per cent. on the capital invested. This announcement led the Springfield (Mass.) *Republican* to ask whether his company would also agree to preserve to the employees of the service the hours and wages now accorded by the government; and it then facetiously added: "We shall next have syndicates offering to do the policing of the country on a private monopoly basis, and then taking charge of public education." Mr. Tucker made clear the position of Anarchism on this point:

I understand that there was some doubt in Chicago whether the millionaire refered to "meant business" and was entitled to serious consideration. But suppose a like offer to be made by a known and entirely competent and responsible or corporation; would congress and Teddy [President Roosevelt] entertain it for a moment? Would the intelligent and earnest *Republican* urge them to accept it? If not, why not? The hint in regard to the employees is rather unfortunate. The government has not been a good employer in the postal service, as everybody knows. It pays low wages, requires hard work, and forbids the clerks and mail-carriers to bother congress or to agitate politically against unfriendly individuals in that body. A private corporation could not in these days do much worse.

But suppose further that the aforesaid responsible bidder should agree to raise the wages and shorten the hours of the employees, and to refer disputes to arbitrators named by Teddy himself; would the *Republican then* favor acceptance of the offer? I doubt it. But why not? What would be its objection? As to the remark about the private police and private education it is not the paradox, the *reductio ad absurdum*, our friend imagines it to be. Under healthy economic and political conditions private enterprise in those spheres would be not only "possible," but eminently desirable. And Anarchists contemplate even a private police without the least consciousness of particular audacity.

LIBERTY OR AUTHORITY

It has always been difficult to induce the superficial thinker to distinguish between things libertarian and things authoritarian. Hence even trained economists have frequently confused State Socialism and Communism with Anarchism. In the following article the editor of *Liberty* proceeded to clarify the subject for one who had failed to make the proper discrimination:

PROFESSOR SUMNER, who occupies the chair of political economy at Yale, addressed recently the New Haven Equal Rights Debating Club. He told the State Socialists and Communists of that city much wholesome truth. But, as far as I can learn from the newspaper reports, which may of course have left out, as usual, the most important things that the speaker said, he made no discrimination in his criticisms. He appears to have entirely ignored the fact that the Anarchistic Socialists are the most unflinching champions in existence of his own pet principle of *laissez faire*. He branded Socialism as the summit of absurdity, utterly failing to note that one great school of Socialism says "Amen" whenever he scolds government for invading the individual, and only regrets that he doesn't scold it oftener and more uniformly.

Referring to Karl Marx's position that the employee is forced to give up a part of his product to the employer (which, by the way, was Proudhon's position before it was Marx's, and Josiah Warren's before it was Proudhon's), Professor Sumner asked why the employee does not, then, go to work for himself, and answered the question very truthfully by saying that it is because he has no capital. But he did not proceed to tell why he has no capital and how he can get some. Yet this is the vital point in dispute between Anarchism and privilege, between Socialism and so-called political economy. He did indeed recommend the time dishonored virtues of industry and economy as a means of getting capital, but every observing person knows that the most industrious and economical persons are precisely the ones who have no capital and can get none. Industry and economy will begin to accumulate capital when idleness and extravagance lose their power to steal it, and not before.

Professor Sumner also told Herr Most and his followers that their proposition to have the employee get capital by forcible seizure is the most short-sighted economic measure possible to conceive of. Here again he is entirely wise and sound. Not that there may not be circumstances when such seizure would be advisable as a political, war, or terroristic measure calculated to induce political changes that will give freedom to natural economic processes; but as a directly economic measure it must always and inevitably be, not only futile, but reactionary. In opposition to all arbitrary distribution I stand with Professor Sumner with all my heart and mind. And so does every logical Anarchist.

But, if the employee cannot at present get capital by industry and economy, and if it will do him no good to get it by force, how is he to get it with benefit to himself and injury to no other? Why don't you tell us that, Professor Sumner? You will, to be sure, send us a stray shot somewhere near the mark when, in answer to a question why shoemakers have no shoes, you said that, where such a condition of things prevailed, it was due to some evil work of the government,—said evil work being manifest at present in the currency and taxation. But what is the precise nature of the evils thus manifest? Tell me that definitely, and then I will tell you whether you are a consistent man.

I fancy that, if I should ask you what the great evil in our taxation is, you would answer that it is the protective tariff. Now, the protective tariff is an evil certainly; and an outrage; but, so far as it affects the power of the laborer to accumulate capital, it is a comparatively small one. In fact, its abolition, unaccompanied by the abolition of the banking monopoly, would take away from very large classes of laborers not only what little chance they now have of getting capital, but also their power of sustaining the lives of themselves and their families. The amount abstracted from labor's pockets by the protective tariff and by all other methods of getting governmental revenue is simply one of the smaller drains on industry. The amount of capital which it is thus prevented from getting will hardly be worth considering until the larger drains are stopped. As far as taxation goes, the great evils involved in it are to be found, not in the material damage done to labor by a loss of earnings, but in the assumption of the right to take men's property without their consent, and in the use of this property to pay the salaries of the officials through whom, and the expenses of the machine through which, labor is oppressed and ground down. Are you heroic enough, Professor Sumner, to adopt this application of *laissez faire*? I summon you to it under penalty of conviction of an infidelity to logic which ought to oust you from your position as a teacher of youth.

If taxation, then (leaving out the enormous mischief that it does as an instrument of tyranny), is only one of the minor methods of keeping capital from labor, what evil is there in the currency that constitutes the major method? Your answer to this question, Professor Sumner, will again test your consistency. But I am not so sure what it will be in this case as I was in the other. If you answer it as most of your fellow-professors would, you will say that the great evil in the currency is the robbery of labor through a dishonest silver dollar. But this is a greater bugbear than the protective tariff. The silver dollar is just as honest and just as dishonest as the gold dollar, and neither of them is dishonest or a robber of labor except so far as it is a monopoly dollar. Both, however being monopoly dollars, and all our other dollars being monopoly dollars, labor is being robbed by them all to an extent perfectly appalling. And right here is to be found the real reason why labor cannot get capital. It is because its wages are kept low and its credit rendered next to valueless by a financial system that makes the issue of currency a monopoly and a privilege, the result of which is the maintenance of interest, rent, and profits at rates ruinous to labor and destructive to business. And the only way that labor can ever get capital is by striking down this monopoly and making the issue of money as free as the manufacture of shoes. To demonetize silver or gold will not help labor; *what labor needs is the monetization of all marketable wealth.* Or, at least, the *opportunity* of such monetization. This can only be secured by absolutely free competition in banking. Again I ask you, Profesor Sumner, does your anxiety lest the individual be interfered with cover the field of finance? Are you willing that the individual shall be "let alone" in the exercise of his right to make his own money and offer it in open market to be taken by those who choose? To this test I send you a second summons under the same penalty that I have already hung over your head in case you fail to respond to the first. The columns of *Liberty* are open for your answer.

Before you make it, let me urge you to consistency. The battle between free trade and protection is simply one phase of the battle between Anarchism and State Socialism. To be a consistent free trader is to be an Anarchist; to be a consistent protectionist is to be a State Socialist. You are assailing that form of State Socialism known as protection with a vigor equalled by no other man, but you are rendering your blows of little effect by maintaining, or encouraging the belief that you maintain, those forms of State Socialism known as compulsory taxation and the banking monopoly. You assail Marx and Most mercilessly, but fail to protest against the most dangerous manifestations of their philosophy. Why pursue this confusing course? In reason's name, be one thing or the other! Cease your indiscriminate railing at Socialism, for to be consistent you must be Socialist yourself, either of the Anarchistic or the governmental sort: either be a State, Socialist and denounce liberty everywhere and always, or be an Anarchist and denounce authority everywhere and always; else you must consent to be taken for what you will appear to be,—an impotent hybrid.

Herbert Spencer was prone to err in a similar manner, and he was no more immune than Professor Sumner to Mr. Tucker's shafts of criticism:

Liberty welcomes and criticises in the same breath the series of papers by Herbert Spencer on "The New Toryism," "The Coming Slavery," "The Sins of Legislators," etc., now running in the *Popular Science Monthly* and the English *Contemporary Review*. They are very true, very important, and very misleading. They are true for the most part in what they say, and false and misleading in what they fail to say. Mr. Spencer convicts legislators of undeniable and enormous sins in meddling with and curtailing and destroying the people's rights. Their sins are sins of commission. But Mr. Spencer's sin of omission is quite as grave. He is one of those persons who are making a wholesale onslaught on Socialism as the incarnation of the doctrine of State omnipotence carried to its highest power. And I am not sure that he is quite honest in this. I begin to be a little suspicious of him. It seems as if he had forgotten the teachings of his earlier writings, and had become a champion of the capitalistic class. It will be noticed that in these later articles, amid his multitudinous illustrations (of which he is as prodigal as ever) of the evils of legislation, he in every instance cites some law passed, ostensibly at least, to protect labor, alleviate suffering, or promote the people's welfare. He demonstrates beyond dispute the lamentable failure in this direction. But never once does he call attention to the far more deadly and deep-seated evils growing out of the innumerable laws creating privilege and sustaining monopoly. You must not protect the weak against the strong, he seems to say, but freely supply all the weapons needed by the strong to oppress the weak. He is greatly shocked that the rich should be directly taxed to support the poor, but that the poor should be indirectly taxed and bled to make the rich richer does not outrage his delicate sensibilities in the least. Poverty is increased by the poor laws, says Mr. Spencer. Granted; but what about the *rich* laws that caused and still cause the poverty to which the poor laws add? That is by far the more important question; yet Mr. Spencer tries to blink it out of sight.

A very acute criticism of Mr. Spencer's position has been made recently before the Manhattan Liberal Club by Stephen Pearl Andrews. He shows that Mr. Spencer is not the radical *laissez faire* philosopher which he pretends to be; that the only true believers in *laissez faire* are the Anarchists; that individualism must be supplemented by the doctrines of equity and courtesy; and that, while State Socialism is just as dangerous and tyrannical as Mr. Spencer pictures it, "there is a higher and nobler form of Socialism which is not only not slavery, but which is our only means of rescue from all sorts and degrees of slavery." All this is straight to the mark,—telling thrusts, which Mr. Spencer can never parry.

But the English philosopher is doing good, after all. His disciples are men of independent mind, more numerous every day, who accept his fundamental truths and carry them to their logical conclusions. A notable instance is Auberon Herbert, formerly a member of the House of Commons, but now retired from political life. While an enthusiastic adherent of the Spencerian philosophy, he is fast outstripping his master. In a recent essay entitled "A Politician in Sight of Haven," written, as the London *Spectator* says, with an unsurpassable charm of style, Mr. Herbert explodes the majority lie, ridicules physical force as a solution of social problems, strips government of every function except the police, and recognizes even that only as an evil of brief necessity, and in conclusion proposes the adoption of *voluntary taxation* with a calmness and confidence which must have taken Mr. Spencer's breath away. To be sure, Mr. Herbert is as violent as his master against Socialism, but in his case only because he honestly supposes that compulsory Socialism is the only Socialism, and not at all from any sympathy with legal monopoly or capitalistic privilege in any form.

Mr. Willis Hudspeth, in a communication to *Liberty*, stated that an Anarchist paper defines an Individualist to be "one who believes in the principle of recognizing the right of every non-aggressive individual to the full control of his person and property"; and he then inquired how, if that were correct, does Anarchism conflict with Socialism or Individualism. Mr. Tucker answered his question in this manner:

THE definition offered of Individualism might not be accepted by all Individualists, but it will do very well as a definition of Anarchism. When my correspondent speaks of Socialism I understand him to mean State Socialism and Nationalism, and not that Anarchistic Socialism which *Liberty* represents. I shall answer him on this supposition. He wishes to know, then, how State Socialism and Nationalism would restrict the non-aggressive individual in the full control of his person and property. In a thousand and one ways. I will tell him one, and leave him to find out the thousand. The principal plank in the platform of State Socialism and Nationalism is the confiscation of *all* capital by the State. What becomes, in that case, of the property of any individual, whether he be aggressive or non-aggressive? What becomes also of private industry? Evidently it is totally destroyed. What becomes then of the personal liberty of those non-aggressive individuals who are thus prevented from carrying on business for themselves or from assuming relations between themselves as employer and employee if they prefer, and who are obliged to become employees of the State against their will? State Socialism and Nationalism mean the utter destruction of human liberty and private property.

LIBERTY AND LABOR

The industrial problem has always been an acute one in Great Britain, and the politicians have been struggling with it for a great many years. From time to time the editor of *Liberty* recorded and commented upon the efforts of the more clear-sighted economists in that country to solve the problem, hence his welcome of a new book on the subject:

AUBERON HERBERT, whose essay, "A Politician in Sight of Haven," creates such an enthusiasm for Liberty in the minds of all thinking people who read it, has recently published still another book of similar purport and purpose. He calls it "The Right and Wrong of Compulsion by the State: A Statement of the Moral Principles of the Party of Individual Liberty, and the Political Measures Founded Upon Them." It consists of a series of papers written for Joseph Cowen's paper, the Newcastle *Chronicle*, supplemented by a letter to the London *Times* on the English factory acts. Dedicated to Mr. Cowen's constituents, "The Workmen of Tyneside," it appeals with equal force to workmen the world over, and their welfare and their children's will depend upon the readiness with which they accept and the bravery with which they adhere to its all-important counsel. The book is a magificent assault on the majority idea, a searching exposure of the inherent evil of State systems, and a glorious assertion of the inestimable benefits of voluntary action and free competition, reaching its climax in the emphatic declaration that "this question of power exercised by some men over other men is the greatest of all questions, the one that concerns the very foundations of society," upon the answer to which "must ultimately depend all ideas of right and wrong." This is a bold and, at first sight, an astonishing claim; but it is a true one, nevertheless, and the fact that Mr. Herbert makes it so confidently shows that he is inspired by the same idea that gave birth to this journal, caused it to be christened *Liberty*, and determined it to labor first and foremost for Anarchy, or the Abolition of the State. This is no fitful outburst on Mr. Herbert's part. He evidently has enlisted for a campaign which will end only with victory. The book in question seems to be the second in a series of "Anti-Force Papers," which promises to include special papers dealing more elaborately, but in the light of the same general principle, with the matters of compulsory taxation, compulsory education, land ownership, professional monopolies, prohibitory liquor laws, legislation against vice, State regulation of love regulations, etc., etc. I know no more inspiring spectacle in England than that of this man of exceptionally high social position doing battle almost single-handed with the giant monster, government, and showing in it a mental rigor and vigor and a wealth of moral fervor rarely equalled in any cause. Its only parallel at the present day is to be found in the splendid attitude of Mr. Ruskin, whose earnest eloquence in behalf of economic equity rivals Mr. Herbert's in behalf of individual liberty.

This thought leads to the other, that each of these men lacks the truth that the other possesses. Mr. Ruskin sees very clearly the economic principle which makes all forms of usury unrighteous and wages for work the only true method of sustaining life, but he never perceives for a moment that individual human beings have sovereign rights over themselves. Mr. Herbert proves beyond question that the government of man by man is utterly without justification, but is quite ignorant of the fact that interest, rent, and profits will find no place in the perfect economic order. Mr. Ruskin's error is by far the more serious of the two, because the realization of Mr. Herbert's ideas would inevitably result in the equity that Mr. Ruskin sees, whereas this equity can never be achieved for any length of time without an at least partial fulfilment of individual liberty. Nevertheless it cannot be gainsaid that Mr. Herbert's failure to see the economic results of his ideas considerably impairs his power of carrying them home to men's hearts. Unfortunately, there are many people whom the most perfect deductive reasoning fails to convince. The beauty of a great principle and its harmonizing influence wherever it touches they are unable to appreciate. They can only see certain great and manifest wrongs, and they demand that these shall be righted. Unless they are clearly shown the connection between these wrongs and their real causes, they are almost sure to associate them with imaginary causes and to try the most futile and sometimes disastrous remedies. Now, the one great wrong that these people see today is the fact that industry and poverty commonly go hand in hand and are associated in the same persons, and the one thing that they are determined upon, regardless of everything else whatsoever, is that hereafter those who do the work of this world shall enjoy the wealth of this world. It is a righteous determination, and in it is to be found the true significance of the State-Socialistic movement which Mr. Herbert very properly condemns and yet only half understands. To meet it is the first necessity incumbent upon the friends of Liberty. It is sure that the workers can never permanently secure themselves in the control of their products except through the method of Liberty; but it is almost equally sure that, unless they are shown what Liberty will do for them in this respect, they will try every other method before they try Liberty. The necessity of showing them this Mr. Herbert, to be sure, dimly sees, but, the light not having dawned on himself, he cannot show it to others. He has to content himself, therefore, with such inadequate, unscientific, and partially charitable proposals as the formation of voluntary associations to furnish work to the unemployed. The working people will never thus be satisfied, and they ought not to be.

But Mr. Herbert can satisfy them if he can convince them of all that is implied in his advocacy of "complete free trade in all things." To many special phases of this free trade he does call marked attention, but never, I believe, to the most important of all, free trade in banking. If he would only dwell upon the evils of the money-issuing monopoly and emphasize with his great power the fact that competition, in this as in other matters, would give us all that is needed of the best possible article at the lowest possible price, thereby steadily reducing interest and rent to zero, putting capital within the comfortable reach of all deserving and enterprising people, and causing the greatest liberation on record of heretofore restricted energies, the laborers might then begin to see that here lies their only hope; that Liberty, after all, and not Government, is to be their saviour; that their first duty is to abolish the credit monopoly and let credit organize itself; that then they will have to ask nobody for work, but everybody will be asking work of them; and that then, instead of having to take whatever pittance they can get, they will be in a position to exact wages equivalent to their product, under which condition of things the reign of justice will be upon us and labor will have its own. Then Mr. Herbert's work for Liberty will no longer be a struggle, but an unmixed pleasure. He will no longer have to breast the current by urging workmen to self-denial; he can successfully appeal to their self-interest, the tide will turn, and he will be borne onward with it to the ends that he desires.

COMPETITION AND CO-OPERATION

"Is competition or coöperation the truest expression of that mutual trust and fraternal good-will which alone can replace present forms of authority, usages and customs as the social bond of union?" asked W. T. Horn, in a communication to *Liberty*. Here is the editor's answer:

THE supposition that competition means war rests upon old notions and false phrases that have been long current, but are rapidly passing into the limbo of exploded fallacies. Competition means war only when it is in some way restricted, either in scope or intensity,—that is, when it is not perfectly free competition; for then its benefits are won by one class at the expense of another, instead of by all at the expense of nature's forces. When universal and unrestricted, competition means the most perfect peace and the truest coöperation; for then it becomes simply a test of forces resulting in their most advantageous utilization. As soon as the demand for labor begins to exceed the supply, making it an easy matter for every one to get work at wages equal to his product, it is for the interest of all (including his immediate competitors) that the best man should win; which is another way of saying that, where freedom prevails, competition and coöperation are identical. For further proof and elaboration of this proposition I refer Mr. Horn to Andrew's "Science of Society" and Fowler's pamphlets on "Coöperation." The real problem, then, is to make the demand for labor greater than the supply, and this can only be done through competition in the supply of money or use of credit. This is abundantly shown in Greene's "Mutual Banking" and the financial writings of Proudhon and Spooner. My correspondent seems filled with the sentiment of good-fellowship, but ignorant of the science thereof, and even of the fact that there is such a science. He will find this science expounded in the works already named. If, after studying and mastering these, he still should have any doubts, *Liberty* will then try to set them at rest.

What the person who goes out into the work-a-day world will see there depends very much upon the power of his mental vision. If that is strong enough to enable him to see that the evils around him are caused by a prohibition of competition in certain directions, it is not unlikely that he will be filled with a "wish to foster competition." Such, however, will not be the case with a man who so misapprehends competition as to suppose that monopoly is its soul. Instead of its soul, it is its antithesis.

Whatever the reason for which men strive for wealth, as a general thing they get it, not by competition, but by the application of force to the suppression of certain kinds of competition,—in other words, by governmental institution and protection of monopoly.

Inasmuch as the monopolist is the victor, it is true that to deny him the spoils of victory is to sheathe the sword of *monopoly*. But you do not thereby sheathe the sword of competition (if you insist on calling it a sword), because competition yields no spoils to the victor, but only wages to the laborer.

When my correspondent says that all monopolies are "resultants of a competition as *free* as nature could make it," he makes competition inclusive of the struggle between invasive forces, whereas he ought to know that free competition, in the economic sense of the phrase, implies the suppression of invasive forces, leaving a free field for the exercise of those that are non-invasive.

If a man were to declare that, when the benefits of *labor* cease to be won by one class at the expense of another and when they are shared by all at the expense of nature's forces, *labor* loses its *raison d'être* and dies, his sanity would not long remain unquestioned; but the folly of such an utterance is not lessened an iota by the substitution of the word *competition* for the word *labor*. As long as the gastric juice continues to insist upon its rights, I fancy that neither labor nor competition will lack a *raison d'être*, even though the laborer and competitor should find himself under the necessity of wresting his "spoils" from the bosom of his mother earth instead of from the pocket of his brother man.

In Mrs. Glass's recipe for cooking a hare, the first thing was to catch the hare. So in Mr. Horn's recipe for the solution of economic forms in ethical concepts, the first thing is to get the concepts. Now, the concepts of mutual confidence and good-fellowship are not to be obtained by preaching,—otherwise the church militant would long ago have become the church triumphant; or by force,—otherwise progress would have gone hand in hand with authority instead of with liberty; but only by unrestricted freedom,—that is, by competition, the necessary condition of confidence, fellowship, and coöperation, which can never come as long as monopoly, "the economic expression of hostility and mastership," continues to exist.

LIBERTY AND THE BOYCOTT

LONDON *Jus* does not see clearly in the matter of boycotting. "Every man," is says, "has a perfect right to refuse to hold intercourse with any other man or class from whom he chooses to keep aloof. But where does liberty come in when several persons conspire together to put pressure upon another to induce or coerce him (by threats expressed or implied) to refrain also from intercourse with the boycotted man? It is not that the boycotted man has grounds of legal complaint against those who voluntarily put him in coventry. His complaint is against those who compel (under whatsoever sanction) third persons to do likewise. Surely the distinction is specific." Specific, yes, but not rational. The line of real distinction does not run in the direction which *Jus* tries to give it. Its course does not lie between the second person and a third person, but between the threats of invasion and the threats of ostracism by which either the second or a third person is coerced or induced. All boycotting, no matter of what person, consists either in the utterance of a threat or in its execution. A man has a right to threaten what he has a right to execute. The boundary-line of justifiable boycotting is fixed by the nature of the threat used. B and C, laborers, are entitled to quit buying shoes of A, a manufacturer, for any reason whatever or for no reason at all. Therefore they are entitled to say to A: "If you do not discharge the nonunion men in your employ, we will quit buying shoes of you." Similarly they are entitled to quit buying clothes of D, a tailor. Therefore they are entitled to say to D: "If you do not coöperate with us in endeavoring to induce A to discharge his non-union employees,—that is, if you do not quit buying shoes of him,—we will quit buying clothes of you." But B and C are not entitled to burn A's shop or D's shop. Hence they are not entitled to say to A that they will burn his shop unless he discharges his non-union employees, or to D that they will burn his shop unless he withdraws his patronage from A. Is it not clear that the rightful attitude of B and C depends wholly upon the question whether or not the attitude is invasive in itself, and not at all upon the question whether the object of it is A or D?

In reply, *Jus*, being convinced by the argument, cheerfully acknowledged its error, but asserted that the principle did not apply when two or more persons conspired to conduct a boycott, saying, "That which may not be illegal or even wrong in one person becomes both illegal and morally wrong when in a crowd of persons." Mr. Tucker then proceeded to demolish that contention:

Jus still thinks, however, that something may be said on the other side, and declares that there are some things that one person may rightfully do which become illegal and immoral when done by a crowd. I should like to have *Jus* give an instance. There are some invasive acts or threats which cannot be executed by individuals, but require crowds—or conspiracies, if you will—for their acccomplishment. But the guilt still arises from the invasive character of the act, and not from the fact of conspiracy. No individual has a right to do any act which is invasive, but any number of individuals may rightfully "conspire" to commit any act which is non-invasive. *Jus* acknowledges the force of *Liberty's* argument that A may as properly boycott C as B. Further consideration, I think, will compel it to acknowledge that A and B combined may as properly boycott C as may A alone or B alone.

In these days of boycott trials a great deal of nonsense is being talked and written regarding "blackmail." This is a question which the principle of Liberty settles at once. It may be well to state the verdict boldly and baldly. Here it is: Any individual may place any condition he chooses, provided the condition be not in itself invasive, upon the doing or not doing of anything which he has a right to do or not do; but no individual can rightfully be a party to any bargain which makes a necessarily invasive condition incumbent upon any of the contracting parties. From which it follows that an individual may rightfully "extort" money from another by "threatening" him with certain consequences, provided those consequences are of such a nature that he can cause them without infringing upon anybody's rights. Such "extortion" is generally rather mean business, but there are circumstances under which the most high-minded of men might resort to it without doing violence to his instincts, and under no circumstances is it invasive and therefore wrongful, unless the act threatened is invasive and therefore wrongful. Therefore to punish men who have taken money for lifting a boycott is oppression pure and simple. Whatever may be the "common law" or the "statute law" of blackmail, this—to use Mr. Spooner's phrase—is the *natural law* that governs it.

The courts are at last beginning to take rational views on the question of peaceable picketing and peaceable boycotting. Several refreshing decisions have been rendered within a short time in which the principle is recognized that what one man may legitimately do several men may do in concert. But even the most independent and intelligent of the judges still stultify themselves by attempting baseless distinctions between self-regarding boycotts and purely sympathetic boycotts. A, they say, may boycott B, if he has any grievance against him, but he may not ask C to boycott B and threaten to boycott *him* in turn in the event of refusal. When they undertake to defend this position, they fail miserably, of course, and the truth is that they shrink from the clear logic of the principle which they lay down at the outset. But let us not expect too much of them at once. "It is the first step that is difficult." Having accepted a sound principle, its corollaries will force themselves on them.

ANARCHISM AND COPYRIGHT

Not alone on the land question did Mr. Tucker find himself in disagreement with Henry George. In his newspaper, the *Standard* of June 23, 1888, the latter discussed with a correspondent the question of property in ideas. The editor of *Liberty* thus took exception to his arguments:

MR. GEORGE, taking his stand upon the principle that productive labor is the true basis of the right of property, argues through three columns, with all the consummate ability for which credit should be given him, to the triumphant vindication of the position that there can rightfully be no such thing as the exclusive ownership of an idea.

No man, he says, "can justly claim ownership in natural laws, nor in any of the relations which may be perceived by the human mind, nor in any of the potentialities which nature holds for it. . . . Ownership comes from production. It cannot come from discovery. Discovery can give no right of ownership. . . . No man can discover anything which, so to speak, was not put there to be discovered, and which some one else might not in time have discovered. If he finds it, it was not lost. It, or its potentiality, existed before he came. It was there to be found. . . . In the production of any material thing—a machine, for instance—there are two separable parts,—the abstract idea of principle, which may be usually expressed by drawing, by writing, or by word of mouth; and the concrete form of the particular machine itself, which is produced by bringing together in certain relations certain quantities and qualities of matter, such as wood, steel, brass, brick, rubber, cloth, etc. There are two modes in which labor goes to the making of the machine,—the one in ascertaining the principle on which such machines can be made to work; the other in obtaining from their natural reservoirs and bringing together and fashioning into shape the quantities and qualities of matter which in their combination constitute the concrete machine. In the first mode labor is expended in discovery. In the second mode it is expended in production. The work of discovery may be done once for all, as in the case of the discovery in prehistoric time of the principle or idea of the wheelbarrow. But the work of production is required afresh in the case of each particular thing. No matter how many thousand millions of wheelbarrows have been produced, it requires fresh labor of production to make another one. . . . The natural reward of labor expended in discovery is in the use that can be made of the discovery without interference with the right of any one else to use it. But to this natural reward our patent laws endeavor to add an artificial reward. Although the effect of giving to the discoverers of useful devices or processes an absolute right to their exclusive use would be to burden all industry with most grievous monopolies, and to greatly retard, if not put a stop to, further inventions, yet the theory of our patent laws is that we can stimulate discoveries by giving a modified right of ownership in their use for a term of years. In this we seek by special laws to give a special reward to labor expended in discovery, which does not belong to it of natural right, and is of the nature of a bounty. But as for labor expended in the second of these modes,—in the production of the machine by the bringing together in certain relations of certain quantities and qualities of matter,—we need no special laws to reward that. Absolute ownership attaches to the results of such labor, not by special law, but by common law. And if all human laws were abolished, men would still hold that, whether it were a wheelbarrow or a phonograph, the concrete thing belonged to the man who produced it. And this, not for a term of years, but in perpetuity. It would pass at his death to his heirs or to those to whom he devised it."

The whole of the preceding paragraph is quoted from Mr. George's article. I regard it as conclusive, unanswerable. It proceeds, it will be noticed, entirely by the method of *ergo*. But it is time for the philosopher to disappear. He has done his part of the work, which was the demolition of patents. Now it is the prestidigitator's turn. It remains for him to justify copyright,—that is, property, not in the ideas set forth in a book, but in the manner of expressing them. So juggler George steps upon the scene. *Presto!* he exclaims: "Over and above any 'labor of discovery' expended in thinking out *what* to say, is the 'labor of production' expended on *how* to say it." Observe how cunningly it is taken for granted here that the task of giving literary expression to an idea is labor of production rather than labor of discovery. But is it so? Right here comes in the juggler's trick; we will subject it to the philosopher's test. The latter has already been quoted: "*The work of discovery may be done once for all. . . . but the work of production is required afresh in the case of each particular thing.*" Can anything be plainer than that he who does the work of combining words for the expression of an idea saves just that amount of labor to all who thereafter choose to use the same words in the same order to express the same idea, and that this work, not being required afresh in each particular case, is not work of production, and that, not being work of production, it gives no right of property? In quoting Mr. George above I did not have to expend any labor on "how to say" what he had already said. He had saved me that trouble. I simply had to write and print the words on fresh sheets of paper. These sheets of paper belong to me, just as the sheets on which he wrote and printed belong to him. But the particular combination of words belongs to neither of us. He discovered it, it is true, but that fact gives him no right to it. Why not? Because, to use his own phrases, this combination of words "existed potentially before he came"; "it was there to be found"; and if he had not found it, some one else would or might have done so. The work of copying or printing books is analogous to the production of wheelbarrows, but the original work of the author, whether in thinking or composing, is analogous to the *invention* of the wheelbarrow; and the same argument that demolishes the right of the inventor demolishes the right of the author. The method of expressing an idea is itself an idea, and therefore not appropriable.

THE END

BIBLIOGRAPHY

Out of a great number of books that could be cited as showing a tendency of modern thought toward the ideals of Individualist Anarchism, the following are those that bear most directly on the subject, and, in some instances may be considered as source books. Where they are available, their reading in connection with the present volume will serve to enlighten the student of individual liberty.

Proudhon was the greatest figure of the middle period of the nineteenth century. He was the first thinker to fully apply the principle of liberty directly to all economic conditions. His "General Idea of the Revolution in the Nineteenth Century" (Freedom Press, 127 Ossulston Street, London, N. W. 1, England) describes the changes impending and the direction they must take. He predicted the growing power of the financial capitalist, and history has abundantly borne him out. His influence in France has lasted to this day. "What Is Property?"—one of his greatest works and the first translated into English—also may be had from the Freedom Press.

John Stuart Mill was one of the first to see clearly the real meaning of liberty. His essay, "On Liberty," although first published over sixty-five years ago, is so fundamental in its substance that it is quite applicable to present conditions. Moreover, he discussed denials of liberty in the United States as well as in England. For a long time out of print, this essay is fortunately now to be had in the Big Blue Book series of the Haldeman-Julius Company, Girard, Kansas.

William B. Greene, working independently in America, reached the same conclusions as Proudhon in France. In his pamphlet on "Mutual Banking" (published by Henry Cohen, 426 California Building, Los Angeles, California) he attacks, first, the state banks of his day. The intricate processes of exchange and the part played by money and credit are described with such simplicity and yet so correctly that his arguments have not suffered by the lapse of time and are as fully pertinent today as they were when written. He clearly points the way to the abolition of interest.

A brief exposition of some of Proudhon's ideas, brought down to date and linked up with present conditions, is embodied in "The Economics of Liberty," by John Beverly Robinson (supplied by Freedom Press, 127 Ossulston Street, London, N. W. 1). With the exception of some digressions into irrelevancies, it is thought-provoking and valuable.

Individualist Anarchism, especially as expounded by Tucker, is fundamentally egoistic, which makes Max Stirner's masterpiece, "The Ego and His Own" (also to be had from Freedom Press), a book that should be read in connection with any exposition of individual liberty, since it contains the essence of the egoistic philosophy. Another book on the same subject, more modern and less voluminous, but unfortunately not now to be had except in a few public libraries, is James L. Walker's "The Philosophy of Egoism." Walker, under the pen name of Tak Kak, was a frequent editorial contributor to *Liberty*.

Henry D. Thoreau, though not properly labeled an anarchist, was certainly a free spirit, and his essay, "On the Duty of Civil Disobedience," will be found to contain many inspiring thoughts for the person who is seeking to understand individual liberty. His "Walden," to a certain extent, may be similarly described.

Josiah Warren's "True Civilization" and Stephen Pearl Andrews' development of the same theme in "The Science of Society" would, were both books not out of print, provide profitable reading for those interested in the ideas set forth in this volume. "Instead of a Book" was dedicated to Warren, and Tucker frequently referred to him as his "master."

Lysander Spooner was one of the most prolific of writers on the subject of liberty and its application to the everyday problems of life, but he too suffers from being wholly out of print. One of his greatest works, "Trial by Jury," was edited and abridged by Victor Yarros and published under the title of "Free Political Institutions," but this too can no longer be had from booksellers. If it can be borrowed or found on second-hand book counters, it should be studied.

"Josiah Warren," by William Bailie (Small, Maynard & Company, Boston), is a biography which deals sympathetically and understandingly with Warren's ideas, and, aside from Tucker's writings, is the best exposition of those ideas now in print.

Francis D. Tandy's "Voluntary Socialism" (alas! also out of print) is designed to show how individual liberty can be applied to conditions as they exist today. It is valuable.

On the financial question Hugo Bilgram's "The Cause of Business Depressions" (Lippincott, Philadelphia) is of importance, especially as exploding the fallacy of the volume theory of money and as showing that interest has no reason for being. As giving a detailed history of the evolution of industry and banking in Great Britain, Charles P. Isaacs' "The Menace of the Money Power" (Jonathan Cape, 11 Gower Street, London) is excellent. It shows how Scotland formerly prospered under a comparatively free system of banking.

INDEX

www.ingramcontent.com/pod-product-compliance
Lightning Source LLC
Chambersburg PA
CBHW082129290526

45794CB00008B/2975